CREATION
The
CUTTING
EDGE

Edited By

Henry M. Morris, Ph.D. and Donald H. Rohrer, B.S.

*The Modern Conflict Between
Creationists and Evolutionary Humanists*

*Highlights of Acts & Facts
Creationist News Articles, Plus All The
ICR "Impact Series" for 1980-1981*

CREATION-LIFE PUBLISHERS
San Diego, California

Creation—The Cutting Edge

Copyright © 1982

Creation-Life Publishers
P. O. Box 15666
San Diego, California 92115

ISBN 0-89051-088-1
Library of Congress Catalog Card No. 82-83646

Cataloging in Publication Data

Morris, Henry Madison, 1918 -   ed.
    Creation—the cutting edge.
    Partial reprints from *Acts & Facts* 1980 and 1981. Fifth in a
series.
    1. Creation.   2. Bible and Science.
I. Rohrer, Donald H., 1946-   jt. ed.   II. Title.
                        213   82-83646

Cover Design: G. A. Bradley

Printed in the United States of America

Contents

Introduction

An amazing development is under way in the academic world. Meetings are being called, committees being formed, plans of action devised and alarms being sounded up and down the land. The academic establishment is being supported in this crusade by all the powers of the news media, with editorial columnists, news commentators, and ordinary reporters all being enlisted to help turn back a bold assault on the citadels of wisdom and learning.

Who is this fearsome foe against which such unprecedented defenses must be erected? Is it the Marxists? The pornographers? The occultists? No, of course not! Academic freedom must be preserved, so these groups must all be accommodated and defended, not opposed.

It is the creationists! *This* movement *must* be stopped, at all costs. Professor Delos B. McKown, Head of Auburn University's Philosophy Department, formerly a preacher and now a self-appointed defender of the scientific establishment, has solemnly proclaimed the following.

> . . . old time religion [is] something that educated people, both believers and non-believers, had thought was safely behind us in the old times, where it belongs. But, alas, modern, scientific, progressive America is witnessing a reactivation of biblical literalism, fundamentalism, and evangelicalism that almost defies belief . . . . But, of all the recent manifestations of old-time religion, I can think of none more impertinent than that of the Institute for Creation Research, which is devoted to destroying the ideas of cosmic and organic evolution. The mischief this organization is prepared to do to the life and earth sciences

in elementary and secondary schools defies the scientific
imagination.[1]

Dr. McKown is only one of a growing host of such alarmists
today, and probably not a very important one at that. Much
more imposing is the array of scientific, political, and educational organizations that are organizing for an all-out battle
against teaching the concept of creation in the schools and other
institutions of our country. The prestigious National Academy
of Sciences called a meeting of leading scientists and educators
in Washington on October 19, 1981, to discuss ways of dealing
with those who oppose evolutionism. The next day a similar
meeting was sponsored by the National Association of Biology
Teachers.

The largest and most influential scientific organization, the
American Association for Advancement of Science, has held a
number of councils, as well as lecture sessions at its conventions,
and has published a long series of critical articles in its journals.
It has formed local Committees of Correspondence in every
state, their function being to combat creationism wherever it
surfaces at the local level.

The list of organizations that have become active in the fight
against the Creator goes on and on—the American Humanist
Association, the American Civil Liberties Union, the National
Science Teachers Association, the American Geological Institute
(incorporating all the societies in the geological field), the
American Institute of Biological Sciences, the American An-
thropological Association, and many others.

Among the proposals emanating from these deliberations are
the following: (1) write and distribute books, articles, and pam-
phlets criticizing creationists and creationism; (2) *don't* participate in any more creation-evolution debates with creationist
scientists; (3) help prepare and support the most appropriate
debaters when debates are unavoidable; (4) organize an Institute
for Evolution Research "to counter the San Diego-based Institute for Creation Research"; (5) develop a national consor-

---

1.   D. R. McKown, "Contemporary Religion versus Science," *Chemtech.*
     June 1981, p. 336.

tium of organizations of all types, even including churches and other religious institutions, united to fight creation; (6) develop a strong program of political action to lobby legislatures, departments of education, and school boards; (7) initiate a nationwide series of short courses, designed to equip teachers to promote the evolutionist position in their classes; (8) prepare evolution television specials for broadcast on P.B.S.; (9) try to get every scientist and science teacher to contribute $10 annually for the work of the consortium.

The above are only a few of the many suggestions developed at these meetings. Some of these, along with many others, were presented in a paper "Countering the Creationists" by long-time anti-creationist John A. Moore, biologist at the University of California at Riverside. Dr. Moore made a very important point in conclusion: "If we do not resolve our problems with the creationists, we have only ourselves to blame. Let's remember, the greatest resource of all is available to us—the educational system of the nation."

Evolutionists, unfortunately, *do* seem to control our educational system, as well as our courts and news media today, and all these resources are being mobilized to do battle with the fearful menace of creation!

Somehow the term "overkill" comes to mind. According to the conventional wisdom, creationists are an insignificant fundamentalist sect, and scientific creationism, according to Harvard's Stephen Jay Gould, is merely a "nonsense term."

There would be a much simpler, quicker, and less expensive way to stop the creation movement, of course, but none of these evolutionary strategists seem to have thought of it. All they would have to do would be to provide one single documented *proof* of evolution, or even a few unequivocal scientific evidences!

In the meantime, there is another word that also comes to mind—*"Why?"* *"Why* do the . . . people imagine a vain thing? . . . [taking] counsel together against the Lord, . . . saying, Let us break their bands asunder, and cast away their cords from us" (Psalm 2:1-3). If evolution is such an assured fact of science and creation is scientific nonsense, why are they so afraid of allowing young people to evaluate the facts for themselves? On the other hand, if there could indeed be a Creator, and if He really could have created the universe, it is sad and foolish for educators to withhold this vital information from the young people whose training has been committed into their hands. The founding fathers of our nation, those who wrote the Declaration of Independence and the Bill of Rights, certainly never intended such a thing.

This intensifying and well-orchestrated battle against the creation movement is the underlying theme of this present volume, which is the fifth in the series of biennial anthologies published by the Institute for Creation Research. The titles of these volumes, and the two-year periods covered by each of them are as follows:

Creation: Acts/Facts/Impacts (1972 - 1973)
The Battle For Creation (1974 - 1975)
Up With Creation (1976 - 1977)
The Decade of Creation (1978 - 1979)
Creation—The Cutting Edge (1980 - 1981)

These five volumes comprise a fascinating on-going history of the modern creationist revival, featuring particularly the activities of the ICR scientists as they have led in this battle. All of the popular "Impact Series" articles, published monthly in the ICR *Acts and Facts* periodical, are also available for permanent reference use in these volumes.

As the creation movement has grown in impact and outreach, the initial reaction of the giant evolutionary establishment was to ignore it. Later, this attitude of aloofness changed to one of sarcasm and ridicule. But now it has erupted into full mobilization for battle! At least, we now have their attention.

At the same time, there have been multitudes of young people, and even hundreds of scientists, who have been won to creationism. Many of them were nominal Christians, but were lukewarm and doubting Christians because they were confused by their long indoctrination in evolution and the obvious contradiction of this philosophy with the Bible and Christianity. Many others have first become Christians as a direct result of first coming to believe in creation. There are still a goodly number of others who have now become creationists, but have not yet taken the step of personal commitment to saving faith in their Creator and Savior, the Lord Jesus Christ.

In any case, the ministry of creationism is primarily a ministry of ground preparation and seed-sowing, in the confidence that the Lord will eventually bring much fruit to perfection as a result. Using another figure, it has been called the *Cutting Edge* of the Gospel, the sharp weapon of foundational truth, in the great battle for the eternal souls of men and women for whom Christ died. Even though the opposition may be powerful, the ultimate victory is sure, because the God of creation is also the God of redemption, the Lord of the harvest, and triumphant King of Kings.

Chapter 1

The Impact of Creation

This chapter consists of the twenty-four articles appearing in the popular "Impact Series," a regular feature of the ICR periodical *Acts and Facts,* published in 1980 and 1981. These brief studies in creationism have indeed been having a profound impact in almost every area of modern life and thought. Many readers have expressed the view that assembling them in biennial anthologies such as this has made them even more useful.

The reader will find some of these articles quite technical, others very easy. Various fields of science are included, in addition to questions of Biblical exegesis, history, education, and other fields. A total of sixteen different authors have contributed. This variety is intentional, as it helps emphasize the fact that creationism is of interest and concern to people in all walks of life—scientists, teachers, preachers, homemakers, students, lawyers, doctors, businessmen, and everyone else.

IMPACT ARTICLES

No. 79, January 1980
Origin of Limestone Caves
By Steven A. Austin, Ph.D. *

Introduction

A cave is a natural opening or cavity within the earth, generally extending from the earth's surface to beyond the zone of light. Three genetic classes of caves can be recognized according to the major sculpturing process: (1) caves formed by pressure or flow, (2) caves carved by erosion, and (3) caves dissolved by solution. Those structures formed by mechanical pressure or flow include lava tunnels associated with volcanoes (e.g. Catacombs Cave in Lava Beds National Monument, California) and "badlands caves" excavated from poorly consolidated rock by hydraulic pressure (e.g., small caves of the arid Badlands of South Dakota). The caves carved by erosion include shoreline grottos created by the mechanical action of waves (e.g., La Jolla sea caves near San Diego, California) and rock shelters cut by river meanders (e.g., the massive sandstone alcoves of the famed cliff-dwelling Pueblo Indians). The caves dissolved by solution include ice caves associated with glaciers and the familiar limestone caverns or caves. Limestone caves are, by far, the most common type of caves.

The great size and beauty of limestone caves have made them features of public amazement and wonder. More than 130 caves in the United States are open commercially, and at least 13 national parks and monuments contain caves. The world's longest cave appears to be Kentucky's Mammoth Cave which has more than 240 kilometers (150 miles) of accessible passages. The largest subterranean chamber yet discovered is the Big Room of New Mexico's Carlsbad Caverns. The Big Room is about 400 meters (1,312 feet) long, 200 meters (656 feet) wide, 90 meters (295 feet) high, and contains the Great Dome, a stalagmite 19 meters (62 feet) tall. Gouffre Berger Cave near Grenoble,

---

* Dr. Steven A. Austin is a Research Associate in Geoscience with ICR, as well as Associate Professor of Geology at Christian Heritage College.

France, descends at least 1,100 meters (3,680 feet) below the surface and is the deepest cave yet explored by man. Records of the National Speleological Society of America indicate more than 11,000 caves in the United States, and it appears likely that 100,000 caves exist in the whole earth.

Caves are of interest to the student of the Bible because the Bible lands are rich in limestone caves. In Old Testament times caves often served as refuge or emergency shelter (Genesis 19:30; I Samuel 22:1, 24:1-8; Hebrews 11:37-40). Caves were also used as places of burial (Genesis 23:17; John 11:38). After the great confrontation between Elijah and the prophets of Baal, Elijah lodged in a cave and received the Word of the Lord there (I Kings 19:9-11). Psalms 57 and 142 were composed in a cave by David after he fled from Saul. The famed "Dead Sea Scrolls" were discovered in caves.

A great deal of scientific interest has been generated by caves. Speleology is a multidisciplinary science which deals with the cave environment: cave discovery, exploration, surveying, archaeology, zoology, botany, paleontology, meteorology, and geology. Mineralogists and gem collectors know that caves contain many large and perfect crystals. Paleontologists have found fossils in caves which shed light on the history of man (e.g., Neanderthal man). Geologists have attempted to answer several theoretical and practical questions posed by caves. One of the most difficult problems has been to interpret the history of limestone caves in relation to the Biblical framework for earth history.

Solution of Limestone

Solution cave chemistry can be simply stated: limestone and dolostone, the host rocks for most caves, are dissolved by natural acids (carbonic, sulfuric, and various organic acids) which occur in groundwater. Calcite ($CaCO_3$), the principal mineral comprising limestone, is dissolved in the presence of acid to produce calcium ion (Ca^{++}) and bicarbonate ion (HCO_3^-). Dolomite [$CaMg(CO_3)_2$], the most important mineral in dolostone, is dissolved by acid to produce calcium ion (CA^{++}), magnesium ion (Mg^{++}), and bicarbonate ions (HCO_3^-). If the acid is able to flow through the rock, ions will be removed and a cavity or solution conduit will form.

That many limestone caves formed by the solution process is indicated by four types of geologic evidence.

1. *Modern limestone caves often show evidence of ongoing solution*—the groundwater leaving a cave often has a higher concentration of calcium and bicarbonate ions than the water entering the cave.[1] Dripstone deposits on the interior of caves prove that solution occurs above the cave.

2. *The shapes of bedrock structures in limestone caves often resemble those produced in solution experiments.* For example, the shapes produced at intersections of joints in cave bedrock can be predicted based on the theory of solution kinetics.[2]

3. *The passages in limestone caves usually follow joints, fractures, and the level of the land surface in such a way as to suggest that the permeability of the bedrock has influenced the position of cave passages.* Maps and cross-sections of caves often show the regular spacing and orientation of passageways caused by joints.[3]

4. *Caves resembling those found in limestone and dolostone do not occur in insoluble, non-carbonate rocks.* The apparent causal relationship implies that some characteristic of the rock (i.e., solubility) has affected the occurrence of the caves.

Solution Theories

That solution is a major factor in the formation of limestone caves appears to be well substantiated. The hydrologic conditions and sequence of events leading to cave formation, however, are poorly understood by geologists. The *Encyclopedia Americana* begins its discussion of the origin of solution caves with the following admission:

> The origin of solution caves in limestone and related rocks is complex, and scientists are not in full accord as to the exact sequence of events that lead to the formation of such caves.[4]

The problem is that we are attempting to understand the origin of a cavity for which the evidence of the events forming it has been largely dissolved.

Two basic types of theories concern the water conditions when the cave formed. These are the *vadose* and *phreatic* theories.[5] The vadose theory suggests that solution of the cavity occurred while the limestone was above the level of groundwater (water table) and that the cavity was largely filled with air. The phreatic theory claims that the cavity formed when it was below the level of groundwater when it was completely filled with water.

Non-Solution Processes

Although solution was a major process in the formation of limestone caves, some major problems are encountered if these caves are considered to have formed *only* by solution. The first problem is the origin of the original fracture porosity along which circulation of acidic groundwater could be initiated. The original hairline fractures in the limestone would not transmit water, and therefore, solution conduits would not be expected to form. Davis[6] suggested that groundwater flow could be initiated by tectonic stresses on the rock which opened fractures and created the driving force for fluid flow. The process of "piping" (the production of underground conduits by removal of fine particles by water driven by pressure through poorly consolidated material) may also be important in producing fracture porosity. "Badlands caves" in shaly rocks form by this process.

A second problem for solution theory is the evidence of erosion and abrasion in limestone caves. Many caves contain large amounts of clay, gravel, cobbles, and boulders which could not have been dissolved from the limestone. Instead, the cave-filling material appears to have been transported by moving water from a sediment source outside the cave. These cave deposits show that some caves at one time were essentially "underground rivers," and, as such, could have experienced abrasion and erosion such as occurs in modern channels. The amount of material removed from caves by this process, however, appears to be small compared to that removed by solution.

Factors Affecting Solution

The solubility of calcite and dolomite, and the rate at which solution occurs, are dependent on at least eight factors: amount of carbon dioxide in solution, pH, oxidation of organic matter, temperature, pressure, concentration of added salts, rate of solution flow, and degree of solution mixing. Calcite is more soluble if carbon dioxide is increased, acidity is increased, oxygen and organic matter are increased, temperature is decreased, pressure is increased, concentration of salts is increased, rate of flow is increased, and degree of mixing is increased.[7]

The amount of carbon dioxide (CO_2) in solution is probably the single most important factor affecting solution because carbon dioxide combines with water to produce carbonic acid (H_2CO_3). The air, which normally has a pressure of 1 atmosphere, has a partial pressure of only 0.0003 atmosphere of CO_2. Rain water in equilibrium with air can dissolve very little calcite. Water containing oxygen and decaying organic material, however, can possess 0.1 atmosphere of CO_2 (over 300 times more CO_2 than normal rain water) and is able to dissolve a lot of calcite.[8] It is possible to make undersaturated solutions simply by mixing two types of water having different pressures of CO_2, different salinities, or different temperatures. Undersaturation occurs in the case of CO_2 because a non-linear relationship exists between the partial pressure of CO_2 and the solubility of calcite. A swiftly moving, turbulent flow promotes washing of the limestone walls of its conduit, and is, also, more effective at dissolving calcite.[9]

Rates of Limestone Solution

Because at least eight complex variables determine the rate of solution of limestone, an estimate of solution rates based on the theory of chemical thermodynamics and kinetics would be a monumental task! A better way to estimate solution rates would be to go to the cave environment, measure the various physical and chemical parameters, and relate them to observed solution rates. Unfortunately, the cave environment where solution may be occurring exists deep in the earth, in total darkness, in passages which are completely flooded with water. This environment is very inhospitable to man, and no data are available.

Another way of attacking the problem is to study a large cave-containing area where water chemistry and flow rates are known in order to estimate overall rates. An excellent area for this type of study is the large limestone and dolostone Sinkhole Plain-Mammoth Cave Upland region of central Kentucky. The area is between Green River, Barren River, and Beaver Creek, and comprises several hundred square kilometers. Although it receives 122 centimeters (48 inches) mean annual rainfall[10] and would naturally have about 51 centimeters (20 inches) of average annual runoff,[11] the area has virtually no surface streams! The runoff is channeled into sinkholes which distribute the water into a widespread limestone and dolostone formation which is about 100 meters (330 feet) thick. Caves and solution conduits in the aquifer transport most of the water northward where it discharges at springs into the Green River.

Chemical analyses of the area's groundwater by Thrailkill[12] indicate that mean calcium ion concentration is 49.0 milligram per liter and the mean magnesium ion is 9.7 milligram per liter. Because rain water has only trace amounts of calcium and magnesium, essentially all of the dissolved calcium and magnesium in the groundwater must come from solution of calcite and dolomite. By simple chemical calculation it can be shown that these concentrations represent 0.16 gram of dissolved calcite and dolomite per liter of groundwater.

It is reasonable to assume that about 1.0 meter of the 1.22 meters of mean annual rainfall go into the aquifer. Therefore, each square kilometer (1 million square meters) of central Kentucky receives about 1 million cubic meters of infiltration each year $(1,000,000 \ m^2 \times 1m = 1,000,000 m^3)$. Because a cubic meter of water contains 1 thousand liters, 1 billion liters of water enter the ground through each square kilometer of land surface each year.

The above data can be used to calculate the amount of calcite and dolomite dissolved each year. This is done by multiplying the mass of minerals per liter times the water infiltration rate $(0.16 \ g/l \times 1,000,000,000 \ l/yr = 160,000,000 \ g/yr)$. The answer is 160 million grams (176 tons) of dissolved calcite and dolomite per year over each square kilometer of land surface. If the mass of calcite and dolomite dissolved is divided by the density of the minerals, the volume is obtained $(160,000,000 \ g/yr \div 2,700,000 \ g/m^3 = 59m^3/yr)$. Thus, if the dissolving power of the acid in one square kilometer of central Kentucky is carried in one conduit, a cave 1 meter square and 59 meters long could form in a year![13]

The high rate of solution of limestone and dolostone should be a matter of alarm to uniformitarian geologists. In 2 million years (the assumed duration of the Pleistocene Epoch and the inferred age of many caves), a layer of limestone well over 100 meters thick could be completely dissolved off of Kentucky (assuming present rates and conditions). Any reasonable estimate of the volume of limestone actually removed by solution of Kentucky caves and karst would be insignificant compared to that predicted by an evolutionary model.

The solution data are not at odds with a catastrophist interpretation of earth history. The data of Thrailkill[14] show that the groundwater in central Kentucky is actually *undersaturated* with respect to calcite and dolomite, and that the full dissolving power of the acidic water is not being utilized in attacking the limestone. Calcite is dissolved only to about 55% of saturation and dolomite only to about 14% of saturation.[15] Furthermore, climatic and geomorphic evidence in Kentucky suggests that rates of groundwater flow and rates of solution have not remained unchanged. The more humid, cooler climate of the Pleistocene would have *increased* groundwater flow and *increased* rates of solution. It is also probable that the atmosphere had more CO_2. In the final analysis, there appears to be no major obstacle to a short time period for the solution of limestone caves.

Stalactites, Stalagmites, and Flowstone

The formations which hang from the ceiling of a cave are *stalactites;* those built up above the floor of a cave are *stalagmites;* whereas those sheet-like, layered deposits on the walls or floors are *flowstone.* A *column* forms by the joining of a stalactite and a stalagmite. Together these cave formations are known as *speleothems.*

The origin and age of speleothems is a controversial subject. A popular theory for the origin of caves involves two stages. The first stage was when the cavity was filled with water, and solution of limestone occurred. The second stage was when the cavity or cavern was filled with air, and deposition of speleothems began from solutions depositing calcium carbonate. A less popular theory is that there was only *one* stage in cave formation with solution occurring in the water-filled part of the chamber concurrently with speleothem deposition in the air-filled spaces.

Radiocarbon (C - 14) dating of speleothems has been used by some scientists to support the great age of cave formations.

However, attempts to date the carbonate minerals directly give deceptively old ages because carbon from limestone with infinite radiocarbon age (carbon out of equilibrium with atmospheric carbon) has been incorporated in minerals with atmospheric carbon.

Most of the stalactites and stalagmites in modern caves are not growing, and it appears impossible to estimate their former rate of growth. The ones that are growing may be subject to extreme variation in growth rate.[16] Because the Pleistocene Epoch was a time of higher humidity and rainfall than today, it is probable that more speleothems were growing and that they were growing at faster rates than today. It must be remembered that the rates of deposition of calcite are subject to the same complex environmental factors which affect the rates of solution of calcite (see above discussion). Therefore, some of the great ages for speleothems claimed by cave guides and "spelunkers" may be significantly in error.

A large number of reports concern the rapid growth of stalactites and stalagmites.[17] Most of these observations have been made in tunnels, bridges, dams, mines, or other dated manmade structures which approximate cave conditions. Fisher[18] summarized some of the early literature where stalactite growth averages about 1.25 centimeters (0.5 inch) yearly with some observed to grow over 7.6 centimeters (3 inches) yearly. Stalagmites observed by Fisher grew 0.6 centimer (0.25 inch) in height and 0.9 centimeter (0.36 inch) in diameter at the base each year. At this rate of height increase the 1,900 centimeter tall stalagmite called "Great Dome" in Carlsbad Caverns might grow in less than 4,000 years.

A large stalagmite like Great Dome may contain 100 million cubic centimeters of calcite, which, if accumulated in 4,000 years, would require a deposition rate of 25,000 cubic centimeters (67,000 grams) of calcite yearly. If the dripping water is assumed to deposit 0.5 gram of calcite per liter, 133,000 liters of water would have to drip over the stalagmite each year. Because about 6,000 drops comprise 1 liter, it would take about 800 million drops of water per year to form the stalagmite. This works out to 25 drops of water per second, which is a considerable flow. Whether a stalagmite would be deposited in the above hypothetical situation is not known. One would want to carefully examine the assumptions and the complex environmental factors which might affect stalagmite growth.

In addition to the observations of speleothem growth in cave or cave-like natural environments, some interesting experiments have been performed to simulate stalactite and stalagmite growth in controlled laboratory situations. Williams and Herdklotz[19] are studying the effects of acidity, salinity, temperature, humidity, and other factors on rates of stalactite growth in the laboratory. Their work applies to natural cave environments, and indicates that stalactites can form very rapidly.

A Model for the Origin of Caves

Having examined the processes which can form limestone caves, we are now ready to formulate a model which is consistent with the geologic data and in harmony with a Biblical framework for earth history.[20]

Step 1—Deposition and burial of limestone. The first step for the formation of a cave is obviously to deposit the limestone. Most major limestone strata appear to have accumulated during the Flood. After a lime sediment layer (which later contained a cave) was deposited, it would have been buried rapidly under perhaps several thousand feet of sediments. The weight of overburden would compact the lime sediment and tend to expel interstitial water. Although the fluid pressure would have been great within the sediment, the lack of a direct escape route for the pore water would impede water loss and prevent complete lithification. The major means of water loss was probably through joints which formed during the early stage of compaction while the sediment was only partially consolidated.

Step 2—Deformation and erosion of limestone and overburden. As the Flood waters receded, tectonic activity would deform the sediments and bevel the upper layers down to a new level. The lime sediment layer would again be near the surface. The tectonic forces would induce movement on joints and build up fluid pressure, and the removal of overburden would make compaction in and flow from partially consolidated sediments proceed at faster rates. The pressure gradient would have been highest near the surface, causing sediment to be removed by piping. As the joints were opened, a conduit system for vertical and horizontal flow would have been established.

Step 3—Horizontal groundwater drainage and solution of limestone. After the Flood waters had completely receded, the regional groundwater level would be in disequilibrium and horizontal flow would be significant. Acids from organic decomposition at the surface and at depth would tend to move to just below the water table where the highest horizontal velocities of flow would exist. Solution of newly consolidated limestone would occur chiefly in horizontal conduits at a level just below the water table. The mixing of vadose water (CO_2 rich, oxygen poor, organic rich, and high salinity) would also produce conditions ideal for solution of limestone near the water table. As a result, a cave system would be developed at a certain level.

Step 4—Deposition of speleothems. After the groundwater drainage had been largely accomplished and the caves dissolved out, the water table would be at a lower level and caves would be filled with air, not water. Thus, the final step would be the rapid deposition of stalactites, stalagmites, and flowstone.

Conclusion

Caves are among the most fascinating structures in the earth's crust. The processes which removed material from caves in principle are rather simple, but they were manifest geologically in response to many environmental factors. Deposition in caves was also complex. Although there is much in caves to challenge further study, it appears that they can be interpreted within the basic framework of earth history presented in Scripture.

References

1. Thrailkill, J.F., "Carbonate Chemistry of Aquifer and Stream Water in Kentucky," *Journal of Hydrology,* V. 16, 1972, pp. 93-104.
2. Lange, A. L., "Caves and Cave Systems," in *Encyclopaedia Britannica,* 15th ed., Chicago: Encyclopaedia Britannica, Inc., V. 3, 1977, p. 1026.
3. Moore, G. W., "Limestone Caves," in R. W. Fairbridge (ed.) *The Encyclopedia of Geomorphology,* New York: Reinhold Book Co., 1968, pp. 652-653; Davies, W. E., "Caverns in West Virginia," West Virginia Geol. Survey, Bull. 19A, 1958, p. 330; Thornbury, W. D., *Principles of Geomorphology,* New York: John Wiley, 2nd ed., 1959, pp. 324-331.

4. Davies, W. E., "Cave," in *Encyclopedia Americana,* New York: Americana Corp., V. 6, 1969, p. 101.

5. Further details of these theories can be found in Thornbury, *Principles of Geomorphology,* pp. 324-331 and in Ford, D. C., "The Origin of Limestone Caverns: A Model from the Central Mendip Hills, England," *Nat. Speleological Soc. Bull.,* V. 27, 1965, pp. 109-132.

6. Davis, S. N., "Initiation of Ground Water Flow in Jointed Limestone," *Nat. Speleological Soc. Bull.,* V. 28, 1966, pp. 111-118.

7. Thrailkill, J. V., "Chemical and Hydrologic Factors in the Excavation of Limestone Caves," *Geological Soc. Amer. Bull.,* V. 79, 1968, pp. 19-46; Sipple, R. F. and Glover, E.D., "Solution Alternation of Carbonate Rocks: The Effects of Temperature and Pressure," *Geochimica Cosmochimica Acta,* V. 28, 1964, pp. 1401-1417.

8. Moore, *Encyclopedia of Geomorphology,* pp. 652-653.

9. Kaye, C. A., "The Effect of Solvent Motion on Limestone Solution," *Jour. Geology,* V. 65, 1957, pp. 35-46.

10. U. S. Geological Survey, *The National Atlas of the United States of America,* Washington: Dept. of Interior, 1970, p. 97.

11. *Ibid.,* p. 119.

12. Thrailkill, *Journal of Hydrology,* p. 98. Analyses represent the mean of seven water samples from Mill Hole.

13. For an estimate that a cave 3 by 6 by 120 feet could be dissolved in a single year per square mile, see Swinnerton, A. C., "Origin of Limestone Caverns," *Geological Soc. Amer. Bull.,* V. 43, 1932, pp. 678-679.

14. Thrailkill, *Journal of Hydrology,* p. 98.

15. *Ibid.,* p. 98. Saturation data represent the mean of seven water samples from Mill Hole.

16. Lange, *Encyclopaedia Britannica,* p. 1028.

17. For introduction to various works see several articles in Volumes 14 and 15 of the *Creation Research Society Quarterly,* 1977 and 1978, especially Helmick, L. S., *et al.,* "Rapid Growth of Dripstone Observed," V. 14, 1977, pp. 13-17.

18. Fisher, L. W., "Growth of Stalactites," *American Mineralogist,* V. 19, 1934, pp. 429-431.

19. Williams, E. L., and Kerdklotz, R. J., "Solution and Deposition of Calcium Carbonate in Laboratory Situation," *Creation Research Society Quarterly,* V. 13, 1977, pp. 192-199, V. 15, 1978, pp. 88-91.

20. Williams and Herdklotz (*Ibid.* pp. 197-198) have suggested a similar model. Their model can supplement ideas presented here.

No. 80, February 1980
Does Academic Freedom Apply to Both Secular Humanists and Christians?
By Jerry Bergman, Ph.D. *

A prominent concern among educators in our schools, colleges, and universities is *academic freedom*. Academic freedom is the ability of the instructor to teach what he/she feels is the truth about reality in an intellectually honest and reasonable way. However, a conflict over academic freedom has emerged between proponents of *secular humanism* and those who accept the Christian world view.

The Christian view is based on belief that God made mankind in His image, and that He communicates to us through the Scriptures principles, concepts, and data that we need to build a proper understanding of ourselves, others, and our world. Secular humanism is based on belief that man created God as a projection of his own mind, and that the mind of man is the final arbiter of morality and the only source of information about ourselves, others, and our world.

In the schools secular humanists are allowed to spend a great deal of time presenting their position to students. Yet Christians are discouraged from presenting their position because it is claimed they are *teaching religion*. Many educators assume it is illegal to teach *religion*, for doing so is seen as a violation of separation of church and state. In this controversy, the position of the secular humanists is often labeled *non-religious* and the Christian position *religious*. Then the humanists argue that because their position is labeled *non-religious* or *secular*, it can be taught, and the other side, because it is labeled *religious*, cannot be taught!

---

*   The Author, Dr. Jerry Bergman, is a member of the Department of Educational Foundations & Inquiry at Bowling Green State University in Ohio. His Ph.D. is from Wayne State University in Detroit, majoring in Educational Psychology and Evaluation and Research. He has authored several books and many articles in his field.

ACADEMIC FREEDOM CONFLICT

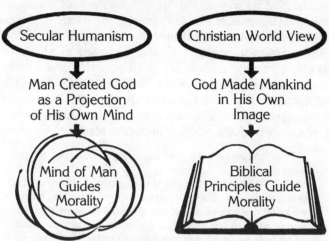

For example, teachers consider it legal to present arguments **against** creation and **for** evolution. In fact, it is often considered inappropriate to criticize evolution, let alone present the creationist position. Rarely do high school or college textbooks discuss the many criticisms and serious problems in evolutionary theory. Only recently have textbooks, such as Stansfield's *The Science of Evolution,* Macmillan, 1977, attempted to be more honest regarding evolution. While Stansfield's textbook does not espouse creationism, it does admit to some of the difficulties in modern evolutionary theory. For example, on page 76 he states:

> During the Cambrian Period there suddenly appeared representatives of nearly all the major groups of animals now recognized. It was as if a giant curtain had been lifted to reveal a world teeming with life in fantastic diversity. The Cambrian "curtain" has become the touchstone of the creation theory. Darwin was aware of the problem this created for evolutionists, and it remains a problem today. Evolutionists keep hoping that new discoveries will eventually fill in the missing pieces of the fossil puzzle, but the chance of success may be less than those of finding the proverbial "needle in the haystack."

There are dozens of books highly critical of evolutionary theory written either by evolutionists or by individuals who at least do not agree with the creationist position. Rarely does this material find its way into college or high school textbooks or libraries. The result is that few students are aware of the many difficulties in evolutionary theory.

The creationist position, if it is discussed at all, is often ridiculed in a way which is not at all objective or scholarly. A number of biologists involved in Ph.D. training programs have told the writer that their graduates are often totally unaware of the existence of viable alternate theories to evolution. One director of a large graduate program in biology stated:

> I personally hold the evolutionary position, but yet lament the fact that the majority of our Ph.D. graduates are frightfully ignorant of many of the serious problems of the evolution theory. These problems will not be solved unless we bring them to the attention of students. Most students assume evolution is proved, the missing link is found, and all we have left is a few rough edges to smooth out. Actually, quite the contrary is true; and many recent discoveries . . . have forced us to reevaluate our basic assumptions.

Students are often grossly ignorant of this research, partly because it does not support the belief structure of humanism. To some degree, the schools serve as apologists for humanism, and therefore also for evolution. They avoid discussing the problems of evolution, possibly because of a fear that the theory will lose credibility if the problems are pointed out. But to strengthen the theory, if that is a worthy goal, the whole theory and each of its many assumptions must be critically examined. In addition, presenting the creationist arguments will help students to understand more objectively what evolutionary theory purports to explain. A good education requires that science students at least be **aware** of the basic theories opposing modern evolution theory. The writer has yet to see an objective presentation of the creationist ideas in **any** standard biology textbook, although, as noted above, a few of the more current books now devote a few pages to creation theory.

The tendency for humanists and the *liberal* press to label ideas which are unpopular as *religion* and thus off limits to teachers is both incorrect and pernicious. Virtually any belief can be labeled *religious,* and virtually anything can be labeled *non-religious.* It is generally thought appropriate for schools to teach "thou shalt not steal, lie, or murder" but inappropriate for them to teach "thou shalt not commit adultery or take the name of God in vain." Somehow the first three prohibitions are not religious, but the last two are. Yet all five are part of the most basic religious law known to the Western world, the Mosaic law covenant. Many concepts commonly taught in the schools clearly have a religious origin. Included would be **the goal of treating others as one would like to be treated, the need to take an occasional break from one's work, to be balanced in all things,** and the **attempt to be fair to all people.**

One of the most ambitious causes of the liberals in recent years has been insuring *equal rights* among all people. Yet this idea was espoused as a religious goal in the writings of the Christian Scriptures over 2,000 years ago. Before the current equal rights trend, this idea would probably have been considered religious; thus, it could not have been taught in the schools. Now that the liberals have espoused this cause, it is no longer seen as a *religious* idea but a *secular* idea. Thus, we can now teach the Christian concept of racial equality. Incidentally, the source of the belief in the equality of man is the Bible, few ancient books espouse this concept, and it is foreign to most non-Christian peoples.

Consider other topics. Rarely do students hear an objective and effective presentation of the case against abortion, homosexuality, or fornication. Again, one side of these issues tends to be labeled *non-religious* and therefore a topic teachers are permitted to discuss, but the other side tends to be labeled *religious,* and off limits in the school. The facts are that, for whatever reason, teachers often indoctrinate their students in **one** side, and many times it is the secular humanist position.

What about teaching religion? The very fact that we usually do not mention religion or religious issues means that we are teaching very definite ideas about religion, especially that religion is not important. A prolonged, conspicuous absence of an idea tends to produce fairly definite attitudes about the idea in most children, and for this reason it is **impossible** for the schools not to teach **something** about religion.

For those concerned about the practicality of this issue, it is clear that religious issues **can** be objectively studied and discussed in the classroom. In Australia, for example, where only 3% of the population attends church regularly, classes in *religious education* are included as an integral part of the school curriculum at all grade levels. An excellent summation of this issue is presented by John Whitehead in *The Separation Illusion* (Mott Media, P.O. Box 236, Milford, Michigan 48042). This book discusses the implication of the fact that religion is going to be taught in the schools in one form or another. It is only a matter of **what** religion is going to be taught, and how it is going to be taught. Once we accept this reality, we can begin to deal with this important area in a manner acceptable to the total community.

Viewing the concept of *religion* broadly, it is impossible to take religion out of the schools because *religion* or its lack, is an integral part of our life and is going to affect our total belief structure and outlook on life. **Anything** that affects our belief structure is going to affect us *religiously*. Religion is a belief structure, and **all** fields of knowledge are based upon belief structures, even though some fields of knowledge include more empirical content than others.

To say that the schools can teach the entire world of knowledge but must exclude religion is censorship of the worst sort. One is not truly free to teach unless one is free to bring **all** areas of knowledge to bear on a subject. There is no academic freedom where every area of knowledge can be taught except one, especially when that one pervades, to some extent, **all** other areas of knowledge.

Parents are rightfully concerned that teachers may attempt to indoctrinate students with a specific religious belief. This is a special concern if the student's religious beliefs happen to be different from the teacher's. While teachers may have some influence on the life of certain students, it must be remembered that students are intelligent, reasoning, thinking persons, and do not gullibly accept all that a teacher may say. Indeed, the experience of many teachers is such that it is **quite difficult** to help students accept even **well-accepted** axioms of science. The writer has had difficulty helping students understand the validity of such basic concepts as the influence of our environment on behavior and the importance of understanding other cultures in order to reduce ethnocentrism.

If a child has strongly ingrained prejudices against certain groups, most teachers find it very difficult to overcome these prejudices. Likewise, if a student holds certain religious beliefs, it is not likely that one teacher is going to be able to change those beliefs. Even if the student is clearly right, confrontation with a teacher may encourage the student to search further into his own beliefs to insure that they are valid. If schools are to be a place where students can debate important questions, it would seem that eliminating religious questions would shelter students from an important area of debate which is crucial for living a well-rounded life. It has been said that the only things important in life are religion and politics. Although this is no doubt an exaggeration of the truth, it seems desirable to spend a great deal **more** time on these areas, and not less.

Many Christians have noted that those who view homosexuality as an acceptable lifestyle openly teach their position in the school (see "The Gay Movement and the Rights of Children" in the *Journal of Social Issues,* V. 34, No. 2, 1978, pp. 137-148). Yet Christians, afraid of being labeled "ultrarightest," "fanatical," or "uninformed," often stand back and say nothing. This is tragic, for the Christian faith requires that Christians speak up intelligently and cogently in presenting the Christian standpoint on these important issues. Christians must support each other and their right to convey their beliefs. Because all too often Christians do not present their position, students are totally unaware of the "other side" on many social issues facing us today. The situation is such that Christians must no longer be afraid to speak out for their position. If they are right, and have thoroughly studied the issue, they have an **obligation** to present their case. This does not mean that one argues for a position only because it is part of his/her tradition, but that one reasons out a firm Christian stand, and responds according to what he/she feels is right.

There is another reason that Christians should speak out. Bondage, sadomasochism, pedophilia, and incest are now being pushed as acceptable sexual behavior by some liberals. The writer is increasingly coming across articles and books which support the position that incest, for example, is not a sexual deviation, but is a normal, healthful, and indeed, can "be a very beautiful relationship as long as the proper steps are taken to prevent conception." This may seem shocking to some, but the crusade for full acceptance of homosexuality likewise seemed shocking just a few years ago. Today, even in nominally Christian publications, articles approving homosexuality as an acceptable life style are common, or there are even arguments that homosexuals fully qualify as ministers of God (see *Christianity and Crisis*, V. 37, Nos. 9, 10). The same could also occur with incest, and there are several signs that this is already taking place. For example, one "Christian" journal argued that there is nothing wrong with incest, even incest with young children. The journal felt that society's outdated cultural taboos are the problem and "once these are overcome, we can enjoy sexual pleasures with people of the same sex, the opposite sex, animals, children, or any other sexual object, and then enjoy the best of **all** of the sexual worlds. A person well adjusted sexually is one who can fully enjoy the **full range of sexual behavior** available to mankind today requiring full sexual adjustment without any hangups caused by outdated religious concepts. And our schools are the main tool used to teach the young people this human freedom." (Emphasis added.)

If Christians did openly speak out in defense of their beliefs, it is likely that there would be repercussions in many schools, including denial of tenure (as has already happened in a number of cases) and outright firings. The case of a Christian teacher who lost his job in a private religious school because he taught creationism in his science classes received much publicity recently. There have been many similar cases throughout the country, although, interestingly, most of these have been in religious schools.

The plight of Christian teachers should merit the attention of a Christian organization such as the Christian Legal Society. A group of attorneys familiar with the law should be able to help their brothers fight for academic freedom. Furthermore, legal publications could inform Christians of their rights and the legal recourses available in case they are threatened with loss of their jobs or are denied the freedom to express a Christian viewpoint. Of course, it is necessary to act tactfully and respectfully, showing awareness that differing positions generally each have some merit. The efforts in many schools to silence one side totally are clearly inappropriate and demand an intelligent, but kind and calm, response.

In addition, Christians must not be afraid of responding by letter to material which seems inaccurately presented, biased, or incorrect. The writer has often come across position statements which contain glaring errors which it seems were deliberately penned to justify a certain position on an issue. For example, the writer responded by letter to an article in *McCall's Magazine* about homosexuality, part of which is printed below:

> I am totally at a loss as to how you arrived at your conclusions in your article on "How School Principals Feel About Homosexuality" (June 1978 issue). You state that 7% of the principals reported complaints of homosexual contact between teachers and students compared to 13% complaining of heterosexual contact. This is a ratio of 35 complaints about homosexuality out of every 100 complaints. In view of the fact that according to the best estimates, 5% of the population are exclusively homosexuals, your data would indicate that homosexuals are 7 times more likely to seduce students than heterosexuals. Yet you conclude that "homosexual teachers are less likely to molest students than heterosexual teachers." In spite of the fact that I have a Ph.D. in research and statistics, I am unable to understand your conclusions. Further, I realize that many writers are anxious to serve as apologists for homosexuality and, possibly as a result of these efforts, I have noticed a number of gross statistical and thinking fallacies in their reasoning. Please respond to the above comments.

Over one year later, *McCall's* has not replied to my letter. Hopefully, they will at least be aware of this problem and, perhaps, less likely to make this error in the future. While it is difficult for Christians to respond to a large number of articles, we could intelligently respond to blatant errors, or at least ill-founded attacks against Christianity. If each Christian did so, there would probably be far less publicly accepted incorrect information. Although this would undoubtedly not solve the problem of fair treatment for differing views, it should help considerably.

In particular, there is a clear legal freedom to teach the traditional Christian values, as at least one among other viewpoints. To take advantage of this freedom by voice or letter, it is imperative that Christians be well informed, well read, and insistent on their rights. There are excellent works put out by Christian book publishers written by reputable scholars on almost any area that would concern an educator. This awareness is necessary in order for a Christian to properly **"make a defense for the faith that is within us."**

No. 81, March 1980
Theistic Evolution and the Day-Age Theory
By Richard Niessen *

The Alleged Basis for the Day-Age Theory

Two elements are essential in any evolutionary scheme, whether it be theistic or atheistic: long periods of time and the assumed validity of the **molecules-to-man** evolutionary scenario. Atheists care little for the biblical account, except to ridicule its statements. Theistic evolutionists, however, profess a certain allegiance to the Scriptures and must attempt to harmonize the biblical account with the evolutionary scenario. The biblical text, at least to the unbiased observer, indicates a universe and earth that were formed in six days; evolutionists suppose at least six billion years. The mechanism by which theistic evolutionists harmonize the two is known as the **day-age theory.**

The key term in this attempted harmony is the word **day** as it

---

*   The author, Mr. Richard Niessen, is Associate Professor of Apologetics at Christian Heritage College, El Cajon, California, and is a popular lecturer on Bible-science topics. He received his B.A., Th.B. (with honors) from the Northeastern Bible College, N.J.; his M.A. (cum laude) was earned at Trinity Evangelical Divinity School, Illinois; and he is currently a Ph.D. candidate.

is used in Genesis 1. The Hebrew word for **day** is *yom,* and, we are reminded, it is used in a variety of ways: (1) the daylight period in the diurnal cycle as in Genesis 1:5, 14, 16, 18; (2) a normal 24-hour period; and (3) an indefinite time period as in Psalm 90:10.

A passage that is invariably appealed to is II Peter 3:8: "One day is with the Lord as a thousand years and a thousand years as one day." Also, it is claimed that too much activity took place on the sixth day (Genesis 2) to fit into a normal day: Adam's naming of thousands of animals, his perception of his loneliness, and the subsequent creation of Eve.

The claim, then, is that the **days** of Genesis 1 are really long periods of time, which correspond to the major periods of evolutionary geological history.

A Refutation of the Day-Age Theory

Most Bible-believing creationists maintain the day-age theory is an unbiblical option for the following reasons:

An improper interpretation of II Peter 3:8.

It is axiomatic in hermeneutics (the science of biblical interpretation) that "a text without a context is a pretext." Just as a tape recording can be edited to make the speaker say whatever the editor desires, so the Scriptures can be juggled to suit a person's fancy or predisposition. For example, "And Jesus answered . . . 'What is truth?' " (John 18:37-38). All the above words are straight from the Bible, but a closer examination discloses that it was actually Pilate who uttered the statement, and that the intervening words have been "edited" out.

II Peter 3:3-10 is a unit. The context speaks of scoffers in the last days who will ridicule the second coming of Christ. Their rationale is uniformitarian in nature: Jesus promised to come quickly, He has not come yet, therefore He is not going to come at all. Peter refutes these uniformitarian assumptions with a reference to the Flood and the certainty of judgment for these scoffers. Then, responding to the charge that Christ has failed to fulfill His promise, Peter writes the words in question, and concludes by reaffirming the certainty of the second coming of Christ.

Verse 8 was never intended to be a mathematical formula of $1 = 1000$ or $1000 = 1$. The point is that God created time, as well as the universe, and therefore stands above it (cf. Heb. 1:2). While we mortals think 1000 years is a long time, God can scan 1000 years of history—past and future—as quickly as we can scan from one end of the horizon to the other. The verse could have equally been worded, "Five minutes is with the Lord as ten thousand years," and still have conveyed the same message. Note the use of the word as, describing similarity, is not the same as an equal sign. Conversely, God is able to do in one day what would normally require a thousand years to accomplish. A pertinent suggestion here, in light of the passage's reference to Creation and the Flood, is a possible allusion to the Flood's rapid buildup of the sedimentary layers of the so-called **geologic column.** One day's Flood activity could build up layers of sediments that would normally take a thousand years to form by uniformitarian (slowly acting) processes.

II Peter 3:8 has nothing whatever to do with the length of the creation week. Genesis 1 needs to be interpreted in its own context and not by an irrelevant verse written 1500 years later.

The inadequacy of a thousand-year *day.*

Let us grant, for the sake of discussion, the mathematical formula that the theistic evolutionists desire. In that case, day one is the first thousand years of earth's history, day two the second thousand years, etc. Consistency would logically dictate that each of the six periods be the same length, resulting in a 6000-year period of creation from nothing to Adam. But 6000 years is only a drop in the bucket compared to the time required to make the evolutionary system work. A lack of a vast time period is the death knell of the evolutionary process. So, let us try 1 day equals 10,000 years. No, 60,000 years is not enough time either. How about 1 day equals 100,000 years? 1 million years? 10 million years? 100 million years? 1 billion years? Ah, yes, that does it for the required time! But what does it do to language as a tool to communicate meaningful information? If words have this kind of infinite flexibility, then the art of communication is indeed a lost cause. These tactics would be laughed to scorn if they were attempted in any other field of study. We should certainly not tolerate them in the study of God's Word.

It appears that II Peter 3:8 is merely the wedge used to get the camel's head into the tent. The Hebrew word *olam* was available to communicate the idea of a long time period if Moses had intended to convey that idea. And the Hebrew word *yom* was available had he wanted to convey the idea of a 24-hour day.

The demands of primary word usage.

Every language has certain words that are used in different contexts with different meanings. For example, *Webster's Dictionary* defines the noun **ship** as follows:

> ship (n) 1: a large seagoing boat 2: airplane 3: a ship's officers and crew.

If you were able to see the noun form of ship, in isolation and without a context, which of the three definitions would first come to mind? Obviously the definition listed as #1, or the primary definition of the word. If the context absolutely demanded it, #3 could be used, but it would certainly be an unusual usage of the word.

It is likewise in the biblical languages. The lexicons (Greek and Hebrew dictionaries) list the words and then the definitions in descending order of usage. The translation of Greek and Hebrew is not accomplished by the casting of lots, nor by the spin of a roulette wheel. The primary usage of any term is always given priority in any translation and secondary uses are tried only when the primary usage does not make sense in the context in which the term is set.

The Hebrew word *yom* is used more than 2000 times in the Old Testament. A cursory examination reveals that in over 1900 cases (95%) the word is clearly used of a 24-hour day, or of the daylight portion of a normal day. Many of the other 5% refer to expressions such as "the day of the Lord" (Joel 2:1) which may not be exceptions at all, since the second coming of Christ will occur on one particular day (I Cor. 15:51-52), even though His reign extends over a longer period of time.[1] Therefore, even without a context, an unbiased translator would normally understand the idea of "24-hour period" for the word *yom*.

The demands of context.

Words generally do not hang in space and in isolation from other words. When they appear in writing, they are always surrounded by other words which serve as modifiers and/or clarifiers. Let us take the word **ship** used as an illustration in the last point. It is only necessary to add two words to not only differentiate between the noun and the verb forms, but to clarify which of the uses is intended within that form. For example: "The ship flew." The definite article identifies the form as a noun; the verb identifies the secondary usage of the word as an airplane rather than a boat.

We need not belabor the point by multiplying examples here. If I write: "I spaded the garden on my day off," it is clear from the surrounding words that this activity is confined to one particular day. So it is in Genesis 1: all the surrounding words convey, to the unbiased reader, the idea that each activity is confined to one of the particular 24-hour days of this creation week.

The numerical qualifier demands a 24-hour day.

The word "day" appears over 200 times in the Old Testament with numbers (*i.e.,* first day, second day, etc.). In every single case, without exception, it refers to a 24-hour day. Each of the six days of the creation week is so qualified and therefore the consistency of Old Testament usage requires a 24-hour day in Genesis 1 as well.

The terms "evening and morning" require a 24-hour day.

The words evening (52 times) and **morning** (220 times) always refer to normal days where they are used elsewhere in the Old Testament. The Jewish day **began** in the evening (sunset) and **ended** with the start of the evening the following day. Thus it is appropriate that the sequence is **evening-morning** (of a normal day) rather than **morning-evening** (= start and finish). The literal Hebrew is even more pronounced: "There was evening and there was morning, day one . . . . There was evening and there was morning, day two," etc.

The words "day" and "night" are part of a normal 24-hour day.

In Genesis 1:5, 14-18, the words **day** and **night** are used nine times in such a manner that they can refer only to the light and dark periods of a normal 24-hour day.

Genesis 1:14 distinguishes between days, years, and seasons.

> And God said, "Let there be light-makers in the expanse above to divide the day from the night, and let them be for signs, and for the determination of *seasons* and for *days* and for *years.*"

Clearly the word **days** here represents days, **years** represents years, **seasons** represents seasons.

It is a **red herring** to claim that, if the sun did not appear until the fourth day, there could be no days and nights on the first three days. The Bible clearly says that there was a light source (apparently temporary in nature, Genesis 1:3), that there were periods of alternating light and darkness (1:4-5), and that there were evenings and mornings for those first three days (1:5, 8, 13).

Symbiosis requires a 24-hour day.

Symbiosis is a biological term describing a mutually beneficial relationship between two types of creatures. Of particular interest to us are the species of plants that cannot reproduce apart from the habits of certain insects or birds. For example, the yucca plant is dependent upon the yucca moth, and most flowers require bees or other insects for pollination and reproduction. The *Calvaria* tree, on the Mauritius Islands, was totally dependent upon the dodo bird to ingest its seeds, scarify its hard coating, and excrete the seeds before germination could take place. Since the dodo bird became extinct in 1681, no reproduction of this tree has taken place. In fact, the youngest trees are 300 years old! Many additional examples could be cited.

According to Genesis 1, plants were created on the third day (vv. 9-13), birds on the fifth day (vv. 20-23), and insects on the sixth day (vv. 24-25, 31). Plants could have survived for 48 or 72 hours without the birds and the bees, but could they have survived 2-3 billion years without each other according to the day-age scenario? Many birds eat only insects. Could they have survived a billion years while waiting for the insects to evolve?[2] Hardly.

The survival of the plants and animals requires a 24-hour day.

If each **day** were indeed a billion years, as theistic evolutionists require, then half of that **day** (500 million years) would have been dark. We are explicitly told in verse 5 that the light was called **day** and the darkness was called **night**, and that each day had one period of **light-darkness**. How then would the plants, insects, and animals have survived through each 500-million-year stretch of darkness? Clearly a 24-hour day is called for.

The testimony of the Fourth Commandment.

It is a marvelous thing to observe the unity of the Scriptures and the orderliness with which God carries out His plans. Have you ever wondered why there were six days of creation, rather

than some other number? In the light of the apparently instantaneous creation of the new heavens and new earth of Revelation
21, and the instantaneous nature of the miracles of the New
Testament, why is it that God takes **as long as** six days to create
everything? And why is it that God **rested** on the seventh day?
Was He tired after all this exertion? No, Psalm 33:6-9 state that
"the heavens were made by the Word of the Lord . . . . He
spoke and it was done. He commanded and it stood fast." There
is no hint of exertion here. Genesis 2:2-3 merely means that He
ceased working because the created order was completed, not
because He was tired.

The commentary on these questions is found in Exodus
20:8-11, and it reads as follows:

> verse 8—Remember the sabbath **day**, to keep it holy.
> verse 9—**Six days** you shall *labor* and do all your work,
> verse 10—But the **seventh day** is the sabbath (rest) of the
>   Lord your God. In it you shall not do any
>   work . . .
> verse 11—**For** in **six days** the Lord **made** heaven and earth,
>   the sea, and all that is in them and rested on the
>   **seventh day** . . . .

Verses 8-10 speak of man working six days and ceasing from
his work on the seventh. These are obviously not eons of time,
but normal 24-hour days. A key word in verse 11 is **for**, because
it introduces the rationale or foundation for the previous com-
mand. It continues by equating the time period of creation with
the time period of man's work week (six days plus one day) and
states that God Himself had set the example in Genesis 1. That
indeed is the reason why the creation week was 7 days—no
more, no less. The passage becomes nonsense if it reads: "Work
for six days and rest on the seventh, because God worked for six
billion years and is now resting during the seventh billion-year
period." If God is resting, who parted the waters of the Red Sea
in Exodus 14? And what did Jesus mean in John 5:17 when He
said, "My Father is working until now, and I myself am
working"?

Sometimes the claim is made by theistic evolutionists that we
do not know how long the days were way back in Genesis 1. In
the first place, Genesis 1 was not **way back**, but was only a few
thousand years prior to the writing of Exodus. Since the earth is

constantly slowing down in its rotation, the early earth would have been spinning faster and therefore the days would have been shorter, not longer.

But the day-age people have overlooked something even more obvious here: Genesis 1 and Exodus 20 were written by the same author—Moses—at about the same time (ca. 1500 B.C.). Therefore, the common authorship of both passages is evidence that he had the same time period in mind when he used the word **day**. Furthermore, we might note that the Fourth Commandment was actually written by the finger of God Himself on tablets of stone (Ex. 31:18; 32:16-19; 34:1, 28, 29; Deut. 10:4). If anyone should have known how long the days were, it should be the Creator Himself!

The testimony of the rabbis.

The Talmudic literature contains commentaries on virtually every passage in the Old Testament. The liberties they take in interpreting some passages boggle the imagination and yet one thing is certain: they are unanimous in accepting a normal, 24-hour day for Genesis 1. If there were the slightest grammatical or contextual indicator within that chapter that would point to a longer period, you can be sure they would have spotted it and developed it at length. The fact that they do not is a strong testimony for interpreting the days as normal, 24-hour periods.

The testimony of the church fathers.

It is sometimes claimed that the church fathers believed in long ages for the days in Genesis 1. That is a half truth. The only two who held to this view were Origen and Clement of Alexandria, and they were allegorizers who devised unusual interpretations for every part of Scripture. Their system of allegorizing led to the most unbelievable interpretations, which were bounded only by the limits of their fertile imaginations.

Other early commentators on Genesis 1 include the Epistle of Barnabas, Irenaeus, and Justin Martyr. Their remarks have frequently been misunderstood to mean that they believed in the day-age theory. That is not true. What they were doing was developing an eschatological framework which included a literal 1000-year reign of Christ on earth (the millennium). Their logic followed these lines:

a. God worked for six days and rested on the seventh.

    b. One day is with the Lord as a thousand years (cf.
       II Peter 3:8).
    c. The six days of creation and one day of rest therefore
       typify the six thousand years of human history that will
       be concluded by the one-thousand-year millennium, fol-
       lowed by eternity. Creation took place on 4000 B.C.,
       therefore the millennium should commence on A.D.
       2000, terminate on A.D. 3000, and usher in the timeless
       period of eternity.

Whether of not we agree with their reasoning and the resulting prophetic framework, we conclude that these early church fathers were not denying the literal six-day creation, but were affirming their faith in it.

The view of the Reformers (Luther, Calvin, etc.) is that of a six-day creation, of 24 hours apiece.

Thomas Scott's commentary of 1780 generally mentions varying interpretations where they exist, but says nothing about any possibility of the "days" being other than 24-hour periods.

It is only since the middle of the nineteenth century that commentators began talking about long periods of time within Genesis 1 itself. That is truly amazing! The Pentateuch was written by Moses in 1500 B.C. The day-age theory is not mentioned by any serious biblical scholar until the 1800's A.D. For 3300 years this supposed secret lay hidden awaiting the craftiness of nineteenth-century scholarship to unlock its mysteries and reveal them to a waiting world! Something is wrong here. Either God does not know how to express Himself very clearly, or three thousand years' worth of biblical scholars were blind for failing to see this obvious truth, or . . . the whole day-age theory is nothing more than a modern contrivance.

Is there some event in the mid 1800's that would tie in with this? Indeed, there is. It was at this time that Darwin's *Origin of Species,* Lyell's *Principles of Geology,* and other evolutionary treatises were flooding the marketplace, resulting in a widespread popular acceptance of the major tenets of evolution. Instead of holding their ground and insisting on the authenticity of God's account of origins, many theologians made the evolutionary theory the criterion of truth and practically fell over each other in their wild scramble to compromise the biblical account of origins with the speculations of nineteenth-century atheists and agnostics. Where it comes to a contest between the Bible and the theories of men, it seems that there are always those who will lean over backward to make sure the Bible gets the short end of the stick.

The theological problem of sin and death.

According to theistic evolutionists, plant and animal life flourished and died at least 500 million years before man evolved. Their deaths have been recorded as the fossil remains embedded in the sedimentary rocks of the so-called **geologic column**.

Romans 5:12, however, does not agree: "Therefore as through one man sin entered into the world, and death through sin, so death passed to all men, because all have sinned."

The passage then goes on to identify Adam as the **one man** referred to in verse 12. There is nothing ambiguous about the passage; it means exactly what it says: Adam was the first man, and there was no death prior to the Garden of Eden incident recorded in Genesis 3. Either theistic evolution and its day-age theory are wrong, or Romans 5:12 is in error. There is no harmonizing or fence-straddling here; one must make a choice between holding to theistic evolution or believing the plain statements in the Bible.

There is yet another lesson to be learned from this New Testament passage. There is a tendency among neo-evangelicals today to make a false dichotomy between the Bible's statements of **faith and practice** and statements pertaining to **science and history**. The former, we are told, are accurate; the latter are riddled with errors of fact. This view is also known as the **partial inspiration** or **limited inerrancy** view of inspiration.

Romans 5:12 shows that the above is untenable because the passage bases a theological doctrine (man's sin) upon a historical event (Adam's fall). Likewise, I Cor. 15:45 bases the doctrine of the resurrection upon the historicity of Adam as the first man. Many other examples could be cited, but the lesson is clear: the theology ("faith and practice") of the Christian life is inseparably linked to and interwoven with the historicity and scientific validity of the narrative portions of Scripture. To deny one is to deny the other.

The feasibility of the events of the sixth day.

One problem seems to be: **how could Adam have named all the animals in one day?** There are two factors to consider here.

First, only a limited number of animals are required. The purpose of parading this entourage of animals before Adam appears to have been to demonstrate to him that man was an entirely different order of creation than the animal kingdom and that none of them could ever serve as a physical and psychological companion to him. This obviously eliminates most of the organisms of the earth: insects, mice, lizards, and fish need not even apply for the position. Since God selected the animals here, He probably limited the number of candidates to those who would even conceivably be suitable. The text itself limits them to "all cattle, and to the fowl of the air, and to every beast of the field" (Genesis 2:20).

Second, Adam must have had an extremely high intelligence. Because Adam was capable of using 100 percent of his pre-Fall brain, he would probably have had an IQ of 1500 or better. Furthermore, Adam did not have to learn his vocabulary: God programmed it into his brain at the moment of his creation, and he was created as a fully functioning person. It was therefore with the utmost facility that Adam named the animals that were brought before him.

The second problem is due to a misreading of the biblical text where it says in Genesis 2:18 that "it is not good that the man should be alone." Being alone is not the same as being lonely. The latter requires some time; the former does not.

Unless one is predisposed, because of outside assumptions (evolution), to find fault with the passage, there is nothing inherently unreasonable about the events occurring on one normal 24-hour day, as indicated.

Conclusion

Much could be said about the scientific fallacies of the evolution model and the scientific superiority of the creation model[3] but that is beyond the scope of this essay. The emphasis here has been on the professing Christian who is attempting to unequally yoke together two entirely opposing scenarios (creation and evolution) and who is using an unscriptural methodology (the day-age theory) to accomplish this unholy matrimony.

Ecclesiastes 4:12 speaks about a three-fold cord being not easily broken. This essay has woven together a fifteen-fold cord that is not easily broken. The day-age theory, according to the above evidence, is not permitted by Scripture and is therefore false. Elijah said, "How long will you waver between two opinions . . . " (I Kings 18:21). Each of us needs to decide where he stands on this vital issue.

References

1. There are very few, if any, of these "exceptions" that actually require the meaning of a period of time other than a solar day.
2. Note that the order of the Bible is not the order required by evolution. See the writer's article "Significant Discrepancies Between Theistic Evolution and the Bible," *Christian Heritage Courier,* August, 1979. Also see John C. Whitcomb's book *The Early Earth* (1972), and Henry M. Morris' book *Biblical Cosmology and Modern Science* (1970)—both available from CLP Publishers, P. O. Box 15666, San Diego, CA 92115.
3. See Henry M. Morris, *Scientific Creationism* (San Diego: CLP Publishers, 1974).

No. 82, April 1980
The Sun is Shrinking
By Russell Akridge, Ph.D. *

Observations

Does the size of the sun change over the years? Recently, "John A. Eddy [Harvard-Smithsonian Center for Astrophysics and High Altitude Observatory in Boulder] and Aram A. Boor-

---

* The author, Dr. Russell Akridge, earned his B.S., M.S., and Ph.D. degrees in physics from Georgia Tech. He earned the Th.M. degree from the New Orleans Baptist Theological Seminary. Dr. Akridge is an Assistant Professor of Physics at Oral Roberts University. He has written several articles in the *Creation Research Society Quarterly* in which he shows that the laws of physics support a recent creation.

Dr. Akridge and his wife, Anita, have two children, Floyd and Sheryl. They live in Tulsa, Oklahoma.

nazian [a mathematician with S. Ross and Co. in Boston] have found evidence that the sun has been contracting about 0.1% per century . . . corresponding to a shrinkage rate of about 5 feet per hour."[1] The diameter of the sun is close to one million miles, so that this shrinkage of the sun goes unnoticed over hundreds or even thousands of years. There is no cause for alarm for us or for any of our descendants for centuries to come because the sun shrinks so slowly. Yet the sun does actually appear to shrink. The data Eddy and Boornazian examined spanned a 400-year period of solar observation, so that this shrinkage of the sun, though small, is apparently continual.

Interpretation

What does the shrinkage of the sun have to do with creation and evolution? The sun was larger in the past than it is now by 0.1% per century. A creationist, who may believe that the world was created approximately 6 thousand years ago, has very little to worry about. The sun would have been only 6% larger at creation than it is now. However, if the rate of change of the solar radius remained constant, 100 thousand years ago the sun would be twice the size it is now. One could hardly imagine that any life could exist under such altered conditions. Yet 100 thousand years is a minute amount of time when dealing with evolutionary time scales.[2]

How far back in the past must one go to have a sun so large that its surface touches the surface of the earth? The solar radius changes at 2.5 feet per hour (half the 5 feet per hour change of the solar diameter). The distance from the sun to the earth is 93 million miles, and there are 5,280 feet in one mile. Assuming (by uniformitarian-type reasoning) that the rate of shrinkage has not changed with time, then the surface of the sun would touch the surface of the earth at a time in the past equal to

$$t = \frac{(93{,}000{,}000 \text{ miles } (5{,}280 \text{ ft/mile})}{(2.5 \text{ ft/hr}) (24 \text{ hr/day}) (365 \text{ day/yr})}$$

or approximately 20 million B.C. However, the time scales required for organic evolution range from 500 million years to 2,000 million years.[3] It is amazing that all of this evolutionary development, except the last 20 million years, took place on a planet that was *inside* the sun. By 20 million B.C., all of evolution had occurred except the final stage, the evolution of the primate into man.

One must remember that the 20 million B.C. date is the extreme limit on the time scale for the earth's existence. The time at which the earth first emerged from the shrinking sun is 20 million B.C. A more reasonable limit is the 100 thousand year B.C. limit set by the time at which the size of the sun should have been double its present size.

A further word of explanation is needed about the assumption that the rate of shrinkage of the sun is constant over 100 thousand years or over 20 million years. The shrinkage rate centuries ago would be determined by the balance of solar forces. Since the potential energy of a homogeneous spherical sun varies inversely with the solar radius, the rate of shrinkage would have been greater in the past than it is now. The time at which the sun was twice its present size is less than 100 thousand B.C. The time at which the surface of the sun would touch the earth is much less than 20 million B.C. Therefore, the assumption of a constant shrinkage rate is a conservative assumption.

Solar Energy

The shrinkage of the sun greatly alters what we believe to be the energy source within the sun. The sun shrinks because of its own self-gravitational attraction. As it compresses itself, it heats itself. This heat is then liberated in the form of solar radiation, i.e., sunlight.

Would a 2.5 feet per hour contraction of the solar surface be sufficient to liberate all of the energy that comes from the sun? A crude estimate can be made by assuming the interior of the sun is uniform. The known formula[4] for the gravitational potential energy of two masses m and M a distance r apart is $U = -GmM/r$, where $G = 6.6 \times 10^{-11} jm/kg^2$. The gravitational potential energy of the sun's mass M_s interacting with its own mass M_s is $U = Gm_s^2/R$, where R is the radius of the sun. The solar power produced as the sun shrinks at the rate of $v = R/t$ is[5] $P = U/t = (Gm_s^2/R^2) \cdot (R/t) = GM_s^2v/R^2$. The mass of the sun is $2 \times 10^{30} kg$, the radius of the sun is $7 \times 10^8 m$, and the 2.5 feet/hour rate of shrinkage in the radius of the sun is 2×10^{-4}m/sec. in metric units. The power formula gives a potential solar power of 1×10^{29} watts. This potential gravitational power is hundreds of times *more* than the 4×10^{26} watts of power actually produced by the sun. This figure is an overestimate because the sun is actually far from uniform. The massive interior of the sun is protected by the outer layers of the sun. Only those low density outer layers are thought to contract. Even so, there is plenty of gravitational contraction energy potentially available to account for all or a large part of the sun's energy.

Stellar Evolution Shaken

One thing is certain. *Some* of the sun's energy comes from its gravitational self-collapse. Therefore, not all of this energy comes from thermonuclear fusion. This discovery greatly alters all calculations on the evolution of the sun, because all those calculations attribute practically 100% of the sun's energy over the past 5 billion years to thermonuclear fusion. The discovery that the sun is shrinking may prove to be the downfall of the accepted theory of solar evolution. All accepted theories of the evolution of the stars are based on the assumption that thermonuclear fusion is the energy source for the stars. If this assumption is unjustified for our own star, the sun, it is unjustified for the other stars too. The entire theoretical description of the evolution of the universe may be at stake. With the stakes that high, it is no wonder that the experimental evidence for the shrinkage of the sun is "explained away" by evolutionists. Evolutionists claim that the sun probably undergoes temporary shrinkages and expansions as small fluctuating oscillations on its overall regular evolutionary development.[6] They point to other cyclic solar occurrences such as the 11-year sunspot cycle on the surface of the sun. This claim is made in spite of the evidence that the shrinkage rate of the sun has remained essentially constant over the past 100 years when very accurate measurements have been made on the size of the sun. Less accurate astronomical records spanning the past 400 years indicate the shrinkage rate has remained the same for the past 400 years.

Historically Speaking

Scientists have not always attributed the energy source of the sun to thermonuclear fusion. Prior to the discovery of thermonuclear fusion, Helmholtz predicted that the energy of the sun was supplied by the gravitational collapse of the sun.[7] This model was accepted until the theory of evolution began to dominate the scientific scene. Then Helmholtz's explanation was discarded because it did not provide the vast time span demanded by the theory of organic evolution on the earth. The substitute theory was introduced by Bethe in the 1930's precisely because thermonuclear fusion was the only known energy source that would last over the vast times required by evolution. Science may now be on the verge of disproving the substitute evolutionary model of the sun.

Conclusion

The change in the size of the sun over the past 400 years is important in the study of origins. Over 100 thousand years these changes would have accumulated so much that life of any kind on the earth would have been very difficult, if not impossible. Thus, all life on the earth must be less than 100 thousand years old. The sun, 20 million years ago, would have been so large that it would have engulfed the earth. The earth cannot be more than 20 million years old. Those dates as upper limits rule out any possibility of evolution requiring hundreds of millions of years. However, the tiny change that would have occurred in the sun during the Biblical time since creation would be so small as to go almost unnoticed. Thus, the changes in the sun are consistent with recent creation.

The changes detected in the sun call into question the accepted thermonuclear fusion energy source for the sun. This, in turn, questions the entire theoretical structure upon which the evolutionary theory of astrophysics is built.

References

1. Lubkin, Gloria B., *Physics Today*, V. 32, No. 17, 1979.
2. Ordway, Richard J., *Earth Science and the Environment*, New York: D. Van Nostrand, 1974, p. 130. Fig. 5-23 on this page gives a good illustration of the accepted evolutionary time scale.
3. *Scientific American*, V. 239, No. 3, 1978. All articles in this edition

list the various evolutionary time scales.

4. Halliday, David and Resnick, Robert, *Fundamentals of Physics,* New York: Wiley, 1974, Chapter 14.
5. The exact formula must be derived layer by layer using integral calculus. The result is identical to the formula listed, except that it contains an additional factor. The additional factor is so close to unity that it makes little difference in an estimation.
6. Lubkin, p. 18.
7. Poppy, Willard J. and Wilson, Leland L., *Exploring the Physical Sciences,* Englewood Cliffs: Prentice Hall, 1973, p. 324.

———————————◆———————————

No. 83, May 1980
Noah and Human Etymology
By Bengt Sage*

As traditions of the universal flood spread around the world with the post-Ararat migrations, the venerable name of Noah traveled with them.[1] This seems especially evident by way of the ancient Sanskrit language and the name *Manu.* The Sanskrit term may in turn have come from an equivalent word in the so-called "Proto-Indo-European" language.

Manu was the name of the flood hero in the traditions of India. He, like Noah, is said to have built an ark in which eight people were saved. It is highly probable that Noah and Manu were thus the same individual. "Ma" is an ancient word for "water," so that Manu could mean "Noah of the waters." In the Hebrew Old Testament, the words "water" and "waters"

*   The author, Bengt Sage, is an Australian businessman whose avocation is the study of languages and etymology. He was born in Sweden and, in his younger days, traveled to every continent in the merchant navy. He received a diploma in Bible through correspondence studies in the Spanish language, and became committed to creationism as a result of reading *The Bible and Modern Science* in its Spanish translation.

are both translations of *mayim,* with the syllable *yim* being the standard Hebrew plural ending.

The "ma" prefix could well be the original form of *mar* and *mer* (Spanish and French for "sea," both from the Latin *mare*) and thus of such English words as "marine."

In Sanskrit, the name *Manu* appropriately came to mean "man" or "mankind" (since Manu, or Noah, was the father of all post-flood mankind). The word is related to the Germanic *Mannus,*[2] the founder of the West Germanic peoples. Mannus was mentioned by the Roman historian Tacitus in his book *Germania.*[3] Mannus is also the name of the Lithuanian Noah.[4] Another Sanskrit form *manusa* is closely related to the Swedish *manniska,*[5] both words meaning "human being."

The same name may even be reflected in the Egyptian *Menes* (founder of the first dynasty of Egypt) and *Minos* (founder and first king of Crete). Minos was also said in Greek mythology to be the son of Zeus and ruler of the sea.[6]

The English word "man" is thus also related to the Sanskrit *manu,* as well as its equivalents in other Germanic languages. Gothic, the oldest known Germanic language, used the form *Manna,* and also *gaman* ("fellow man").

The name *Anu* appears in Sumerian as the god of the firmament, and the rainbow was called "the great bow of Anu,"[7] which seems a clear reference to Noah (note Genesis 9:13). In Egyptian mythology *Nu* was the god of waters who sent an inundation to destroy mankind.[8] Nu and his consort *Nut* were deities of the firmament and the rain. Nu was identified with the primeval watery mass of heaven, his name also meaning "sky."[9]

In Africa, the king of the Congo (the Congo Empire once included the entire Congo basin, now incorporating the territories of Angola, Zaire, Cabinda, and the Congo Republic) was called *Mani Congo.* "Mani" was a noble rank given to great chiefs, ministers, governors, priests, and the king himself. This empire, in fact, was once called the Manikongo Empire.[10]

In Europe, the prefix "ma" seems often to have taken the form *da,* which is an old word for "water" or "river." This led to the name "Don" in England and Russia and "Danube" in the Balkans. The first Greeks living in the coastal regions were called *Danaoi,* or "water people."[11] Variants of the name Danube have included Donau, Dunaj, Duna, Dunau, and

Dunay. The root of all of these names is *danu,* which means "river" or "flowing."[12] The Latvian river Dvina was formerly called Duna, so it also is from the same Indo-European root word *danu.* The similarity of *danu* to *manu* is evident.[13]

From India, the Sanskrit "manu" also traveled east. In Japan, "manu" became "maru," a word which is included in the name of most Japanese ships. In ancient Chinese mythology, the god Hakudo Maru came down from heaven to teach people how to make ships. This name could well relate to Noah, the first shipbuilder.

The custom of including "maru" in the names of Japanese ships seems to have started between the 12th and 14th centuries. In the late 16th century, the warlord Hideyoshi built Japan's first really large ship, calling it "Nippon Maru." In Japanese "maru" also seems to mean a round enclosure, or circle of refuge, so that the circle is considered to be a sign of good fortune. Noah's ark, of course, had been the first great enclosure of refuge.

The aboriginals of Japan are called *Ainu,* a word which means "man."[14] The word *mai* denotes "aboriginal man" in some of the Australian aboriginal languages. In Hawaii, *mano* is the word for "shark," as well as the name for the shark god. A hill on the island of Molokai is named Puu Mano ("hill of the shark god").[15] The word for "mountain" is *mauna,* and it may also be that Hawaii's great volcanic mountains *(Mauna Loa,* for example, is the largest and most active volcano in the world) reminded its first settlers of Mount Ararat, also a great volcanic mountain, so that they named such mountains after the name of their ancestor Manu or Noah. Ararat, by the way, is the same as Armenia in the Bible. The prefix "Ar" means "Mountain," so that "Armenia" probably means "the mountain of Meni."

On the American continent, "manu" seems to have been modified into several forms. In the Sioux language, it took the form *minne,* meaning "water." Thus, Minneapolis means "city of water," Minnesota means "sky blue water," etc. In the Assiniboine language, "minnetoba" meant "water prairie." This name is preserved in the Canadian province of Manitoba. However, this word may also have been derived from the Cree and Ojibiva-Saulteaux languages, in which "manitoba" meant "the place of the Great Spirit." *Manitou* ("the Great Spirit") was the chief god among Algonquins.[16]

Even in South America can be found traces of the ancient name Manu. The name of Managua, the capital of Nicaragua, comes from the Nahuatl *managuac,* which means "surrounded by ponds."

Francisco Lopez de Gomara, secretary to the Conqueror Cortez, has given an account of the fabled city of Manoa, supposed to be the capital of El Dorado, the city of gold. Manoa (meaning "Noah's water") was said to be a dead city high in the Sierra Parina between Brazil and Venezuela.[17] The Brazilian city Manaus on the Amazon River was named after the aboriginal Indian tribe Manau which once dominated the region. In Bolivia there is a town of Manoa and a river called Manu in Peru. In fact, several rivers include "manu" in their names—Muymanu, Tahuamanu, Pariamanu, Tacuatimanu, etc. In the Department of Madre de Dios, where all these rivers are located, "manu" is understood to mean "river" or "water." One of the provinces of this department is, in fact, named Manu and another Tahuamanu.

The Egyptian hieroglyph for "water" was written as a wavy line. When the alphabet was invented, this symbol became the letter "m," representing *mayim,* the Semitic word for "water." In the Phoenician of 1300-1000 B.C. it was called *Mem,* which was later called *Mu* in Greek and finally *Em* among the Romans.[18,19]

Another reflection of the name Noah may have been the Assyrian word for "rain," *zunnu.*[20] Janus, the two-headed god (from which the name of our month of January is derived) was regarded by the earliest inhabitants of Italy as both the father of the world and the inventor of ships, later as the god of portals. All of these concepts would be appropriate for Noah. It is not impossible that the name Janus could originally have been a combination of "Jah" and "Noah," meaning "Noah's Lord."

In Norse mythology, Njord was the god of ships, living at Noatun, the harbor of ships. In this language, the syllable "noa" is related to the Icelandic *nor,* meaning "ship."[21]

Similarly the original Sanskrit word for "ship" is *nau.* This root has developed even in English into such words as "navy," "nautical," "nausea," etc.[22] This word could very well be still another variant of "Noah," the first master shipbuilder. Further, there is Ino, a sea-goddess in Greek mythology, and the Greek word *naiade,* meaning "river nymph."[23] Many other examples might be cited.

Thus, Noah and the waters of the great Flood are not only recalled in the ancient traditions of all nations, but their names have also become incorporated in many and varied ways into the very languages of his descendants. The trails are tenuous and often almost obliterated, so that some of the inferred connections are speculative and possibly mistaken, but the correlations are too numerous to be only coincidental, thus adding yet one more evidence for the historicity of the worldwide Flood.

References

1. This study is necessarily exploratory and somewhat speculative. Nevertheless, it is fascinating, and the etymological correlations seem too numerous and detailed to be coincidental.
2. See the *Oxford Dictionary of English Etymology.*
3. Tacitus, *The Agricula and the Germania,* Middlesex, England: Penguin Books, Ltd., 1970, p. 102.
4. Kolosimo, Peter, *Not of This World,* London, England: Sphere Books, Ltd., 1975, p. 171.
5. See the *Syensk Etymologisk Ordbok.*
6. Ceram, C. W., *Gods, Graves and Scholars,* Middlesex, England: Penguin Pelican Books, 1974, pp. 79-83.
7. Sandars, N. K., *The Epic of Gilgamesh,* Middlesex, England: Penguin Classics, 1960.
8. Tomas, Andrew, *Atlantis from Legend to Discovery,* London: Sphere Books, Ltd., 1972, p. 25.
9. Spence, Lewis, *Myths and Legends of Ancient Egypt,* London: George C. Harrap & Co., Ltd., 1915.
10. Hall, Richard, *Discovery of Africa,* Melbourne, Australia: Sun Books, Ltd., 1970, p. 67.
11. See article on *El Correo,* published by Unesco, April 1960, p. 27.
12. See *National Geographic Magazine,* October 1977, p. 458.
13. There is no actual documentation of a phonetic change from "ma" to "da," although such would have been quite possible, especially in view of the similar meanings of their derivatives.
14. Furneaux, Rupert, *Ancient Mysteries,* London: Futura Publications, Ltd., 1976.
15. Pukui, Mary Kawens, and Elbert, Samuel H., *Place Names of Hawaii,* Honolulu: University of Hawaii Press, 1966.
16. See brochure published by Manitoba Historical Society in Winnipeg, Canada.

17. Kolosimo, Peter, *Timeless Earth,* London: Sphere Books, Ltd., 1974, pp. 136, 215.
18. Laird, Charlton, *The Miracle of Language,* New York: Fawcett World Library, 1967, p. 177.
19. Pei, Mario, *Language for Everybody,* New York: Pocket Books, Inc., 1958, p. 182.
20. Cleator, P. E., *Lost Languages,* New York: New American Library of World Literature, 1962, p. 105.
21. Filby, Frederick A., *The Flood Reconsidered,* London: Pickering and Inglis, 1970, pp. 55-57.
22. Hellquist, Elof, *Svensk Etmologisk Ordbok,* Lund, Sweden: C.W.K. Gleerups Forlag, 1966, p. 701.
23. Cuerber, H. A., *The Myths of Greece and Rome,* London: George G. Harrap and Co., Ltd., 1948, p. 235.

No. 84, June 1980

Extinction

By Kenneth B. Cumming, Ph.D. *

Jay Williams[1] tells about an old woman who was living out the last days of her life. Surrounded by white walls, upon a white bed, in care of doctors and nurses, this dark-skinned relict fought off death with all her primitive vitality. She rebuked her attendants and intermittently broke forth in song and chants. But inevitably she collapsed onto her pillows and whispered, *"Bury me behind the mountains."* And so she died, but her skeleton was placed instead in a city museum, for she was the

* The author, Dr. Kenneth B. Cumming, is Chairman of the Biology Department at Christian Heritage College and Research Associate in Bioscience for ICR. He has a Ph.D. in Biology from Harvard University, as well as extensive research, teaching, and administrative experience with the federal government and in three universities.

last of her kin. With her passing, the Tasmanian people became extinct.

Extinction is like that. It is the absolute terminus for a formerly recognized group of organisms. When mortality exceeds natality for a sufficient time to bring the total number of individuals of a species to *zero* or *one* (for those organisms which reproduce sexually), then extinction is pronounced.[2]

Since life began, many organisms have been lost from the biosphere through extinction. Some people feel that this is a normal expectation of life—a parade of passing species. It is to be expected that new "species" and higher taxa (levels of classification) will progressively evolve to displace existing or waning groups. On the other hand, some feel that this happening represents a net loss to the total biota. This latter group says no new "kinds" are being formed. Consequently, when populations of unique organisms die out, that genome is gone forever.

If extinction is part of the natural order, why save endangered species? The money and effort put into protecting, restoring, and sustaining a few minor species of plants and animals becomes a questionable national effort. Indeed, if we are a part of the evolving cosmos, we should look forward to the new order and help the evolutionary process! When we stop the parade, we slow down evolution (i.e., we are keeping critical niches occupied too long). The evolutionist requires extinction; it is like throwing out the slum dwellers for urban renewal.

Congress addressed these issues, and in their wisdom they concluded that endangered and threatened species of fish, wildlife, and plants *"are of aesthetic, ecological, educational, historical, and scientific value to the nation and its people."*[3] Perhaps protecting organisms is good stewardship of finite resources. Whatever one's view of the matter, the observation remains true that many more species are being lost in our time than are being formed, and this pace appears to be accelerating.

Extinction can occur as a result of any of three principal pressures: *mortality/natality imbalance, loss of critical habitat,* and *minimum population density.* Three examples are cited: Dodos in historical times were found only on a few small islands in the Indian Ocean. When man wiped them out of their tiny refuges, no replacements were available to rekindle the species— mortality exceeded natality. A pair of ivory-billed woodpeckers is said to require a territory of 5 km² of primeval bottomland forest. A viable population probably needed 160 km². Much of this type of appropriate habitat has gone and, to our knowledge, so has the bird. Theoretical limits appear to exist for some species in that when the numbers dwindle below that limit, genetic variability is lost to such an extent that ultimate extinction is assured. There is a failure to mate for social reasons below a certain population density. The whooping crane and California condor may have passed below this level—certainly the passenger pigeon did.

The record of extinctions in the United States is startling. Since the arrival of the settlers in America in the early 1600s, over 500 species and subspecies of native biota have passed on. Another 170 animals are designated "endangered" today. The rate of loss roughly follows the national population increase.

Paleontologically speaking, there are two chief classes of extinctions: those for which the paleontologist has a satisfactory explanation, and those for which he has none.[4] There are extinctions in historical times which are due to depredations of man or stronger animals upon weaker ones. Before those times in the distant past there were even greater exterminations which apparently affected organisms globally but do not have obvious causes. In the geological record these are associated with the late Cambrian, Ordovician, Devonian, Permian, and Cretaceous strata. Since these latter events were worldwide, they must have had worldwide causes. Two explanations can be offered: either catastrophes or subtle and insidious global reactions.

Newell[5] says that man was the exterminator in historical times. A few species of large mammals dropped out of the fossil record in North America at the height of the last glaciation, and some of these (perhaps the giant sloth and saber-toothed cat in California) may have been due to over-hunting by man. The rate of extinction picked up rapidly when the climate became milder and glaciers began shrinking. Many large herbivores and carnivores existed worldwide through a great range in climate, yet they died out in only a few hundred years. In recent times about 75 percent of the North American herbivores have disappeared, and most of the ecological niches have not yet been filled. Glaciation was apparently *not* important for these extinctions.

Some investigators have suggested that the large mammals

may have been hunted out of existence by prehistoric man using fire as a weapon. The wipe-out coincided with rapid growth in agriculture.

Correlating extinctions to ancient earth's history has been a scientific mystery according to Baker and Allen.[6] The fossil record contains mass extinctions in many layers. As an example of mass extinction, two-thirds of the trilobite families disappeared at the end of the Cambrian Period. Nearly one-half of the then-known animal species became extinct at the close of the Permian Period! A large extinction of reptiles also occurred at the end of the Triassic. The dinosaur extinction is the best known of all disappearances, and it occurred at the close of the Cretaceous Period in a relatively short period of time.

Many postulates have been put forward to account for mass extinctions of organisms. One such postulate is that a nearby supernova might have showered the earth with bursts of high-energy radiation. Since water is a good shield against radiation, we would expect to find the land organisms to be more affected than the marine ones. Yet, we know that for certain periods most of the extinctions occurred in the sea. Postulates on the change in the earth's magnetic field suffer the same limitations.

Another postulate is that a "biological drive" became exhausted. There is no direct evidence for any such force in nature or that extinction is a result of its exhaustion.

Mountain building has been suggested as a cause. Attempts to relate mountain building periods to times of mass extinction have led to conflicting conclusions. Further, the greatest periods of mass extinction are said to have occurred during geologically quiet times.

Climate change is the most popular explanation for the observed extinctions. It was assumed that sudden changes in climate would quickly eliminate vast numbers of organisms that could not adapt. Perhaps the dinosaurs were not able to handle cold-prevailing climates. But fossil plants do not show such changes to have occurred at the time this hypothesis would predict them.

Fluctuations in the sea level have been well documented. It is known that an increase or decrease of only a few feet would cover or expose large areas of land. The correlation is that diversification is greatest during times of flooding and extinctions greatly increased during withdrawals. However, the worldwide effect would imply massive continental coverage rather than coastal swamping.

Many hypotheses have been offered but none seem to hold a majority opinion. What do the data show over geologic time? Valentine[7] has studied the states of the marine biosphere over time by examining the fossil record for various benthic taxa. He has minimized the bias of incomplete fossil records by using only well-skeletonized taxa. Further, the benthic shelf environment was selected because it is the best-represented major environment in the fossil record, and also the environment most resistant to major forces of change.

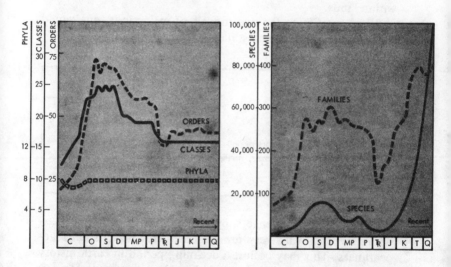

Diversity levels of taxa including estimated diversity levels of species of well-skeletonized marine shelf invertebrates during the Phanerozoic, plotted by epoch. (After Valentine, 1973.)

Notice that the greatest numbers of classes and orders occurred early in the geological record with phyla remaining essentially the same throughout. Families had a similar curve up to the Triassic strata, but the number has increased with time to the present, as have the number of species. The curves show evidence of mass extinctions that speak of worldwide catastrophes especially associated with the Triassic. Valentine says, "In summary, the most likely causes of mass extinction appear to be those factors which are natural regulators of diversity under normal circumstances and which have effects that pervade the entire planet." His catastrophe is related to tectonic processes.

The creationist views these data as evidence supporting an early highly diverse set of higher taxa which are declining in numbers with time. Definite data in the geological record point to a worldwide catastrophe especially in the Triassic and Jurassic strata. Subsequent diversification of benthic families, genera, and species since then is probably due to horizontal variation within kinds.

When comparing the two models of extinctions, one would make predictions something like the following:

	CREATION	EVOLUTION
Initial Number of Taxa	Large	Few
Number of Taxa With Time		
Higher Taxa (phyla, class order)	Decreasing	Increasing
Lower Taxa (family, genus, species)	Variable	Variable
Geological Events	Catastrophes	Uniformity
Niche Replacement With "New" Taxa	Limited	Extensive

Our present experience supports a rapid extinction of taxonomic groups with very few documented "new" species appearances. This may be just a declining period in earth history for biota, but man's impact on the biosphere appears to force us to project an extended period of losses under the human population increase and technological pressure. *Many more organisms will probably join the Tasmanians before new organisms take their place—if they ever do.*

References

1. Williams, Jay, *Fall of the Sparrow,* Oxford, England: Oxford University Press, 1951, p. 158.
2. Opler, Paul, "The Parade of Passing Species: A Survey of Extinc-

tion in the U.S.," *The Science Teacher,* V. 44, No. 1, 1977.

3. United States Congress, "The Endangered Species Act of 1973," Public Law 93-205, U.S. Government Printing Office, 1973.

4. Stokes, William, "Extinction and Replacement," *Essentials of Earth History,* Englewood Cliffs, New Jersey: Prentice-Hall, Inc. 1973, pp. 48-485.

5. Newell, Norman, "Crises in the History of Life," *Scientific American,* V. 200, 1963, pp. 76-94.

6. Baker, Jeffrey and Garland Allen, "The Evolution of Animals," *The Study of Biology,* Reading, Mass.: Addison-Wesley Publishing Co., 1968, pp. 577-597.

7. Valentine, James, "The Biosphere Level," *Evolutionary Paleoecology of the Marine Biosphere,* Englewood Cliffs, New Jersey: Prentice-Hall, Inc., 1973, pp. 373-408.

No. 85, July 1980
The Tenets of Creationism
*By Henry M. Morris, Ph.D. ***

Creationism can be studied and taught in any of three basic forms, as follows:

Scientific creationism (no reliance on Biblical revelation, utilizing *only scientific data* to support and expound the creation model).

Biblical creationism (no reliance on scientific data, using *only the Bible* to expound and defend the creation model).

Scientific Biblical creationism (full reliance on *Biblical revelation* but *also* using *scientific data* to support and develop the creation model).

---

*   The author, Dr. Henry M. Morris, is the Director of the Institute for Creation Research and the author of numerous other articles and books.

These are not contradictory systems, of course, but supplementary, each appropriate for certain applications. For example, creationists should *not* advocate that Biblical creationism be taught in public schools, both because of judicial restrictions against religion in such schools and also (more importantly) because teachers who do not *believe* the Bible should not be asked to *teach* the Bible. It is both legal and desirable, however, that *scientific* creationism be taught in public schools as a valid alternative to evolutionism.

In a Sunday School class, on the other hand, dedicated to teaching the Scriptures and "all the counsel of God," Biblical creationism should be strongly expounded and emphasized as the foundation of all other doctrine. In a Christian school or college, where the world of God is studied in light of the Word of God, it is appropriate and very important to demonstrate that Biblical creationism and scientific creationism are fully compatible, two sides of the same coin, as it were. The creation revelation in Scripture is thus supported by all true facts of nature; the combined study can properly be called scientific Biblical creationism. All three systems, of course, contrast sharply and explicitly with the evolution model.

The evolution and creation models, in their simplest forms, can be outlined as follows:[1]

Evolution Model	Creation Model
1. Continuing naturalistic origin	1. Completed supernaturalistic origin
2. Net present increase in complexity	2. Net present decrease in complexity
3. Earth history dominated by uniformitarianism	3. Earth history dominated by catastrophism

The evolution model, as outlined above, is in very general terms. It can be expanded and modified in a number of ways to correspond to particular types of evolutionism (atheistic evolution, theistic evolution, Lamarckianism, neo-Darwinism, punctuated equilibrium, etc.).

The same is true of the creation model, with the Biblical record giving additional specific information which could never be determined from science alone. The three key items in the creation model above are then modified as follows.

Biblical Creation Model

1. Creation completed by supernatural processes in six days.
2. Creation in the bondage of decay because of sin and the curse.
3. Earth history dominated by the great flood of Noah's day.

Creationists do not propose that the public schools teach six-day creation, the fall of man, and the Noachian flood. They do maintain, however, that they should teach the evidence for a complex complete creation, the universal principle of decay (in contrast to the evolutionary assumption of increasing organization), and the worldwide evidences of recent catastrophism. All of these are implicit in observable scientific data and should certainly be included in public education.

Both the scientific creation model and the Biblical creation model can be considerably expanded to incorporate many key events of creation and earth history, in terms of both scientific observation on the one hand and Biblical doctrine on the other. These can, in fact, be developed as a series of formal tenets[2] of scientific creationism and Biblical creationism, respectively, as listed below.

Tenets of Scientific Creationism

1. The physical universe of space, time, matter, and energy has not always existed, but was supernaturally created by a transcendent personal Creator who alone has existed from eternity.

2. The phenomenon of biological life did not develop by natural processes from inanimate systems but was specially and supernaturally created by the Creator.

3. Each of the major kinds of plants and animals was created functionally complete from the beginning and did not evolve from some other kind of organism. Changes in basic kinds since their first creation are limited to "horizontal" changes (varia-

tion) within the kinds, or "downward" changes (e.g., harmful mutations, extinctions).

4. The first human beings did not evolve from an animal ancestry, but were specially created in fully human form from the start. Furthermore, the "spiritual" nature of man (self-image, moral consciousness, abstract reasoning, language, will, religious nature, etc.) is itself a supernaturally created entity distinct from mere biological life.

5. Earth pre-history, as preserved especially in the crustal rocks and fossil deposits, is primarily a record of catastrophic intensities of natural processes, operating largely within uniform natural laws, rather than one of uniformitarian process rates. There is therefore no *a priori* reason for not considering the many scientific evidences for a relatively recent creation of the earth and the universe, in addition to the scientific evidences that most of the earth's fossiliferous sediments were formed in an even more recent global hydraulic cataclysm.

6. Processes today operate primarily within fixed natural laws and relatively uniform process rates. Since these were themselves originally created and are daily maintained by their Creator, however, there is always the possibility of miraculous intervention in these laws or processes by their Creator. Evidences for such intervention must be scrutinized critically, however, because there must be clear and adequate reason for any such action on the part of the Creator.

7. The universe and life have somehow been impaired since the completion of creation, so that imperfections in structure, disease, aging, extinctions, and other such phenomena are the result of "negative" changes in properties and processes occurring in an originally perfect created order.

8. Since the universe and its primary components were created perfect for their purposes in the beginning by a competent and volitional Creator, and since the Creator does remain active in this now-decaying creation, there does exist ultimate purpose and meaning in the universe. Teleological considerations, therefore, are appropriate in scientific studies whenever they are consistent with the actual data of observation, and it is reasonable to assume that the creation presently awaits the consummation of the Creator's purpose.

9. Although people are finite and scientific data concerning

origins are always circumstantial and incomplete, the human mind (if open to the possibility of creation) is able to explore the manifestation of that Creator rationally and scientifically and to reach an intelligent decision regarding one's place in the Creator's plan.

Tenets of Biblical Creationism

1. The Creator of the universe is a triune God—Father, Son, and Holy Spirit. There is only one eternal and transcendent God, the source of all being and meaning, and He exists in three Persons, each of Whom participated in the work of creation.

2. The Bible, consisting of the thirty-nine canonical books of the Old Testament and the twenty-seven canonical books of the New Testament, is the divinely-inspired revelation of the Creator to man. Its unique, plenary, verbal inspiration guarantees that these writings, as originally and miraculously given, are infallible and completely authoritative on all matters with which they deal, free from error of any sort, scientific and historical as well as moral and theological.

3. All things in the universe were created and made by God in the six literal days of the creation week described in Genesis 1:1 - 2:3, and confirmed in Exodus 20:8-11. The creation record is factual, historical, and perspicuous; thus all theories of origins or development which involve evolution in any form are false. All things which now exist are sustained and ordered by God's providential care. However, a part of the spiritual creation, Satan and his angels, rebelled against God after the creation and are attempting to thwart His divine purposes in creation.

4. The first human beings, Adam and Eve, were specially created by God, and all other men and women are their descendants. In Adam, mankind was instructed to exercise "dominion" over all other created organisms, and over the earth itself (an implicit commission for true science, technology, commerce, fine art, and education), but the temptation by Satan and the entrance of sin brought God's curse on that dominion and on mankind, culminating in death and separation from God as the natural and proper consequence.

5. The Biblical record of primeval earth history in Genesis 1 - 11 is fully historical and perspicuous, including the creation

and fall of man, the curse on the creation and its subjection to the bondage of decay, the promised Redeemer, the worldwide cataclysmic deluge in the days of Noah, the post-diluvian renewal of man's commission to subdue the earth (now augmented by the institution of human government), and the origin of nations and languages at the tower of Babel.

6. The alienation of man from his Creator because of sin can only be remedied by the Creator Himself, Who became man in the person of the Lord Jesus Christ, through miraculous conception and virgin birth. In Christ were indissolubly united perfect sinless humanity and full deity, so that His substitutionary death is the only necessary and sufficient price of man's redemption. That the redemption was completely efficacious is assured by His bodily resurrection from the dead and ascension into heaven; the resurrection of Christ is thus the focal point of history, assuring the consummation of God's purposes in creation.

7. The final restoration of creation's perfection is yet future, but individuals can immediately be restored to fellowship with their Creator, on the basis of His redemptive work on their behalf, receiving forgiveness and eternal life solely through personal trust in the Lord Jesus Christ, accepting Him not only as estranged Creator, but also as reconciling Redeemer and coming King. Those who reject Him, however, or who neglect to believe on Him, thereby continue in their state of rebellion and must ultimately be consigned to the everlasting fire prepared for the devil and his angels.

8. The eventual accomplishment of God's eternal purposes in creation, with the removal of His curse and the restoration of all things to divine perfection, will take place at the personal bodily return to the earth of Jesus Christ to judge and purge sin and to establish His eternal kingdom.

9. Each believer should participate in the "ministry of reconciliation," by seeking both to bring individuals back to God in Christ (the "Great Commission") and to "subdue the earth" for God's glory (the Edenic-Noahic Commission). The three institutions established by the Creator for the implementation of His purposes in this world (home, government, church) should be honored and supported as such.

Even though the tenets of scientific creationism can be expounded quite independently of the tenets of Biblical creationism, the two systems are completely compatible. All the genuine facts of science support Biblical creationism, and all statements in the Bible are consistent with scientific creationism. Either system can be taught independently of the other or the two can be taught concurrently, as the individual situation may warrant.

References

1. See *Scientific Creationism,* ed. Henry M. Morris (San Diego: CLP Publishers, 1974), p. 12.
2. These tenets have recently been adopted by the staff of the Institute for Creation Research and incorporated permanently in its By-Laws.

No. 86, August 1980
The ICR Scientists

Today there are thousands of scientists who are creationists and who repudiate any form of evolution in their analysis and use of scientific data. Creationist scientists can now be found in literally every discipline of science and their numbers are increasing rapidly. In the Creation Research Society (2717 Cranbrook Road, Ann Arbor, Michigan 48104) alone there are over 650 scientist members with either doctor's or master's degrees in some field of natural science. Among the additional 2,000 + sustaining members of the Society, many are also scientists with bachelor's degrees, in addition to numerous social scientists and other highly educated people with postgraduate degrees in their own fields. Evolutionists are finding it increasingly difficult to maintain the *fiction* that evolution is "science" and creation is "religion." When news media personnel and others make such statements today, they merely reveal their own liberal social philosophies—not their awareness of scientific facts!

We are pleased and proud to have 24 of these creationist scientists directly associated with the Institute for Creation Research, either as full-time staff members, regional representatives, or members of our Technical Advisory Board. All of these scientists have excellent scientific credentials, are highly knowledgeable in scientific issues related to the creation/evolution question, and are capable spokesmen for creationism in both its scientific and Biblical aspects. In addition, all are thorough-going Christians, believing in full Biblical inerrancy and authority, and are active members of various local churches.

All of these scientists are in demand as speakers and writers on creationist topics. For information to those who may wish to contact them for such purposes in their own communities, we are publishing herewith brief resumés of each scientist, together with their photos and mailing addresses.

ICR Staff Scientists

The nine ICR staff scientists all follow established guidelines related to costs and other arrangements, with all honoraria and profits from book sales going into the ICR ministry rather than to the speakers. A sheet outlining these guidelines is available on request. These scientists can all be reached at ICR headquarters (2100 Greenfield Drive, El Cajon, California 92021; phone (714) 440-2443).

1. **Henry M. Morris** is the Founder and Director of the Institute for Creation Research. He has a B.S. degree from Rice University and M.S. and Ph.D. degrees from the University of Minnesota, majoring in engineering hydraulics and hydrology, minoring in geology and mathematics. He has served on the faculties of Rice University, University of Minnesota, University of Southwestern Louisiana and Southern Illinois University. From 1957 to 1970 he was Head of the Department of Civil Engineering at the Virginia Polytechnic Institute and State University. In 1970 he helped to

found Christian Heritage College, where he served as Professor of Apologetics and Academic Vice President until 1978, and then as President from 1978 to 1980. He was one of the ten founding members of the Creation Research Society, serving later as its president for five years. He is author of six books in hydraulics/hydrology, and 24 books in creationism/Bible/apologetics.

2. **Duane T. Gish** is Associate Director of ICR, as well as Adjunct Professor of Natural Science at Christian Heritage College. He has the B.S. in Chemistry from UCLA and a Ph.D. in Biochemistry from the University of California (Berkeley). He served on post-doctoral research appointments at Berkeley and Cornell, and then for many years as a research biochemist with the Upjohn Company in Michigan. He also was one of the founding members of the Creation Research Society, where he met Dr. Morris, whom he later joined in San Diego in 1971. He is author of the popular ICR books *Evolution? The Fossils Say NO!* and *Dinosaurs: Those Terrible Lizards,* as well as numerous other papers and books.

3. **Richard B. Bliss** serves as Director of Curriculum Development for ICR, as well as Head of the Education Department at Christian Heritage College. He has the B.S. in Biology, as well as an M.S., from the University of Wisconsin, along with a doctorate in Science Education from the University of Sarasota. He spent over 23 years in high school science teaching, as well as serving as an adjunct professor at the University of Wisconsin. He was Director of Science Education for the outstanding Racine, Wisconsin, Unified School District before joining ICR in 1976. He is author or co-author of several of ICR's published modules for teaching the two-model approach to origins in the schools.

4. Harold S. Slusher is Head of the Physical Sciences Department (comprising both Geophysics and Physics/Math majors) at Christian Heritage College as well as Research Associate in Geophysics and Astronomy at ICR. He also holds a joint appointment on the physics faculty at the University of Texas (El Paso), where he has served as Director of the university's seismic observatory. He has the B.S. from the University of Tennessee, the M.S. (Geophysics) from the University of Oklahoma, and has completed residence work for the Ph.D. He holds an honorary D.Sc. from Indiana Christian University. He is a Director of the Creation Research Society and served as co-editor of its biology textbook. He is author or co-author of five ICR Technical Monographs.

5. Gary E. Parker is Research Associate in Bioscience with ICR as well as Professor of Biology at Christian Heritage College. He has the A.B. degree in Biology from Wabash College, and the M.S. and Ed.D. degrees from Ball State University. He is author of five widely used programmed-learning biology textbooks and has served on the biology faculties at Eastern Baptist College and Dordt College. He is author or co-author of several ICR booklets and teaching modules, and has completed the manuscript for a college-level biology textbook, which is being published in topical installments. He also serves as Director of the ICR Museum of Creation and Earth History.

6. Kenneth B. Cumming is Academic Vice President, Head of the Department of Biological Sciences at Christian Heritage College, as well as Research Associate in Biology and Ecology at the Institute for Creation Research. He holds degrees from Tufts and Harvard in Biology and the Ph.D. in Ecology from Harvard University. He has been on the faculties at the Virginia Polytechnic Institute and State University and the University of Wisconsin, as well as holding a number of important governmental positions, most recently as Chief of Program Operations in the Office of Biological Services in Washington, D.C. He is author of numerous technical articles.

7. **Steven A. Austin** is Research Associate in Geology with ICR, as well as Associate Professor of Geology at Christian Heritage College. He has the B.S. from the University of Washington, M.S. from San Jose State University, and Ph.D. from the Pennsylvania State University, all in geology. He has published several articles in professional geological journals, as well as numerous papers on scientific creationism. He is a specialist in the geology of coal and has established a coal research laboratory at the Institute for Creation Research.

8. **Theodore W. Rybka** is Associate Professor in Physics and Mathematics at Christian Heritage College, as well as Research Associate in Physics with the Institute for Creation Research. He has the B.S. in Physics from the University of British Columbia, the M.S. in Nuclear Physics from the University of Saskatchewan, and the Ph.D. in Solid State Physics from the University of Oklahoma. He has published several technical articles in professional physics journals.

9. **John D. Morris** is Field Scientist for ICR, as well as Associate Professor in Earth Science and Apologetics for Christian Heritage College. He has the B.S. in Civil Engineering from Virginia Polytechnic Institute, the M.S. and the Ph.D. in Geological Engineering from the University of Oklahoma. He worked several years as an engineer for the City of Los Angeles and has taught at Oklahoma University. He was in charge of ICR's research expeditions to Mount Ararat in search of Noah's Ark and has made extensive field studies of

the Paluxy River footprints in Texas. He is author of three ICR books, *Adventure on Ararat, The Ark on Ararat,* and *Tracking Those Incredible Dinosaurs.*

Hardin Simmons. For many years he was Director of the Schellenger Research Laboratories. Mailing address is 2115 N. Kansas Street, El Paso. Texas 79902.

3. **William J. Bauer** is President of the Bauer Engineering Company of Chicago, which has designed many of the major engineering systems in Chicago and around the world. He has a Ph.D. in Hydraulics from the University of Iowa and is author of numerous technical papers. He is a frequent and effective speaker on scientific creationism. Address is 20 N. Wacker Drive, Chicago, Illinois 60606.

4. **Edward Blick** is Professor of Aerospace, Mechanical, and Nuclear Engineering at the University of Oklahoma and formerly Associate Dean of Engineering there. He received his Ph.D. in Engineering Science from Oklahoma University, and has published many important research papers in the fields of aerodynamics and biomechanics. Dr. Blick is co-author of the textbook *Fluid Mechanics and Heat Transfer.* He is also author of a widely distributed booklet on scientific creationism and the Bible. Address is 7006 Lago Ranchero Drive, Norman, Oklahoma 73071.

5. **David R. Boylan** is Professor of Chemical Engineering at Iowa State University and has served as Director of Iowa State's Engineering Research Institute. His B.S. is from the University of Kansas and his Ph.D. from Iowa State University. He is a member of the Board of Directors of the Creation Research Society and also serves on the Board of Regents of Christian Heritage College. He is a distinguished engineering teacher, practitioner, and administrator. Mailing address is 1516 Stafford, Ames, Iowa 50010.

6. **Malcolm Cutchins** is Professor of Aerospace Engineering at Auburn University, where he has twice won Auburn's Outstanding Faculty Award. He received his Ph.D. in Engineering Mechanics from the Virginia Polytechnic Institute and State University and has authored many excellent research papers. He was recognized by the journal *Industrial Research* for "developing one of the 100 most significant new technical products of 1973." Address is 701 Sanders, Auburn, Alabama 36830.

7. **Donald B. DeYoung** is Chairman of the Department of Physical Sciences at Grace College in Indiana. He served one year (while on sabbatical) at Christian Heritage College, as Visiting Professor of Physics and is now ICR's Midwest Regional Representative. His Ph.D. is from Iowa State University. He is co-author of an excellent creationist astronomy reference book *The Origin of the Moon*, as well as a number of ICR "Impact" articles. Address is 1111 Ranch Road, Warsaw, Indiana 46580.

8. **Donald Hamann** is Professor of Food Technology at North Carolina State University. He received his Ph.D. in 1967 from Virginia Polytechnic Institute and State University and has served on the Agricultural Engineering faculties at South Dakota State University and Virginia Tech. He holds several patents in his field and has published many papers. He has organized a group of scientists in the Raleigh-Durham-Chapel Hill area known as TASC (Triangle Association for Scientific Creation). Address is 4205 Weaver Drive, Raleigh, North Carolina 27609.

9. **Harold R. Henry** is Professor and Chairman of the Department of Civil and Mining Engineering at the University of Alabama in Tuscaloosa. He has degrees from Georgia Tech and the University of Iowa, as well as a Ph.D. in Fluid Mechanics from Columbia University. He has served on the faculties at Georgia Tech, Columbia, and Michigan State University. Address is 9 Lenora Drive, Tuscaloosa, Alabama 35401.

10. **Joseph Henson** is Head of the Science Division at Bob Jones University in South Carolina. As a biologist, he is also very active in Christian camping ministries, as well as speaking in creation seminars and debates. His Ph.D. in Entomology was received from Clemson University in 1967. Address is 109 Twinbrook Drive, Greenville, South Carolina 29607.

11. **Lane P. Lester** is now an Associate Professor of Biology at Liberty Baptist College in Virginia, also serving as ICR's Southeast Regional Representative. He has the Ph.D. in Genetics from Purdue University and has served on the biology faculties at the University of Tennessee (Chattanooga) and Christian Heritage College. Also, he spent a year on the writing faculty of the Biological Sciences Curriculum Study Center at the University of Colorado. Address is 413 Woodland Circle, Lynchburg, Virginia 24502.

12. **David N. Menton** is Associate Professor of Anatomy at Washington University School of Medicine in St. Louis. His Ph.D. degree (Biology) was received from Brown University in 1966, with a B.S. from Mankato State University in 1959. He has authored over 18 technical publications in professional journals and received the American Academy of Dermatology's Silver Award for Original Investiga-

tion. He is a member of Sigma Xi and various scientific societies. He has also been a leader in the Missouri Association for Scientific Creation. Address is 11 S. Tealbrook Drive, St. Louis, Missouri 63141.

13. **John R. Meyer** has degrees in Bible and Chemistry and received his Ph.D. in Zoology from the State University of Iowa. He served as a Post-doctoral Fellow at the University of Colorado and as Assistant Professor of Physiology and Biophysics at the University of Louisville Medical School. He is now Professor of Biology at Los Angeles Baptist College and is a member of the Board of Directors of the Creation Research Society. Address is 27117 Langside Avenue, Canyon Country, California 91351

14. **John N. Moore** is Professor of Natural Science at Michigan State University, where he received his M.S. (Biology) and Ed.D. degrees. He has authored several booklets and articles on creationism and served as editor of the Creation Research Society biology textbook. He is a Director of the CRS and has spent many years as Managing Editor of its *Quarterly*. He has also spent a sabbatical at Christian Heritage College and been a faculty member in several ICR Summer Institutes on Scientific Creationism. Address is 1158 Marigold Avenue, East Lansing, Michigan 48823.

15. **Jean Sloat Morton** holds five degrees from three institutions, District of Columbia Teachers' College, American University, and George Washington University. Her Ph.D. from George Washington is in Cellular Studies, with her dissertation at Washington's Smithsonian Institution. She has taught biology at American University and George Washington University and has served as a consultant in microbiology. She is author of an outstanding book *Science in the Bible* (Moody, 1978) and has written numerous

science instructional units for various grade levels. Address is P.O. Box 597, Picayune, Mississippi 39466.

In addition to these scientists, one of America's outstanding theologians, **Dr. John C. Whitcomb** (Grace Seminary) is a member of ICR's Technical Advisory Board. **David Watson**, British theologian, educator, author, and missionary, is Director of ICR's Midwest Center (207 Washington North, Wheaton, Illinois 60187), **Dr. Philip Passon**, biochemist, is President of the ICR Midwest Center which has a list of excellent scientist speakers in the Chicago area.

There are, of course, many other fine creationist scientists in the Creation Research Society and other creationist organizations. Many of these are excellent speakers and writers, but it is not practicable to attempt a complete listing here. Our ICR scientists, however, are among the best representatives of the type of men and women who are being used today in such an effective manner nationwide to restore creationism to a respected place in science. They can be recommended with confidence to any who wish to sponsor local creation seminars or similar meetings in their own areas.

No. 87, September 1980
The Origin of Mammals
By Duane T. Gish, Ph.D. *

According to the neo-Darwinian interpretation of evolution, all living forms have arisen from a single form of life by slow gradual changes. Thus, the time between the origin of life and

---

* The author, Dr. Duane T. Gish, is the Associate Director of the Institute for Creation Research and Professor of Natural Sciences at Christian Heritage College, El Cajon, California. He is the author of several other related articles and books and is in demand as a speaker on scientific creationism throughout the world.

the abrupt appearance in the fossil record of the many complex invertebrate forms of life is now estimated to have been nearly three billion years. The time required for one of these invertebrates to evolve into the vertebrates, or fishes, has been estimated at about 100 million years, and it is believed that the evolution of the fish into an amphibian required about 30 million years. The essence of the neo-Darwinian view is the slow gradual evolution of one plant or animal into another by the gradual accumulation of micromutations through natural selection of favored variants.

If this view of evolution is true, the fossil record should produce an enormous number of transitional forms. Natural history museums should be overflowing with undoubted intermediate forms. About 250,000 fossil species have been collected and classified. These fossils have been collected at random from rocks that are supposed to represent all of the geological periods of earth history. Applying evolution theory and the laws of probability, most of these 250,000 species should represent transitional forms. Thus, if evolution theory is true, there should be no doubt, question, or debate as to the fact of evolution.

Such is not the case at all, however. The fossil record was actually an embarrassment to Darwin, and some paleontologists are willing to admit that it looks even worse from an evolutionary point of view today than it did in Darwin's time.[1] Some even appear to admit that there is, in fact, little, if any, evidence for transitional forms in the fossil records. Kitts, for example, states, "Despite the bright promise that paleontology provides a means of 'seeing' evolution, it has presented some nasty difficulties for evolutionists, the most notorious of which is the presence of 'gaps' in the fossil record. Evolution requires intermediate forms between species and paleontology does not provide them." More and more paleontologists seem to be coming to the point where they are now willing to admit that this is indeed the case and are seeking to devise a mechanism for evolution that will tolerate, even predict, systematic gaps in the fossil record.

Other evolutionists remain steadfastly wedded to neo-Darwinism. They argue that there are examples of transitional forms in the fossil records, and that even if examples of gradual change are few, these few examples eliminate the necessity of seeking mechanisms for evolution other than neo-Darwinism. The examples most often cited are the reptile-to-bird transition (*Archaeopteryx* is the sole suggested intermediate), the so-called horse series, and the reptile-mammal transition.

Of the latter, Olson has said, "The reptilian-mammalian transition has by far the finest record of showing the origin of a new class."[2] Others claim that there are forms that stand perfectly on the reptilian-mammalian boundary. In an "Impact" article to be published soon, we will examine in some detail the "mammal-like" reptiles that some paleontologists believe represent transitional forms between reptiles and mammals. In the present article we wish to review the general nature of the evidence related to the origin of mammals.

The creatures included within the class Mammalia are a diverse group. All are warm-blooded and the females possess mammary glands for suckling the young. The mammals comprise 32 orders, most of which are placental mammals, but which also include the Monotremata, which embrace the egg-laying spiny anteater and the egg-laying duckbilled platypus, and the Marsupialia, which include the opposums and the pouched marsupials, such as the kangaroo and wallabies.

It is interesting to note that while claiming that intermediate forms for the reptile-to-mammal transition have been found, some evolutionists admit that no immediate ancestors for any of the 32 mammalian orders have been discovered. Thus, George Gaylord Simpson, after stating that nowhere in the world is there any trace of a fossil that would close the considerable gap between *Hyracotherium* ("Eohippus"), which evolutionists assume was the first horse, and its supposed ancestral order Condylarthra, goes on to say, "This is true of all the thirty-two orders of mammals . . . . The earliest and most primitive known members of every order already have the basic ordinal characters, and in no case is an approximately continuous sequence from one order to another known. In most cases the break is so sharp and the gap so large that the origin of the order is speculative and much disputed."[3]

The marine mammals thus abruptly appear in the fossil record as whales, dolphins, sea-cows, etc. For example, in one of Romer's concluding statements in his discussion of the subungulates (conies, elephants, sea cows), he says " . . . conies, proboscideans, and sirenians were already distinct groups at the time when they first appear in the fossil record."[4] Olson states that if we seek the ancestries of the marine mammals we run into a blank wall as far as intermediate stages between land and sea are concerned.[5] His remark included the seals, dolphins, and whales. There simply are no transitional forms in the fossil record between the marine mammals and their supposed land mammal ancestors.

Romer suggests that whales may have descended from a primitive carnivore,[6] although concerning the Sirenia (sea cows) and the Cetacea (whales, dolphins) he admits that, "We are ignorant of their terrestrial forebears and cannot be sure of their place of origin."[7] It is interesting to note that many of the so-called "primitive" carnivorous mammals had about 40 teeth differentiated into incisors, canines, premolars, and molars. The porpoises, dolphins, and whales, however, may possess teeth far in excess of that number (one porpoise has 300), and the teeth of these marine mammals are usually simple pegs or wedges and are not differentiated into incisors, canines, premolars, and molars.

Würsig has suggested recently, on the other hand, that dolphins may have evolved from land mammals resembling the even-toed ungulates of today such as cattle, pigs, and buffaloes.[8] It is quite entertaining, starting with cows, pigs, or buffaloes, to attempt to visualize what the intermediates may have looked like. Starting with a cow, one could even imagine one line of descent which prematurely became extinct, due to what might be called an "udder-failure"!

Bats (of the order Chiroptera), the only flying mammal, are especially interesting. Evolutionists assume, of course, that bats must have evolved from a non-flying mammal. There is not one shred of evidence in the fossil record, however to support such speculations, for, as Romer says, "Bats appear full fledged in both hemispheres in the Middle Eocene . . . . "[9]

On the cover page of *Science* of December 9, 1966 (Vol. 154), appears a picture of what the author (Glenn L. Jepsen) of the accompanying article (pp. 1333-1339) describes as the oldest known bat. He reports that it was found in Early Eocene deposits, which are dated by evolutionists at about 50 million years. While stating that this bat possessed a few "primitive" characteristics, Jepsen states that it was fully developed, an "anatomically precocious" contemporary of Eohippus. Thus, bats appear fully-formed, with no trace of ancestors or intermediate forms, as a contemporary of Eohippus, supposedly the ancestor of horses. According to Jepsen this leaves many questions unanswered, including when, from what, where, and how did bats originate?

Horses comprise one of the most interesting mammalian groups as far as the question of origins is concerned. Almost all students are familiar with the story of horse "evolution," beginning with *Hyracotherium* (Eohippus), a dog-sized "horse" with four toes on the front feet, passing via straight-line evolution through three-toed varieties, and ending with the modern one-toed *Equus*. But while subscribing to the evolution of the horse in general, Birdsell proclaims that, "Much of this story is incorrect . . . . "[10] Others hold the same view. George Gaylord Simpson, for example, has declared that several generations of students have been misinformed about the real meaning of the evolution of the horse.[11] These authors believe that the evolution of the horse is much more complicated than usually portrayed and is more like a series of bushes, perhaps, than like a tree.

To us the family tree of the horse appears to be merely a scenario put together from non-equivalent parts. Nowhere, for example, are there intermediate forms documenting transition from a non-horse ancestor (supposedly a condylarth) with five toes on each foot, to *Hyracotherium* with four toes on the front foot and three on the rear. Neither are there transitional forms between the four-toed *Hyracotherium* and the three-toed *Miohippus,* or between the latter, equipped with browsing teeth, and the three-toed *Merychippus,* equipped with high-crowned grazing teeth. Finally, the one-toed grazers, such as *Equus*, appear abruptly with no intermediates showing gradual evolution from the three-toed grazers.

Thus, Birdsell tells this story in the following way (note that when an evolutionist uses such terms as "sudden," "abrupt," or "rapid" with reference to transitions, he is usually inferring that no transitional forms have been found): "The evolution of the foot mechanisms proceeded by rapid and abrupt changes rather than gradual ones. The transition from the form of foot shown by miniature Eohippus to larger consistently three-toed *Miohippus* was so abrupt that it even left no record in the fossil deposits . . . . their foot structure [those of *Miohippus*] changed very rapidly to a three-toed sprung foot in which the pad disappeared and the two side toes became essentially functionless. Finally, in the Pliocene the line leading to the modern one-toed grazer went through a rapid loss of the two side toes on each foot."[12] He then goes on to say that this evolution was not gradual but that it had proceeded by rapid jumps. Thus, the continuity required by theory cannot be documented from the fossil record.

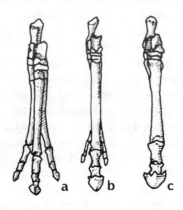

Figure 1. The pes (hindfeet) of (a) "*Eohippus*"; (b) *Merychippus*; (c) *Equus*.

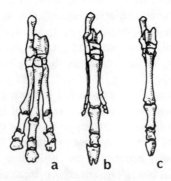

Figure 2. The pes of South American ungulates of the order Litopterna. (a) *Macrauchenia;* (b) *Diadiaphorus;* (c) *Thoatherium.*

A rather astounding and revealing fact is discovered when we compare North American ungulates to South American ungulates. All of us are familiar with the series shown in Fig. 1. These are the hind feet (pes) of (a) "Eohippus"; (b) *Merychippus,* with reduced lateral toes; and (c) modern *Equus.* Now look at Fig. 2. Illustrated are the pes of the South American ungulates (order Litopterna), (a) *Macrauchenia;* (b) *Diadiaphorus;* and (c) *Thoatherium.* Again we see a three-toed ungulate *(Macrauchenia);* a three-toed hoofed ungulate with reduced laterals *(Diadiaphorus);* and, in this case, a one-toed hoofed ungulate *(Thoatherium* which, Romer says, seems even more horselike than any true horse, for it was single-toed with splints more reduced than those of modern equids.[13]

Do they not thus provide another nice, logical evolutionary series? No, not at all, for they do not occur in this sequence at all! *Diadiaphorus,* the three-toed ungulate with reduced lateral toes, and *Thoatherium,* the one-toed ungulate, were contemporaries in the Miocene epoch. *Macrauchenia,* with pes containing three full-sized toes, is not found until the Pliocene epoch, which followed the Miocene according to the geological column. In fact, it is said that the one-toed *Thoatherium* became extinct in the Miocene before the three-toed *Macrauchenia* made his appearance in the Pliocene.

Thus, if evolutionists would permit the fossil evidence and their usual assumptions concerning geological time to be their guide, they should suppose that in South America a one-toed ungulate gave rise to a three-toed ungulate with reduced lateral toes, which then gave rise to an ungulate with three full-sized toes. This is precisely the opposite of the supposed sequence of events that occurred with North American horses. I don't know any evolutionist who suggests such an evolutionary sequence of events, but why not? Perhaps it is because the three-toed to one-toed sequence for North American horses became so popularized in evolutionary circles that no one dare suggest the reverse transition. Of course there is no more real evidence for transitional forms in South America than there is in North America.

It should also be noted that in the Rattlesnake Formation of the John Day Country of northeastern Oregon, the three-toed horse *Neohipparion* is found with the one-toed horse, *Pliohippus.*[14] No transitional forms between the two are found. In other cases "primitive" species of a genus, such as those of *Merychippus,* are found in geological formations supposedly younger than those containing "advanced" species.[15]

Was *Hyracotherium* (Eohippus) really a horse? *Hyracotherium* was discovered in Europe before "Eohippus" was uncovered in North America and was given the genus designation of *Hyracotherium* by the famous British anatomist and paleontologist, Richard Owen, who was also its discoverer. Later, other specimens were discovered in North America and given the genus name *Eohippus.* It was subsequently concluded that the North American specimens were actually of the same genus as *Hyracotherium.* The latter thus has priority, so Eohippus is not a valid name for these creatures. It is most commonly used, however, undoubtedly because the name Eohippus means "dawn horse" while *Hyracotherium* was chosen by Owen because of the resemblance of this creature to creatures of the genus *Hyrax* (cony, daman).

Although *Hyracotherium,* or Eohippus, was unlike modern horses, both morphologically and in habitat, this creature was chosen to stand at the base of the horses by the American paleontologist Marsh, and others, and this scheme became solidly entrenched both in popular circles and in scientific status after a lecture in New York City by Thomas H. Huxley and the publication of Marsh's studies.[16]

Nilsson has pointed out that while *Hyracotherium* has little or no resemblance to horses, it apparently was morphologically and in habitat similar to living creatures of the genus *Hyrax.*[17] *Hyrax,* like *Hyracotherium,* is about the size of a rabbit or fox. *Hyrax,* also like *Hyracotherium,* has four toes on the front feet and three on the rear. The cheek teeth of these two creatures share many similarities and are more like those of rhinoceri than those of horses. The habitat and way of life of *Hyrax* are also similar to those postulated for *Hyracotherium.* Thus, Nilsson maintains, although *Hyracotherium* does not resemble present-day horses in any way, they were, apparently, remarkably similar to the present-day *Hyrax.*

Others also doubt whether *Hyracotherium* was related to the horse. For example, Kerkut states, "In the first place it is not clear that *Hyracotherium* was the ancestral horse. Thus Simpson (1945) states, 'Matthew has shown and insisted that

Hyracotherium (including Eohippus) is so primitive that it is not much more definitely equid than tapirid, rhinocerotid, etc., but it is customary to place it at the root of the equid group.' ''[18] In other words, *Hyracotherium* is not any more like a horse than it is similar to a tapir or a rhinoceros, and thus just as justifiably it could have been chosen as the ancestral rhinoceros or tapir. It seems, then, that the objectivity of those involved in the construction of the phylogenetic tree of the horse was questionable from the very start, and that the "horse" on which the entire family tree of the horse rests was not a horse at all.

No definitive work on horses has been published since the publication of Kerkut's book that would materially affect his conclusion that, "In some ways it looks as if the pattern of horse evolution might be even as chaotic as that proposed by Osborn (1937, 1943) for the evolution of the Proboscidea, where 'in almost no instance is any known form considered to be a descendant from any other known form; every subordinate grouping is assumed to have sprung, quite separately and usually without any known intermediate stage, from hypothetical common ancestors in the Early Eocene or Late Cretaceous' (Romer 1949).''[18] If indeed "horse evolution" is that chaotic and patchy, this classic case for evolution is without real merit. The actual evidence, on the other hand, neatly fits the Creation Model.

The order Rodentia should provide evolutionists with a group of mammals ideal for documenting evolutionary transitions. In number of species and genera, the rodents exceed all other mammalian orders combined. They flourish under almost all conditions. Surely, if any group of animals could supply transitional forms, this group could.

As to their origin, Romer has said, "The origin of the rodents is obscure. When they first appear, in the late Paleocene, in the genus *Paramys,* we are already dealing with a typical, if rather primitive, true rodent, with the definitive ordinal characters well developed. Presumably, of course, they had arisen from some basal, insectivorous, placental stock; but no transitional forms are known."[19]

Furthermore, transitional forms between the basic rodent types are not found in the fossil record. For example, Romer says, "... the beavers are presumably derived from some primitive sciuromorph stock, but there are no annectant types between such forms and the oldest Oligocene castoroids to prove direct relationship."[19]

Speaking of the Hystricidae, the Old World porcupines, Romer says, "There are a few fossil forms, back to the Miocene and possibly late Oligocene, but these give no indication of relationship of hystricids to other rodent types."

Commenting on the "rock rat," *Petromus,* Romer says, "Almost nothing is known of the ancestry or possible descendants." Of the lagomorphs (hares and rabbits), once placed in a suborder of the rodents, but now placed in a separate order, Lagomorpha, Romer must admit that, "The lagomorphs show no close approach to other placental groups, and the ordinal characters are well developed in even the oldest known forms."

Thus we see that the order Rodentia, which should supply an excellent case for evolution, if evolution really did occur, offers powerful evidence against the evolutionary hypothesis.

The order Primates is of special interest since that is the order within which our own species, *Homo sapiens,* is placed. We do not consider the order Primates to be a natural group at all, since prosimians, monkeys, apes, and men each were separately created and did not share a common ancestor. Evolutionists, on the other hand, believe that all of these creatures have shared a common ancestor, and that they shared this common ancestry more recently than they shared their common ancestry with any other animal.

The primates are supposed to have evolved from an insectivorous ancestor, more particularly a creature resembling the tree shrew. There is no evidence whatever in the fossil record, however, to support such an idea, for no transitional forms can be found. Elwyn Simons, a leading evolutionary paleoanthropologist, admits that, "In spite of recent finds, the time and place of origin of order Primates remains shrouded in mystery."[20] Romer states that the early lemurs (lemur-like creatures were supposed to be among the first primates) appear "apparently as immigrants from some unknown area."[21] He suggests this since paleontologists have no indication in the fossil record how lemurs (and thus the primates) arose. Kelso states " . . . the transition from insectivore to primate is not documented by fossils. The basis of knowledge about the transition is by inference from living forms."[22]

It is thus evident that when evolutionists seek for the origin of the primate order in the fossil record they encounter a blank wall. Furthermore, recent studies appear to invalidate earlier conclusions that tree shrews (tupaiids) are closely related to living primates. Campbell, who has reviewed this recent work, states, "I have attempted to indicate the large number of recent studies where results indicate that a close relationship between tupaiids and primates is unlikely."[23] He then goes on to say that the innate attractiveness of including the tree shrew in the sequence tree shrew-lemur-tarsier-ape-man may have been in large measure responsible for its acceptance.

We see, then, that there is no evidence to link the primates to the tree shrews (or to any other supposed ancestor), either in the fossil record or among living creatures. The primates stand distinctly apart from all other groups.

This review, certainly brief and incomplete, should nevertheless be sufficient to document the fact that mammals cannot be linked to reptiles or to any other group. Since it can be shown that each of the 32 orders of mammals are separate and distinct groups set apart from one another and from all other creatures by unbridged gaps, it seems evident that collectively as mammals they are set apart as well.

References

1. Raup, David M., *Field Museum of Natural History Bulletin,* Vol. 50, 1979, p. 25.
2. Olson, E. C., *The Evolution of Life,* New York: The New American Library, 1965, p. 207.
3. Simpson, G. G., *Tempo and Mode in Evolution,* New York: Columbia University Press, 1944, p. 105.
4. Romer, A. S., *Vertebrate Paleontology,* 3rd Ed., Chicago: Univ. of Chicago Press, 1966, p. 254.
5. Olson, E. C., p. 178.
6. Romer, A. S., p. 297
7. Romer, A. S., p. 339.
8. Würsig, B., *Scientific American,* Vol. 240, 1979, p. 136.
9. Romer, A. S., p. 338.
10. Birdsell, J. B., *Human Evolution,* Chicago: Rand McNally College Pub. Co., 1975, p. 169.
11. Simpson, G. G., *The Major Features of Evolution,* New York: Columbia Univ. Press, 1953, p. 259.

12. Birdsell, J. B., p. 170.
13. Romer, A. S., pp. 260-261.
14. Nevins, S., *Creation Research Society Quarterly,* Vol. 10, 1974, p. 196.
15. Gregory, J. T., *University of California Publications in Geological Sciences,* Vol. 26, 1942, p. 428.
16. Cousins, F. W., *Creation Research Society Quarterly,* Vol. 7, 1971, p. 102.
17. Nilsson, H., *Synthetische Artbildung,* Verlag CWE Gleerup, Lund, Sweden, 1954. (See F. W. Cousins, Ref. 16, for a summary on the horse.)
18. Kerkut, G. A., *Implications of Evolution,* New York: Pergamon Press, 1960, p. 149.
19. Romer, A. S., p. 303. The following quotes from Romer are in the section pp. 304-310.
20. Simons, E. L., *Annals New York Academy of Sciences,* Vol. 167, 1969, p. 319.
21. Romer, A. S., p. 218.
22. Kelso, A. J., *Physical Anthropology,* 2nd Ed., New York: J. B. Lippincott, 1974, p. 142.
23. Campbell, C. B. G., *Science,* Vol. 153, 1966, p. 436.

———————————◆———————————

No. 88, October 1980
Creation, Selection, and Variation
By Gary E. Parker, Ed.D. *

Horses only 15 inches high, 141 tree species in a single acre of tropical rain forest—what spectacular variety we see among living things, both variation within kind and the stupendous number of different kinds. Most of us are awed by the spectacular variation in color, size, form, features, and function we

———————————————————

* The author, Dr. Gary E. Parker, is a Research Associate in Bioscience at the Institute for Creation Research and teaches Genetics and Biosystematics at Christian Heritage College, El Cajon, California. He is the senior author of several programmed instruction textbooks in biology.

see, both within and among the incredible diversity of living things that grace our planet. Why so much variation?

To the first scientists of the modern era, the answer seemed obvious. After all, we normally associate lavish use of color and form, subtle variations on a theme, and prolific production with the work of master artists and craftsmen. Wouldn't we expect lavish beauty and abundance from the Author of Life, whose creative talents we so feebly reflect?

This incredible diversity also made a striking impression on the unsettled young mind of an amateur naturalist as he sailed around the world aboard *H.M.S. Beagle*.[1] Although Charles Darwin was aware of the evidence of creation, what struck him more was the awful waste in nature, the continual struggle for survival that the over-abundant offspring of each kind faced in the competition for limited food and resources. Failing to understand this struggle for survival as the corruption of an originally harmonious created order, Darwin elevated the survival of the fittest to the place of Creator instead: " . . . from the war of nature, from famine and death . . . the production of higher animals directly follows." That is what Darwin wrote in summarizing his concept of the *Origin of Species by Means of Natural Selection*.[2]

Natural selection was an instant success as a new religion (a "religion without revelation," to use Julian Huxley's phrase), and it had a revolutionary impact on our cultural view of man and society ("Social Darwinism"). Indeed, the well-known historian-philosopher, Will Durant, said in a recent interview that the present pagan era in human history began in 1859 with the publication of Darwin's *Origin*.[3]

But in spite of its success as a new cultural religion, Darwinism failed completely as a scientific explanation for origins. Darwin, a much more astute scientist than most of his devotees, recognized three major problem areas himself: perfection of adaptation, the origin of variation, and the fossil evidence.

Consider the eye, for example, "with all its inimitable contrivances," as Darwin called them, which can admit different amounts of light, focus at different distances, and correct spherical and chromatic abberation. Consider also the splitting of pigment molecules that must be coupled to nerve impulse initiation, and consider that none of these impulses has any meaning apart from millions of neurons integrated into interpretive centers in the brain. Each of these features of optic structure and function is a complex trait itself, and none of these separate components would have any meaning or "survival value," until nearly all were put together in a functioning whole of compounded complexities. No wonder Darwin wrote: "To suppose that the eye, . . . could have been formed by natural selection, seems, I freely confess, absurd in the highest degree."

Yet compound traits whose separate parts would have no survival value are the rule, not the exception. It is easy to multiply examples: the sending and the receiving-interpreting parts of echo location mechanisms in porpoises and platypuses, umbilical vein and ductus venosus relationships in fetal blood circulation, enolase/triose isomerase/2,3-diphosphoglyceric acid in glycolytic metabolism, etc., etc. (No doubt you can think of better examples!)

In such compound traits, the whole is greater by far than the sum of its parts. Structures are given properties of organization they do not have and could not develop on their own—a phenomenon we normally recognize as the result of creative activity. By means of creative design and organization, for example, phosphorus, copper, and glass have been given the ability to talk—to tell jokes, report the news, and to do all the other things we associate with television.

Living things also have properties of organization that clearly transcend the potential of their parts. As Harvard's Richard Lewontin recently summarized it, organisms " . . . appear to have been carefully and artfully designed."[4] He calls the "perfection of organisms" both a challenge to Darwinism and, on a more positive note, "the chief evidence of a Supreme Designer."

Once a complex trait or combination has originated, however, it is easy to cite, and even to elaborate in great detail, its "fitness" or survival value. (This sport is sometimes considered the epitome of academic erudition!) But how did the trait originate whose fitness value is being considered?

Darwin thought it came from the "direct and indirect action of the conditions of life," and "from use and disuse." Thus Darwin, just like Lamarck (with whom he is often *falsely* contrasted), believed that the giraffe's long neck originated by stretching for leaves in trees. The enlarged neck, he thought, produced more "pangenes" that allowed this acquired trait to be inherited.

The discovery of Mendelian genetics rendered classic Darwinism untenable at the turn of the century, and the neo-Darwinists turned from pangenes to mutations to explain origins. But orthodox textbook extrapolation from mutation-selection to evolution failed the mathematical tests of the 1960's, and the harmful effects of mutational load (genetic burden) turned away other evolutionists in the 1970's.[5] With hope instead in "hopeful monsters," Harvard's Stephen Gould says that scientists of the 1980's are forced to ask, "Is a new and general theory of evolution emerging?"[6]

But the failures of pangenes + selection, of mutations + selection, and of hopeful monsters + selection does not mean that there is anything wrong with the concept of natural selection itself. In fact, natural selection works fine—*if* a species has great genetic variability "built right into it" by plan, purpose, and special creation. To use Lewontin's example, plants growing in a region that becomes progressively drier can respond by developing deeper roots and a thicker waxy cuticle on their stems and leaves, "but only if their gene pool contains genetic variation for root length or cuticle thickness." This is why Lewontin can also say: "Whereas greater relative adaptation leads to natural selection, natural selection does not necessarily lead to greater adaptation." If adaptations originated in special acts of creation, then natural selection can help to explain how the created kinds multiplied and filled the earth in such tremendous ecologic and geographic variety.

As a matter of little-known fact, Edward Blyth published the theory of natural selection 24 years before his fellow Englishman, Charles Darwin.[7] Why isn't Blyth's name a household word? Why is he not buried in Westminster Abbey? Perhaps it is simply because Blyth was a creationist, and he made no more out of natural selection than could be observed and supported scientifically. The Darwinists, however, made natural selection (and pangenes) the basis of a new religion, a "religion without revelation."

The Darwinian Revolution of 1859 was not a scientific one (the science had been taken care of 24 years earlier); it was religious and philosophical. In fact, Darwinian zealots extrapolated natural selection into scientific absurdity.

The fossil evidence makes the point most clearly. Darwin, the same astute scientist who recognized both pangenes and complex adaptations as "difficulties with the theory," called the fossil evidence "perhaps the most obvious and serious objection" to extrapolating evolution from natural selection. Given the paucity of fossil data in his time, Darwin tried to blame the conflict between his theory and the fossil facts on faults with the facts—"the imperfection of the geologic record."

"Well, we are now about 120 years after Darwin," writes David Raup of Chicago's famous Field Museum, "and the knowledge of the fossil record has been greatly expanded."[8] Did this wealth of new data produce the "missing links" the Darwinists hoped to find? " . . . ironically," says Raup, "we have even fewer examples of evolutionary transition than we had in Darwin's time. By this I mean that some of the classic cases of darwinian [sic] change in the fossil record, such as the evolution of the horse in North America, have had to be discarded or modified as a result of more detailed information." Rather than forging links in the hypothetical evolutionary chain, the wealth of fossil data has only served to sharpen the boundaries between the created kinds. As Gould says, our ability to classify both living and fossil species distinctly and using the same criteria "fit splendidly with creationist tenets." "But how," he asks, "could a division of the organic world into discrete entities be justified by an evolutionary theory that proclaimed ceaseless change as the fundamental fact of nature?"[9]

" . . . we still have a record which *does* show change," says Raup, "but one that can hardly be looked upon as the most reasonable consequence of natural selection." The change we see is simply variation within the created kinds, plus extinction. In fact, Raup recognizes that the forms of life which died out seem every bit as fit to survive as those that did survive. The losers, he argues, were not slowly lost or transformed by "survival of the fittest"; rather, they succumbed to the whims of chance or catastrophe, a sort of "survival of the luckiest." Creationists who have long accepted the devastating effects of a global flood cannot help but be amused that the facts have finally generated interest among evolutionists in "catastrophe theory" and in "neo-catastrophism."

Darwinian evolution was at odds with the facts of adaptation, genetics, and paleontology right from the start. So, what was the basis for this revolutionary idea and its wildfire acceptance? In the words of Stephen Gould and Niles Eldredge: "Phyletic gradualism [gradual evolution] was an a priori assertion from the start—it was never 'seen' in the rocks; it expressed the cultural and political biases of nineteenth century liberalism."[10] Karl Marx found it interesting to see how easily English scientists saw the "winner-take-all" cut-throat competitiveness of nineteenth century England reflected in (and perhaps justified by) "survival of the fittest" as a law of nature. In Darwinian thinking, even the evolution of cooperation can proceed only over the dead bodies of those that do not cooperate.

Creationists recognize the waste of over-reproduction and the bitter struggle for survival in our present world order. But, unlike evolutionists, creationists do *not* see these processes as a means of creation. Rather, they reflect the corruption of the created order that followed man's sin. In fact, it was the violence that filled the earth which brought on the judgment and cleansing of the Flood (Gen. 6:5).

Against this background of creation, corruption, and catastrophe, natural selection has several positive roles to play in our present world. For one thing, natural selection acts as a brake to slow down the decay in genetic quality caused by mutations. For another, selection (along with genetic drift and habitat choice) helps each created kind to maintain a variety of specialized subtypes in diverse and changing environments. In Darwin's words, natural selection, although it fails to explain the "origin of species," does help to explain "the preservation of favored races in the struggle for life" (the second half of his book's title).

As Lewontin put it, " . . . natural selection over the long run does not seem to improve a species' chance of survival but simply enables it to 'track,' or keep up with, the constantly changing environment." The *observed, conservative* function of natural selection is not nearly so glamorous as the *hypothetical, creative* function assigned to it by evolutionists, but it really is an important, and scientifically verifiable, role. Natural selection is not bad science, even though it makes bad religion.

Raup was no doubt being too harsh when, condemning with faint praise, he wrote: "So natural selection as a process is okay. We are also pretty sure that it goes on in nature although good examples are surprisingly rare." What would Darwin think if he knew that creationists were now finding his theory more useful than some leading evolutionists are?

Still, for creationists, natural selection and the struggle for survival will come to an end when Christ returns and "the wolf and the lamb will lie down together, . . . and they will not hurt or destroy, . . . for the earth will be full of the knowledge of the Lord as the waters cover the sea" (Isaiah 11).

References

1. Asimov, Isaac, "The Voyage of Charles Darwin," *TV Guide,* Jan. 26, 1980, pp. 13-14.
2. Darwin, Charles, *The Origin of Species,* New York: Washington Square Press, 1963, p. 470 (First ed. 1859).
3. Durant, Will, "Historian Will Durant: We Are in the Last Stage of Pagan Period," an article in *The Daily Californian,* El Cajon, CA, for April 8, 1980, p. 5B, by Rogers Worthington of *The Chicago Tribune.*
4. Lewontin, Richard, "Adaptation," *Scientific American,* V. 239, No. 3, 1978, pp. 212-230.
5. For fuller discussion and documentation, see Gary Parker, *Creation: The Facts of Life,* San Diego: CLP Publishers, 1980.
6. Gould, Stephen, "Is a New and General Theory of Evolution Emerging," *Paleobiology,* V. 6, No. 1, 1980, pp. 119-130.
7. Eiseley, Loren, *Darwin and the Mysterious Mr. X,* New York: Dutton Publishing Co., 1979. (See also the book review by Wendell Cochran, "Evolution and Catastrophe," *Geotimes,* V. 24, No. 10, 1979, p. 17.)
8. Raup, David, "Conflicts Between Darwin and Paleontology," *Field Museum of Natural History Bulletin,* V. 50, No. 1, 1979, pp. 22-29.
9. Gould, Stephen, "A Quahog is a Quahog," *Natural History,* V. 88, No. 7, 1979, pp. 18-26.
10. Gould, Stephen, and Eldredge, Niles, "Punctuated Equilibria: The Tempo and Mode of Evolution Reconsidered," *Paleobiology,* V. 3, No. 2, 1977, p. 115.

No. 89, November 1980
Creation, Mutation, and Variation
By Gary E. Parker, Ph.D. *

"Enormous," "tremendous," "staggering"—all these are adjectives used by geneticist Francisco Ayala to describe the amount of variation that can be expressed among the members of a single species.[1] Human beings, for example, range from very tall to very short, very dark to very light, soprano to bass, etc., etc. This tremendous amount of variation within species has been considered a challenge to creationists. Many ask: "How could the created progenitors of each kind possess enough variability among their genes to fill the earth with all the staggering diversity we see today—and to refill it after a global flood only a few thousand years ago?"

If we use Ayala's figures, there would be no problem at all. He cites 6.7% as the average proportion of human genes that show heterozygous allelic variation, e.g., straight vs. curly hair, Ss. On the basis of "only" 6.7% heterozygosity, Ayala calculates that the average human couple could have 10^{2017} children before they would have to have one child identical to another! That number, a one followed by 2017 zeroes, is greater than the number of sand grains by the sea, the number of stars in the sky, or the atoms in the known universe (a "mere" 10^{80})!

A single human couple could have been created with four alleles (two for each person) at each gene position (locus). Just two alleles for vocal cord characteristics, V and v, are responsible for the variation among tenor (VV), baritone (Vv), and bass (vv) singing voices in men, and hormone influences on development result in soprano (VV), mezzo-soprano (Vv), and alto voices (vv) as expressions of the same genes in women. Furthermore, several genes are known to exist in multiple copies, and

---

* The author, Dr. Gary E. Parker, is a Research Associate in Bioscience at the Institute for Creation Research and teaches Genetics and Biosystematics at Christian Heritage College, El Cajon, California. He is the senior author of several programmed instruction textbooks in biology.

some traits, like color, weight, and intelligence, depend on the cumulative effect of genes at two or more loci. Genes of each different copy and at each different locus could exist in four allelic forms, so the potential for diversity is staggering indeed!

Even more exciting is the recent discovery that some genes exist as protein coding segments of DNA separated by non-coding sequences called "introns." In addition to other functions, these introns may serve as "cross-over" points for "mixing and matching" subunits in the protein product.[2] If each subunit of such a gene existed in four allelic forms, consider the staggering amount of variation that one gene with three such subunits could produce! It is quite possible that such a clever—and created—mechanism is the means by which the information to produce millions of specific disease-fighting antibodies can be stored in only a few thousand genes.

Besides the positive contributors to genetic diversity described above, there is also one major negative contributor: *mutation*. Believe it or not, orthodox evolutionists have tried to explain all the staggering variation both within and among species on the basis of these random changes in heredity called "mutation." What we know about mutations, however, makes them entirely unsuitable as any "raw materials for evolutionary progress."

As Ayala says, mutations in fruit flies have produced "extremely short wings, deformed bristles, blindness, and other serious defects." Such mutations impose an increasingly heavy *genetic burden* or *genetic load* on a species. In her genetics textbook, Anna Pai makes it clear that "the word *load* is used intentionally to imply some sort of burden" that drags down the genetic quality of a species.[3] The list of human mutational disorders, or genetic diseases, for example, has already passed 1500, and it is continuing to grow.

By elimination of the unfit, natural selection reduces the harmful effects of mutations on a population, but it cannot solve the evolutionist's genetic burden problem entirely. Most mutations are recessive. That is, like the hemophilia ("bleeder's disease") gene in England's Queen Victoria, the mutant can be carried, undetected by selection, in a person (or plant or animal) with a dominant gene that masks the mutant's effect.

Time, the usual "hero of the plot" for evolutionists, only makes genetic burden *worse*. As time goes on, existing mutants build up to a complex equilibrium point, and new mutations are continually occurring. That is why marriage among close relatives (e.g., Cain and his sister) posed no problem early in human history, even though now, thanks to the increase in mutational load with time, such marriages are considered most unwise. Already, 1% of all children born will require some professional help with genetic problems, and that percentage doubles in first-cousin marriages.

Genetic burden, then, becomes a staggering problem for evolutionists trying to explain the enormous adaptive variation within species on the basis of mutations. For any conceivable favorable mutation, a species must pay the price or bear the burden of more than 1000 harmful mutations of that gene. Against such a background of "genetic decay," any hypothetical favorable mutant in one gene would invariably be coupled to harmful changes in other genes. As mutational load increases with time, the survival of the species will be threatened as matings produce a greater percentage of offspring carrying serious genetic defects.[1,3]

As the source of adaptive variability, then, mutations (and orthodox evolution theories) fail completely. As a source of "negative variability," however, mutations serve only too well. Basing their thinking on what we observe of mutations and their net effect (genetic burden), creationists use mutations to help explain the existence of disease, genetic defects, and other examples of "negative variation" within species.

Mutations are "pathologic" (disease-causing) and only "modify what pre-exists," as French zoologist Pierre-Paul Grassé says, so mutations have "no final evolutionary effect."[4] Instead, mutations point back to creation and to a corruption of the created order. There are 40-plus variants of hemoglobin, for example. All are variants of hemoglobin; that points back to creation. All are less effective oxygen carriers than normal hemoglobin; that points back to a corruption of the created order by time and chance.

At average mutation rates (one per million gene duplications), a human population of one billion would likely produce a thousand variant forms of hemoglobin. Lethal mutants would escape detection, and so would those that produced only minor changes, easily masked by a dominant normal gene. It is likely then, that the 40 or so recognized hemoglobin abnormalities represent only a small fraction of the genetic burden we bear at the hemoglobin position.

According to a new school of thought, "the neutral theory of molecular evolution," much of the staggering variation within species is due to mutations that are either neutral (without effect) or slightly deleterious.[5] Such a theory offers no comfort to the evolutionist trying to build grander life forms from mutations, but it is an expected consequence of the creation-corruption model. Interestingly, says Kimura, the amount of variation within species is too great for selection models of evolution, but too little for the neutral theory. He suggests that recent "genetic bottlenecks" have set back the "molecular clock" that otherwise ticks off mutations at a relatively constant rate. Scientists who recognize the fossil evidence of a recent global flood are not at all surprised, of course, that data suggest a recent "genetic bottleneck" which only a few of each kind survived!

Now, what about the time factor in the creation model? How long would it take, for example, to produce all the different shades of human skin color we have today?

There are several factors that contribute subtle tones to skin colors, but all people have *the same* basic skin coloring agent, the protein called *melanin*. We *all* have melanin skin color, just

MAXIMUM VARIATION

AaBb x AaBb	AB	Ab	aB	ab	
AB	AA BB	AA Bb	Aa BB	Aa Bb	ONLY DARK AABB
Ab	AA Bb	AA bb	Aa Bb	Aa bb	ONLY MEDIUM AAbb or aaBB
aB	Aa BB	Aa Bb	aa BB	aa Bb	
ab	Aa Bb	Aa bb	aa Bb	aa bb	ONLY LIGHT aabb

different amounts of it. (Not a very big difference, is it?) According to Davenport's study in the West Indies, the amount of skin color we have is influenced by at least two pairs of genes, A-a and B-b.

How long would it take AaBb parents to have children with all the variations in skin color we see today? Answer: *one generation*. Just one generation. As shown in the genetic square, one in 16 of the children of AaBb parents would likely have the darkest possible skin color (AABB); one brother or sister in 16 would likely have the lightest skin color (aabb); less than half (6/16) would be medium-skinned like their parents (any two "capital letter" genes); and one-quarter (4/16) would be a shade darker (3 capital letter genes) and a shade lighter (1 capital letter).

What happened as the descendants of our first parents (and of Noah's family) multiplied over the earth? If those with very dark skin color (AABB) moved into the same area and/or chose to marry only those with very dark skin color, then all their children would be *limited* to very dark skin color. Similarly, children of parents with very light skin color (aabb) could have only very light skin, since their parents would have only "small a's and b's" to pass on. Parents with genotypes AAbb or aaBB would be limited to producing only children with medium-skin color. But where people of different backgrounds get back together again, as they do in the West Indies, then their children can once again express the full range of variation.

Except for mutational loss of skin color (albinism), then, the human gene pool would be the same now as it might have been at creation—just four genes, A, a, B, b, no more and no less. Actually, there are probably more gene loci and more alleles involved, which would make it even easier to store genetic variability in our created ancestors. As people multiplied over the earth (especially after Babel), the variation "hidden" in the genes of two average-looking parents came to visible expression in different tribes and tongues and nations.

The same would be true of the other created kinds as well: *generalized* ("average-looking") progenitors created with large and *adaptable* gene pools would break up into a variety of more *specialized* and *adapted* subtypes, as descendants of each created kind multiplied and filled the earth, both after creation and after the Flood.

There is new evidence that members of some species (including the famous peppered moth) may actually "choose" environments suitable for their trait combinations.[6] If "habitat choice" behavior were created (and did not have to originate by time, chance, and random mutations!), it would reduce the genetic burden that results when only one trait expression is "fittest," and it would also greatly *accelerate* the process of diversification *within* species.

Research and new discoveries have made it increasingly easy for creationists to account for phenomenal species diversification within short periods of time. These same discoveries have only magnified problems in orthodox neo-Darwinian thinking. It is encouraging, but not surprising, therefore, that an increasing number of students and professionals in science are accepting the creation model as the more logical inference from scientific observations and principles.

The scientist who is Christian can also look forward to the end of genetic burden, when the creation, now "subjected to futility" will be "set free from its bondage to decay, and obtain the glorious liberty of the children of God" (Romans 8).

References

1. Ayala, Francisco, "The Mechanisms of Evolution," *Scientific American*, V. 239, No. 3, 1978, pp. 56-69.
2. Kolata, Gina, "Genes in Pieces," *Science*, V. 207, No. 4429, 1980, pp. 392-393. (Note also the emphasized quotation on p. 393: "A number of molecular biologists believe there is more to the extra DNA than the evolutionary theories imply.")
3. Pai, Anna, *Foundations of Genetics*, New York: McGraw-Hill Book Co., 1974, pp. 248-249.
4. Grassé, Pierre-Paul, *Evolution of Living Organisms*, New York: Academic Press, 1977, as quoted by William Bauer, "Review of *Evolution of Living Organisms*," *Acts and Facts*, Impact No. 76, 1979.
5. Kimura, Motoo, "The Neutral Theory of Molecular Evolution," *Scientific American*, V. 241, No. 5, 1979, pp. 98-126.
6. Powell, Jeffrey, and Charles Taylor, "Genetic Variation in Diverse Environments," *American Scientist*, V. 67, No. 5, 1979, pp. 590-596.

No. 90, December 1980
Glycolysis and Alcoholic Fermentation
By Jean Sloat Morton, Ph.D. *

When the oxygen supply runs short in heavy or prolonged exercise, muscles obtain most of their energy from an anaerobic (without oxygen) process called *glycolysis*. Yeast cells obtain energy under anaerobic conditions using a very similar process called *alcoholic fermentation*. Glycolysis is the chemical breakdown of glucose to lactic acid. This process makes energy available for cell activity in the form of a high-energy phosphate compound known as adenosine triphosphate (ATP). Alcoholic fermentation is identical to glycolysis except for the final step (Fig. 1). In alcoholic fermentation, pyruvic acid is broken down into ethanol and carbon dioxide. Lactic acid from glycolysis produces a feeling of tiredness; the products of alcoholic fermentation have been used in baking and brewing for centuries.

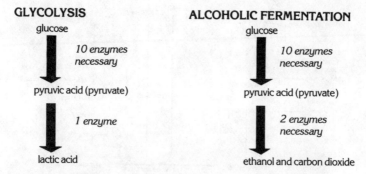

GLYCOLYSIS

glucose

10 enzymes necessary

pyruvic acid (pyruvate)

1 enzyme

lactic acid

ALCOHOLIC FERMENTATION

glucose

10 enzymes necessary

pyruvic acid (pyruvate)

2 enzymes necessary

ethanol and carbon dioxide

Fig. 1. A comparison of two anaerobic energy-harvesting mechanisms.

---

* The author, Dr. Jean Morton, holds a Ph.D. from George Washington University in Cellular Studies and has taught biology at American University and George Washington University, and has served as a consultant in microbiology. She is author of an outstanding book *Science in the Bible* (Moody, 1978) and has written numerous science instructional units for various grade levels. She is a member of ICR's Technical Advisory Board.

Both alcoholic fermentation and glycolysis are anaerobic fermentation processes that begin with the sugar glucose. Glycolysis requires 11 enzymes which degrade glucose to lactic acid (Fig. 2). Alcoholic fermentation follows the same enzymatic pathway for the first 10 steps. The last enzyme of glycolysis, lactate dehydrogenase, is replaced by two enzymes in alcholic fermentation. These two enzymes, pyruvate decarboxylase and alcoholic dehydrogenase, convert pyruvic acid into carbon dioxide and ethanol in alcoholic fermentation.

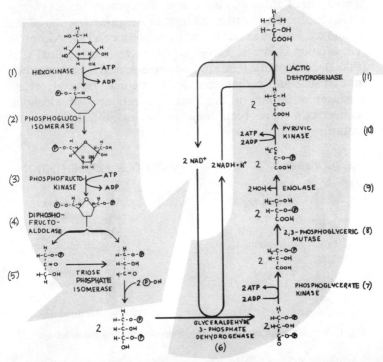

Fig. 2. Notice that ATP is formed at two different locations above (steps 7 & 10). Because there are 2 molecules of the substrates, there will be 2 molecules of ATP formed at both locations, making a total of 4 molecules of ATP. Two molecules of ATP were necessary for priming the original breakdown of glucose (step 1). Therefore, a net gain of 2 molecules of ATP are recognized from the entire breakdown of glucose pyruvate. (4 ATP formed - 2 ATP primers = 2 ATP net overall gain.) Notice also that this final net gain in ATP is not recognized until phosphoenolpyruvate is broken down by pyruvate kinase to form 2 molecules of pyruvate. This means that 10 enzymatic reactions must proceed in sequence, before energy in the form of ATP is obtained.

The most commonly accepted evolutionary scenario states that organisms first arose in an atmosphere lacking oxygen.[1,2] Anaerobic fermentation is supposed to have evolved first and is considered the most ancient pathway for obtaining energy. There are several scientific difficulties, however, with considering fermentations as primitive energy harvesting mechanisms produced by time and chance.

First of all, it takes ATP energy to start the process that will only later generate a net gain in ATP. Two ATPs are put into the glycolytic pathway for priming the reactions, the expenditure of energy by conversion of ATP to ADP being required in the first and third steps of the pathway (Fig. 2). A total of four ATPs are obtained only later in the sequence, making a net gain of two ATPs for each molecule of glucose degraded. The net gain of two ATPs is not realized until the tenth enzyme in the series catalyzes phosphoenolpyruvate to ATP and pyruvic acid (pyruvate). This means that neither glycolysis nor alcoholic fermentation realizes any gain in energy (ATP) until the tenth enzymatic breakdown.

It is purely wishful thinking to suppose that a series of 10 simultaneous, beneficial, additive mutations could produce 10 complex enzymes to work on 10 highly specific substances and that these reactions would occur in sequence. Enzymes are proteins consisting of amino acids united in polypeptide chains. Their complexity may be illustrated by the enzyme glyceraldehyde phosphate dehydrogenase, which is the enzyme that catalyzes the oxidation of phosphoglyceraldehyde in glycolysis and alcoholic fermentation. Glyceraldehyde phosphate dehydrogenase consists of four identical chains, each having 330 amino acid residues. The number of different possible arrangements for the amino acid residues of this enzyme is astronomical.

To illustrate, let us consider a simple protein containing only 100 amino acids. There are 20 different kinds of L-amino acids in proteins, and each can be used repeatedly in chains of 100. Therefore, they could be arranged in 20^{100} or 10^{130} different ways. Even if a hundred million billion (10^{17}) of these combinations could function for a given purpose, there is only one chance in 10^{113} of getting one of these required amino acid sequences in a small protein consisting of 100 amino acids.

By comparison, Sir Arthur Eddington has estimated there are no more than 10^{80} (or $3,145 \times 10^{79}$) particles in the universe. If we assume that the universe is 30 billion years old (or 10^{18} seconds), and that each particle can react at the exaggerated rate of one trillion (10^{12}) times per second, then the total number of events that can occur within the time and matter of our universe is $10^{80} \times 10^{12} \times 10^{18} = 10^{110}$. Even by most generous estimates, therefore, there is not enough time or matter in our universe to "guarantee" production of even one small protein with relative specificity.

If probabilities involving two or more independent events are desired, they can be found by multiplying together the probabilities of each event. Consider the 10 enzymes of the glycolytic pathway. If each of these were a small protein having 100 amino acid residues with some flexibility and a probability of 1 in 10^{113} or 10^{-113}, the probability for arranging the amino acids for the 10 enzymes would be: $P = 10^{-1,130}$ or 1 in $10^{1,130}$.

And 1 in $10^{1,130}$ is only the odds against producing the 10 glycolytic enzymes by chance. It is estimated that the human body contains 25,000 enzymes. If each of these were only a small enzyme consisting of 100 amino acids with a probability of 1 in 10^{-113}, the probability of getting all 25,000 would be $(10^{-113})^{25,000}$, which is 1 chance in $10^{2,825,000}$! The actual probability for arranging the amino acids of the 25,000 enzymes will be much slimmer than our calculations indicate, because most enzymes are far more complex than our illustrative enzyme of 100 amino acids.

Mathematicians usually consider 1 chance in 10^{50} as negligible.[3] In other words, when the exponent is larger than 50, the chances are so slim for such an event ever occurring, that it is considered impossible. In our calculations, 10^{-110} was considered the total number of events that cold occur within the time and matter of our universe. The chances for producing a simple enzyme-protein having 100 amino acid residues was 1 in 10^{113}. The probability for 25,000 enzymes occurring by chance alone was 1 in $10^{2,825,000}$. It is preposterous to think that even one simple enzyme-protein could occur by chance alone, much less the 10 in glycolysis or the 25,000 in the human body!

There are still other problems with the theory of evolution for alcoholic fermentation and glycolytic pathways. It is necessary to account for the numerous complex regulatory mechanisms which control these chemical pathways. For example, phosphofructokinase is a regulatory enzyme which limits the rate of glycolysis. Glycogen phosphorylase is also a regulatory enzyme; it converts glycogen to glucose-1-phosphate and thus makes glycogen available for glycolytic breakdown. In complex organisms there are several hormones such as somatotropin, insulin, glucagon, glucocorticoids, adrenalin, thyroxin, and a host of others which control utilization of glucose. No evolutionary mechanism has ever been proposed to account for these control mechnisms.

In addition to the regulators, complex cofactors are absolutely essential for glycolysis. One of the two key ATP energy harvesting steps in glycolysis requires a dehydrogenase enzyme acting in concert with the "hydrogen shuttle" redox reactant, nicotinamide adenine dinucleotide (NAD^+). To keep the reaction sequence going, the reduced cofactor ($NADH + H^+$) must be continuously regenerated by steps later in the sequence (Fig. 2), and that requires one enzyme in glycolysis (lactic dehydrogenase) and another (alcohol dehydrogenase) in alcoholic fermentation. In the absence of continuously cycled NAD^+, "simple" anaerobic ATP energy harvest would be impossible.

And there are further difficulties yet for evolutionary theory to surmount. At one point, an intermediate in the glycolytic pathway is "stuck" with a phosphate group (needed to make ATP) in the low energy third carbon position. A remarkable enzyme, a "mutase" (Step 8), shifts the phosphate group to the second carbon position—but only in the presence of pre-existent primer amounts of an extraordinary molecule, 2,3-diphosphoglyceric acid. Actually, the shift of the phosphate from the third to the second position using the "mutase" and these "primer" molecules accomplishes nothing notable directly, but it "sets up" the ATP energy-harvesting reaction which occurs two steps later!

In summary, the following items make an evolutionary origin for glycolysis and alcoholic fermentation totally untenable: (1) the extreme improbability of getting even one simple enzyme by random processes; (2) the fact that the overall net gain in energy (ATP) is not recognized until pyruvate formation suggests that the chemical reaction must proceed through at least 10 enzymatic steps and that these steps of necessity must be in sequence; (3) the complex regulatory mechanisms, cofactors, and "primers" necessary for glucose utilization cannot be explained by evolutionary speculation.

On the other hand, the tight fit among complex and interdependent steps—especially the way some reactions take on meaning only in terms of reactions that occur much later in the sequence—seems to point clearly to creation with a teleological purpose, by an Intelligence and Power far greater than man's.

References

1. A. I. Oparin, *Origin of Life,* New York: Dover Pub., Inc., 1965, pp. 225-226.
2. Clark and Synge (eds.), *The Origin of Life on the Earth,* New York: Pergamon Press, 1959, p. 52.
3. Emil Borel, *Probabilities and Life,* New York: Dover Pub., Inc., 1962, p. 28.

No. 91, January 1981
Two Decades of Creation: Past and Future
By Henry M. Morris, Ph.D. *

The year 1980 was the first year of what could well be the most exciting decade in many centuries. Among other encouraging indicators, the signs seem favorable for a much stronger worldwide expansion of creationism than even that which occurred in the seventies. If so, this will be attributable in considerable measure to the strong base of scientific creationism established in the past decade by the wide-ranging activities of

*   The author, Dr. Henry M. Morris, is the Director of the Institute for Creation Research and the author of numerous articles and books.

the Institute for Creation Research. Since ICR is planning in 1981 to institute graduate degree programs in creationist science and education, this is a good time to review not only the work of the past year but also that of the entire past decade since ICR's beginning.

Activities in 1980

The ministry of ICR involves three major functions: (1) publications; (2) research; (3) teaching (including seminars, debates, radio, and all other speaking ministries). The 1980 activities in all three of these categories are summarized below:

A. Publications
  1. R. B. Bliss, G. E. Parker, and D. T. Gish, *Fossils: Key to the Present* (CLP, 1980)
  2. H. M. Morris, *King of Creation* (CLP, 1980)
  3. H. S. Slusher, *Age of the Cosmos* (CLP, 1980)
  4. G. E. Parker, *Creation: The Facts of Life* (CLP, 1980)
  5. J. D. Morris, *Tracking Those Incredible Dinosaurs and the People Who Knew Them* (CLP, 1980)
  6. H. M. Morris, ed. *The Decade of Creation* (CLP, 1980)
  7. 12 issues of ICR *Acts & Facts,* with "Impact Series" articles
  8. 5 articles in professional journals or anthologies
  9. 8 articles in Christian periodicals
B. Research
  1. Field study of geologic catastrophism in Australia
  2. Laboratory study of catastrophic indicators in coal geology
  3. Field studies in Grand Canyon and Anza-Borrego Desert
  4. Theoretical and library research on numerous creation/evolution issues
C. Speaking and Teaching
  1. 10 creation/evolution debates, at Charleston, SC; Kansas City; Iowa State University; Des Moines College; Graceland College; Princeton University; Humboldt State College; Western Washington University; University of Wisconsin (Baraboo); and University of Washington. Total Attendance: 5500.

2. 5 Summer Institutes on Scientific Creationism (week-long, two-credit courses) at Calvary Bible College (Kansas City), Moody Bible Institute (Chicago), Washington Bible College (Lanham, MD), Briercrest Bible Institute (Caronport, Saskatchewan), and Christian Heritage College. Total Enrollment: 400.

3. 6 three-credit courses in Scientific Creationism, at Christian Heritage College. (Total of 270 lecture hours.)

4. 52 weekly radio broadcasts for ICR program "Science, Scripture, and Salvation." Now heard on 85 stations in 33 states, plus overseas.

5. Appearances on more than 20 other radio programs, plus on 6 national telecasts, and at least 10 local television programs, as well as many interviews for newspaper and magazine articles.

6. Appearances in 2 Christian motion picture films.

7. 101 lectures on 32 college and university campuses (in addition to the debates and summer institutes).

8. 75 messages in 53 churches representing 15 or more denominations.

9. 100 lectures at creation seminars in 26 different cities and 19 states.

10. 50 lectures to educational, scientific, political, or civic groups in 26 cities in 14 states.

11. International ministries in Canada and South Korea.

SUMMARY:

Approximately 770 lectures or messages in 23 states, plus Canada and Korea, to audiences totaling over 100,000 (not including radio and television listeners).

Summary of ICR Activities Since 1970

The complex of ministries now associated with the Institute for Creation Research was originally established in September 1970, along with Christian Heritage College. It was reorganized in April 1972 under its present name and has continued to grow in stature and outreach ever since. Thus, in slightly over one decade, a ministry which began with only one scientist working part-time, has grown to international proportions, widely recognized (especially by evolutionists!) as the leading influence in the modern revival of creationism.

A brief summary of part of its ministry during this period would include the following:

1. Publication of 55 significant books, including 9 technical monographs and 14 textbooks now widely used in various schools and colleges.

2. Publication of numerous slide sets, filmstrips, transparencies, and cassettes, which have also been widely used, as well as participating or consulting on 5 significant film productions.

3. Two expeditions to Mount Ararat in search of Noah's Ark, at least 15 field expeditions for geological or archaeological research, plus continuing library and analytical research on a wide-ranging variety of topics.

4. More than 100 formal creation/evolution debates with leading evolutionary scientists, usually held on university campuses (all with favorable results for creationism).

5. Lectures on at least 400 different college and university campuses.

6. Messages in well over 400 different churches

7. Creation seminars or conferences held in 350 cities.

8. 35 Summer Institutes on Scientific Creationism held at 23 different colleges.

9. ICR radio broadcast, "Science, Scripture, and Salvation," produced and distributed weekly since May 1972, plus appearances on at least 300 other radio programs and 200 television programs (including more than 20 network telecasts).

10. Lecture ministries in many other countries (Canada, Australia, New Zealand, England, Ireland, Scotland, Wales, Holland, Germany, Sweden, Norway, Denmark, South Korea, etc.).

11. Translations of ICR publications into at least 10 other languages.

12. Lectures to more than 200 significant gatherings of scientists, teachers, legislators, or other important secular groups.

13. Teaching regular six semester-hour courses in Scientific Creationism and regular six semester-hour courses in Practical Christian Evidences at Christian Heritage College every year since 1970. In addition, ICR staff members have served

as Adjunct Professors at Christian Heritage College, teaching most of its courses in the various sciences.

14. Teaching credit courses in creationism for eight or more other colleges on a visiting-faculty basis.

As a result, there are many more churches, Christian schools, and other institutions today which are teaching creationism to their constituents than was true a decade ago. Many local creationist organizations have been formed all over the country, and in many foreign countries, largely as a result of ICR's impact and publications. The news media, on the other hand, are also widely publicizing these activities now, and often opposing them. The same is true of many humanistically oriented scientific and educational associations, as well as the evolutionary establishment in general.

Over the past decade, ICR speakers have lectured in almost every state, and in at least 15 other countries. The combined attendance at these meetings has exceeded 600,000, not including radio and television audiences. Over a million copies of books by ICR scientists have been distributed.

Hundreds of people have told us during these past ten years, either in person or by letter, that their lives have been changed by this ministry. Many have been brought to saving faith in Christ and many more have been strengthened in their Christian life and witness.

When we contrast the situation at the end of this decade with ICR's fragile foundation at its beginning (or, even more, the almost complete dearth of scientific creationist literature 40 years ago, at the time the writer first became a creationist and began to try to develop a sound scientific case for creation), the prospects for the future with our present strong base look strong and exciting.

ICR Goals for the Future

First of all, we believe that every one of the present activities of ICR, Lord willing, should be continued and expanded. Its unique combination of commitment to creationism in every discipline, and simultaneous commitment to high scientific and personal integrity in all its activities is a much needed emphasis in today's hurting world. However, our present activities, even expanded, will not be enough. A repudiation of evolutionary humanism, and a return to true belief in God as Creator and Sovereign of the Universe is prerequisite to any real solution of human problems, whether those problems are personal, social, or transnational in scope. Since today's dominant belief in evolutionism stems mostly from the schools, and since the teachers in the schools are determined largely by the training of their teachers and the material in their textbooks, it is of first importance that creationist textbooks and training somehow be provided. It is futile and counter-productive to try to force schools by political or other means to teach creationism, when there are no creationist textbooks or graduate schools with which to equip their teachers to do so.

The following goals are, therefore, of transcendent importance. They may well be beyond the reach of ICR or of any other single organization, but we do believe it is essential that we try.

1. Development of an entire spectrum of sound creationist text and reference books, in every subject and at every level, for Christian schools, and of corresponding "two-model" books for non-Christian schools.
2. Development of a true Christian creationist university system, with graduate and professional schools, and with research and extension programs, all oriented toward a real creationist, Christian, Biblical world view.

These may seem like impossible goals, but "with God nothing shall be impossible." There is already an abundance of qualified creationist professionals whom God has raised up, men and women representing all fields of the sciences, and other relevant disciplines, who would be well able to write the needed textbooks and develop the needed graduate and professional programs if they had the opportunity.

In order to do this, however, such people need to be recognized and brought together with their efforts all properly coordinated and underwritten financially. However, the necessary finances have seemed an insurmountable obstacle so far.

But the hour is late, and there will never be a better time than now to trust God to remove the barriers and supply the need. There seems to be no other organization better prepared to attempt this mission (or at least none with a greater burden and sense of need) than ICR and so, as the Lord leads and enables, we plan to move as rapidly as possible toward these goals in 1981 and the critical decade ahead. This decision has been based on much prayer and study extending over several years, as well as clear evidence of the Lord's leading at this time. But the continuing prayers and support of all concerned Christian people everywhere are urgently needed if the goals are to be attained.

No. 92, February 1981
Words: Genetic and Linguistic Problems For Evolution
By Dr. John W. Oller, Jr. *

In 1934, just before his death, the eminent Russian psychologist, Lev S. Vygotsky,[1] concluded his book on *Thought and Language* with a quotation from Faust which insisted that, "In the beginning was the deed." According to Vygotsky, the word came later, crowning the deed. What he had in mind, of course, was the development of intelligence in children. He was not concerned with the ultimate question of how there came to be order in the universe, yet it is the fundamental faith of science that there is order in the universe, and obviously it had to come to be by some means. Vygotsky boldly asserted that order arises from action rather than words. He left God out of the picture and committed himself to the evolutionary doctrine of secularism. One of the Hebrew Psalmists wrote, "Why does the wicked man revile God? Why does he say to himself, 'He won't call me to account' ?" (New International Version, Psalm 10:13). Within a few months after Vygotsky concluded his book, he died. He never saw his thirty-fifth birthday.

Secularists often pay homage to blind chance as the source of the order that science finds in the physical and biological world. Yet they often lament the fact that evolutionary wisdom is not

---

* The author, Dr. Oller, is Professor of Linguistics at the University of New Mexico. His Ph.D. is from the University of Rochester.

maintaining itself, but systematically destroying the very order that it is supposed to have created. Bertrand Russell[2] wept as eloquently as any atheist who ever wielded a pen over the crumbling temple of evolutionary grandeur. He wrote, "All the labors of the ages, all the devotion, all the inspiration, all the noonday brightness of human genius, are destined to extinction in the vast death of the solar system, and . . . the whole temple of man's achievement must inevitably be buried beneath the debris of a universe in ruins . . . " (Russell, 1917).

One can only wonder at the logic of a doctrine which sees chaos as both the beginning and end of the marvelous order that science finds in the universe. How is it that the selfsame principles which supposedly led to the order, are also those which are certainly and permanently destroying it? Vygotsky insisted that actions preceded the formative power of the word, but action without a plan is like a ship without a rudder. There is no reason to suppose that such action could ever result in the order that we find in the universe.

To illustrate the severity of the logical problem for evolutionism, consider the origin of the genetic code. Until 1966 it was more or less popular to poke fun at the notion that the formative power of the *"word"* was fundamentally involved in the origin of order and particularly of life. After 1966, however, with the unraveling of the dictionary of correspondences between the bases in the nucleic acids and the amino acids of the proteins (that is, *"the genetic code"*), the formative power of signfunctions began to have a more respectable scientific status. The opening of John's Gospel, "In the beginning was the Word," came to have a more scientific ring to it.

Even as early as 1963 and 1964, Hinegardner and Engelberg[3,4] published arguments in *Science* showing the extreme implausibility of the claim that the genetic basis of life had evolved in a step by step fashion. The difficulty was that the minutest sorts of changes in the dictionary of correspondences between the words of the nucleic acids and the words of the protein language would be lethal *to all living things*. Because of the apparent universality of the code (see Clark[5], Yĉas[6], and Woese[7]), very minute changes in the code would have devastating effects to all living organisms. This may be why F. H. C. Crick[8] (who shared the Nobel prize with J. D. Watson for work on the structure of DNA) commented in 1966 that he was thinking of offering an annual prize for the worst paper published on the topic of the origin of the genetic code. It seems that in Crick's view, there are far too many who are willing to offer untestable, unscientific claims about how the code came to be.

From a purely logical point of view, the problem is one of words and numbers. There are too many intricacies. As Woese, Yĉas, Clark, and other biologists have been pointing out for some years now, every living cell consists largely of long biological texts. The most basic of these are written in the nucleic acid language. These basic texts are translated into another library of texts in the language of the proteins. Underlying this whole process is the dictionary of correspondences between the two types of texts known as the genetic code.

The code itself may be regarded as part of a grammatical system governing the meaning of strings of words in the nucleic acid language. The nucleic acid texts in their turn are on the one hand the output of the deeper biological grammar, and on the other they are themselves a kind of grammar governing the strings of words that are used to form the texts of the protein language. Similarly, the protein texts have a dual aspect. On the one hand, they are texts output by the nucleic acid *"grammar"* and on the other, they themselves serve a grammatical function in constraining the structure and metabolic functions of the cell. The problem for an evolutionary explanation is how such intricate order could arise by pure chance.

The difficulty can best be appreciated perhaps by examining more closely the linguistic analogy—an analogy which has been proposed unflinchingly by biologists (though it is viewed with some trepidation by many linguists). How is it that such intricately and delicately ordered strings of words got strung together just as they are in order to specify precisely the sorts of biological order that we find in the earth today? The difference between an ant and a human being is apparently determined entirely by the strings of words, and their order, written in the long lineary texts of the nucleic acid macro-molecules.

Suppose that we set aside the equally puzzling problems of how the texts are read, copied, and translated from nucleic acid language into protein language, and simply ask how the texts came to be written in the first place. The difficulty is something like explaining the origin of a library of books. The problem is the words and their orderliness. To obtain a book there must first be an intelligence.

Consider the existence of this line of symbols. Beginning with the word *"Consider,"* it has 47 printed symbols in it (counting the spaces between words as symbols). Suppose we ask, "What is the probability of such a line of text coming to be by pure chance?" For the sake of argument, let us assume that chance produced a thousand typewriters and that each began to crank out lines of text at a rate of a million characters per second.

An ordinary standard typewriter has 44 symbols in lower case and 44 in upper case, plus the space bar. (We will ignore paragraphing, subtitles, and other elements of text that would have to be taken into account in a more complete theory of printed text.) Therefore, on the first strike, the probability of hitting a capital *"C"* is one in 89 (44 + 44 + 1 = 89). The probability of hitting the letters captial *"C"* and then lower case *"o"* would be one in 89 $\times$ 89, or one in 7,921. As we continue to increase the length of the string of characters, the probability of obtaining the desired element by chance decreases as the exponent of 89 increases. The probability of obtaining the 47 characters of the opening sentence of this paragraph in precisely that order would be one in 89^{47}. On the average, a thousand typewriters churning out text at a million characters per second each (for a total of one billion characters per second) would require 8.9×10^{39} seconds to obtain this one 47 character sequence.

It is difficult to appreciate just how large a span of time this is. If the generous value of 20 billion years is taken as an estimate of the age of the universe (following evolutionists), there are only 6.3×10^{17} seconds in all the time from the hypothetical *"big bang"* until now. This value falls short of the required amount of time by a factor of 1.4×10^{22}. That is to say, the amount of time would have to be increased by about fourteen billion trillion times greater than the number of seconds in the supposed age of the universe (according to recent evolutionary doctrine). Therefore, we must conclude that a particular string of *only* 47 typewritten characters could *never* be obtained by chance.

The problem for an evolutionary explanation is, of course, far worse than I have suggested in this rather trivial example. The difficulty is not to explain any string of a mere 47 significant elements, but to explain texts that consists of many millions of such elements. That is, the example of the typewritten string of 47 characters is a reductio ad absurdum. If chaos cannot produce order of such minuscule proportions, how can it be expected to blindly generate all of the order that scientists find in the universe?

If the meaningfulness of experience itself is a miraculous thing, what about man's ability to talk sensibly about experience? Natural discourse logically exceeds the complexity of any knowledge expressible in it. Any knowledge which can be expressed must be less abstract and less complex than the language in which it is expressed.

So we see that in its humblest forms, life is dependent on words, and in its most exalted form, again it is words that bestow distinction. A question of paramount scientific importance is how words come to be strung together in such intricately organized ways either in the biology of the species or in the discourse of ordinary human beings. To posit intelligence in human beings is to suggest an image of God: for if human discourse requires intelligence, how much more must the library of genetic texts that give man this capacity require an Intelligent Creator!

> For since the creation of the world God's invisible qualities—his eternal power and divine nature—have been clearly seen, being understood from what has been made, so that men are without excuse (New International Version, Romans 1:20).

References

1. Vygotsky, Lev, *Thought and Language,* Cambridge, Massachusetts: MIT Press, 1961 ed., 1934.

2. Russell, Bertrand, *Mysticism and Logic,* London: Allen and Unwin, 1917.

3. Hinegardner, T. T. and J. Engelberg, "Rationale for a Universal Genetic Code," *Science,* V. 142, 1963, 1083-1085.

4. Ibid. Comment on a criticism by Woese, V. 144, 1964, p. 1031.

5. Clark, Brian F. C., *The Genetic Code,* London: E. Arnold, 1977.

6. Yĉas, Martynas, *The Biological Code,* Amsterdam: North Holland, 1969.

7.   Woese, Carl R., *The Genetic Code: The Molecular Basis for Genetic Expression,* New York: Harper and Row, 1967.
8.   Crick, F. H. C., "The Genetic Code—Yesterday, Today, Tomorrow," in *Quantitative Biology,* V. 31, 1966, pp. 3-9. Paper presented at the Cold Spring Harbor Symposium.

No. 93, March 1981
Establishing Scientific Guidelines for Origins-Instruction in Public Education*
By Judith Tarr Harding

Two major challenges face creationists who wish to see the scientific content of creationism penetrate into educational circles and public school curricula.

The first task is to find the most efficient means of obtaining a hearing. Approaches will vary according to the organizational structure of each school district. An impressively growing number of creationists are exploring many avenues—editorials, personnel workshops, lectures, writing, etc.

But a second challenge is far more problematic: how does one achieve communicative dialog about the *science* involved in

---

* The material in this article should not be regarded as an official policy or recommendation of ICR, but it represents an approach to school authorities that some have found helpful.

creationism when a good number of educators may not be willing to seriously discuss scientific issues? What if those evaluating curricula expansion insist instead upon debating the philosophical-religious overtones of a creationist explanation as an infringement of the separation of church and state? Deadlocks are then inevitable.

A teacher workshop in Baltimore County (Winter, 1978) stalemated at this precise juncture. Creationists were graciously allowed a 40-minute presentation, during which time comments were confined to scientific material. (Previous months were spent preparing supplemental written materials for take-home review after the workshop.) A teacher-panel with questions and answers followed that barely skimmed scientific issues. Most of that time was consumed with topics unrelated to a science workshop—a critique of Christian Heritage College, the religious dignity of evolutionists, the size of Noah's ark, textbook controversies, etc.!

Many creationists have been disappointed by such *a priori* dismissal of creationism as a valid scientific model. Such unfortunate communication breakdowns show the imperative of developing clear guidelines by which groups can assess creationist material in a scientific manner. Initially, certain philosophical tenets must be thought through, before scientific material is even introduced. If at all possible, it would be well if the following suggested criteria, formulated into a ballot, were *voted upon* by educators BEFORE any scientific data is presented for evaluation.

PROCEDURAL AGREEMENTS TO BE USED IN ESTABLISHING SCIENTIFIC REQUIREMENTS FOR ORIGINS MODELS

A vote of "no" indicates that our group will *not* use such an argument as grounds for rejecting either evolution or creation as suitable curricula material, provided that either origins model can meet the scientific requirements we will collectively establish. A vote of "yes" means such logic *may* be used as we evaluate the scientific content of our origins curricula.

YES ____ NO ✔ 1. Is evolutionary theory a teaching that is strictly a matter of science, with no other influence on the philosophical or religious beliefs of others?

2. Should the religious views of evolutionists, or the uses to which evolutionary theory has been employed politically, philosophically, or religously. . .

YES ____ NO ✔ a) dictate its suitability for public education, or

YES ____ NO ✔ b) determine its scientific validity?

YES ____ NO ✔ 3. Does evolutionary theory have empirical proof for all its postulates?

YES ____ NO ✔ 4. Should scientific creation be rejected for curricula on the grounds of one or more of the first four questions just cited (inserting "creation" for "evolution")?

YES ____ NO ✔ 5. Do the approaches catalogued in Table I constitute *scientific* arguments that should be resorted to in evaluating any model of origins as a valid science model?

YES ____ NO ✔ 6. Should evolutionary theory be taught in classrooms as the only correct view, without giving scientific material for any other view?

YES ____ NO ✔ 7. Does the rational approach involved in the scientific method rule out any hypothesis concerning origins before the evidence amassed to support that hypothesis has been heard?

YES ✔ NO ____ 8. Do both evolutionary and creationist views allow for belief in God or other religious inferences?

YES ✔ NO ____ 9. The main evolutionary hypothesis (based on observable natural phenomena) to be supported by classroom data is that natural laws, acting mechanistically through time, have produced the variety of organisms we see.

YES ✔ NO ____ 10. Does this evolutionary hypothesis have philosophical-religious inferences?

YES ✔ NO ____ 11. The main creationist hypothesis (based on observable natural phenomena) to be supported by classroom data is design -- pre-programmed pattern.

YES ✔ NO ____ 12. Does this creationist hypothesis have philosophical-religious inferences?

YES ✔ NO ____ 13. The hypothesis of design can be inferred from empirical evidence, not just religious writings (e.g., ecological interdependence, mathematical probabilities of cell assemblage, synchronization of chemical activities within a cell, etc.). (This question should be explored further as scientific guidelines are set.)

YES ✔ NO ____ 14. Many evolutionist educators believe in God, or have other philosophical beliefs regarding the nature of the world, but avoid state-church conflicts by limiting their teaching to empirical evidence.

YES ✔ NO ____ 15. If you answered #14 "yes," is it parallel logic to grant that those of creationist persuasion could maintain church-state separation in the same manner as an evolutionist teacher might, so long as they teach both views of origins and limit their approach to empirical evidence?

If educators are willing to try a ballot approach, the above questions may clear up erroneous concepts that exist in the minds of a policy-making group concerning which many creationists may not be aware. If the evaluators agree to use the ballot approach, the next decision is to set rules that qualify any origins view as a scientific model. The following three guidelines seem logically applicable. The same general principles could also be used to solidify the evolutionary model as a science model.

I.   Can the chief creationist hypothesis—design (pre-programmed pattern) be inferred from empirical data without reference to religious writings? (The complexities involved in the origin of a single cell must be thoroughly discussed.)

II. Can this design hypothesis incorporate the major known empirical data used by evolutionists and creationists into a coherent system? (Scientifically demonstrable facts—empirical evidence—must be separated from ideas that may have logical supporting evidence, depending on one's interpretation. If, for example, the creationist hypothesis were to deny that fossils are arranged in depositional sequences in many instances, it would be ignoring obvious, empirical evidence. However, uniformity of process rates and dating methods must be shown to admit varied interpretations and conflicting data. They do not fall into the category of hard-core scientific *proof*.)

III. Can these data (including the need for local or more widespread catastrophism to interpret the fossil record) be drawn from the visible world, and not from religious writings?

Those who believe that the catastrophism of the creationist model can only be inferred from the Genesis flood account should bear in mind that:

1. Almost all fossils are buried in sedimentary strata.
2. The process of fossilization requires some form of catastrophism in most cases: i.e., quick burial (often of whole herds) in aqueous sediment or volcanic outpourings, to prevent destruction of remains by decay.
3. A scientific attempt is made to explain *worldwide* climate changes and glaciation. Such drastic changes, documented by geologic history, cannot be adequately accounted for by local catastrophic events, and thus the model postulates larger-scaled events.
4. A scientific hypothesis of catastrophism seems needed to explain anomalous fossils and "out-of-order" geologic layers of thousands of square miles, where physical evidence for over-thrusting is lacking.
5. An examination of the geologic column shows earmarks of fixed life forms without transitional forms, and catastrophic annihilation.

No one should assume that agreement upon the logical sequences of the first ballot will be easily achieved, and that further discussion of evidence related to the three scientific assessment guidelines will always be objective dialog. If educators will consent to use the ballot approach, however, it will help objectivity on both sides.

Educators should remember at all times that *science is a communications system*. Scientific "facts" are not in themselves magic wands to settle issues. "Facts" are perceived by each listener through his own sets of educational experiences, interpretive systems, biases, skepticism, and motivational stance. Motivation is extremely crucial; when all has been argued and set forth, the educator may simply yawn and reply, "So . . . who cares?"

Such varied interpretive equipment is brought into an arena of almost endless scientific arguments for or against either view. Complicating the situation even further, deep religious-philosophical world-life beliefs are operating in each individual. Misunderstandings and skepticism are not surprising! (See Table I)

TABLE I
IDEOLOGICAL STALEMATES
IN THE ORIGINS DEBATE

1. **ABUSE OF A THEORY**
   Creationist: "Evolution has been used to support many evils, such as Communism, Nazi-ism, racism, etc."

   Evolutionist: "Creationists are divisive, and resort to name-calling, quoting out of context, and other dubious tactics."

2. *A PRIORI* **ASSUMPTIONS**
   Creationist: "Evolution begins by the unproven assumption that a mechanistic view is the only approach that can be considered scientific. This fosters a climate of freedom *from* religion by recognizing scientific respectability only for those who adopt a mechanistic view that leaves God out (even if one believes in God) in order to be 'strictly scientific.' "

Evolutionist: "Creationism expects me to believe that God had to make [or, the world was made] as creationists conceive it, rather than what my study of comparative morphology, fossils, etc., convinces me is true."

3. **AUTHORITY**
Creationist: "My church (or synagogue) teaches creation, so this must be the right view."
Evolutionist: "How many scientists do you know in major universities who support creationism?"

4. **DOGMATISM**
Creationist: "Only creationism should be taught, as it is the true view. Evolution claims to be the only scientific view by defining 'scientific' as those who agree with evolutionary ideas."
Evolutionist: "Only evolution should be taught, as it is established fact. Creationism is not science; it's religion."

5. **FALSIFIABILITY**
Creationist: "No evolutionist can *prove* lifeless matter became living, without aid of any Designer."
Evolutionist: "No creationist can *prove* a single act of direct creation occurred."

6. **INSENSITIVITY TO BELIEFS AND VALUES OF OTHERS**
Creationist: "Evolutionary theory is ridiculous."
Evolutionist: "It's a waste of time for creationists to get so upset over a scientific theory that we spend so little time on in education anyway. The issue's not that important."

7. **MAJORITY FACTORS**
Creationist: "Most great scientific advances were at one time minority views."
Evolutionist: "The majority of scientists believe evolution."

8. **MISTRUST AND MISREPRESENTATION**
Creationist: "Evolutionists do not deal honestly with scientific facts."
Evolutionist: "No competent scientist takes any theory other than evolution seriously. Creationism represents a fringe minority threatened by a changing scientific world."

9. **MOTIVES**
Creationist: "The fact that so many major evolutionary writers emphasize the lack of purpose, dependence upon chance, and reliance upon evolution in providential ways, proves the unsuitability of the theory for public education, as it influences in atheistic or agnostic beliefs."

Evolutionist: "The fact that you see so many references to
                   religious beliefs in creationist publications
                   proves that the Creationist Movement is only
                   concerned with defending certain forms of
                   religion. It has no scientific significance."

10. **PAST HISTORY**
Creationist: "Modern evolutionism is merely a sophisti-
                  cated form of ancient Egyptian and Greek
                  mythological evolutionary ideas."
Evolutionist: "Creationism is merely a revival of the old,
                  defunct catastrophism taught in pre-
                  Darwinian days, and of former ideas about
                  Genesis."

11. **PRIORITIES**
Creationist: (Probably in a parochial setting) — "We teach
                  only creation, because it is the true view."
Evolutionist: "We teach only evolution, since it is the true
                  view."

12. **RELIGIOUS STEREOTYPING**
Creationist: "Most evolutionists are atheists."
Evolutionist: "Most creationists are fanatics."

13. **RELIGIOUS VIEWS**
Creationist: "Evolution presents a mechanistic, natural-
                  istic view of man's origin that conflicts with
                  my belief that man was created in the image
                  of God, and with the reasons Scripture
                  assigns for suffering and death in the world."
Evolutionist: "Creation incorporates an unproven religious
                  idea that should not be forced upon anyone.
                  My view of religion does not require a *fiat*
                  creation."

14. **RIDICULE**
Creationist: "The cow just magically grew a tail, and be-
                  came a whale."
Evolutionist: "To hear a creationist tell it, everybody's
                  against him — the research of 100 years, and
                  careful scientists are all whacky."

15. **SECONDARY SCIENTIFIC ASSUMPTIONS**
Creationist: "Evolutionists salvage their theory by un-
                  proven secondary assumptions."
Evolutionist: "Creationists salvage their theory by un-
                  proven secondary assumptions."

If, however, a solid majority vote on the proposed ballots can
be achieved, the stage is at least set for better communication.
The creationist's task is then to *carefully confine* his workshop
or petitionary material to the three scientific assessment
guidelines. The first ballot can be used as a sort of parliamentary

reference point if discussion strays from the science of origins into sociological opinions about origins.

Since the Scopes trial, origins in public education has been riddled with communication barriers. Hopefully the approach just set forth could minimize the unfortunate tactics of the past—innuendo, mud-slinging, ridicule. Perhaps the use of such parliamentary scientific rules could stimulate personal scientific growth through more dispassionate investigation into diverse scientific views.

———————◆———————

No. 94, April 1981
Materialism, Animism, and Evolutionism
By Magnus Verbrugge, M.D. *

Man's Substitute for God

Man has been wrestling with the question of creation ever since he himself was created. Although orthodox Jews, Christians, and Muslims traditionally have been creationists, relatively few modern scientists are creationists, and some claim that this rejection of the Creator is the result of modern scientific discoveries. Actually, however, the negation of God as Creator is as old as man's sin.

The ancient Hindus for example, believed that their god, Brahma, was merely an aspect of reality that somehow reshaped existing material over and over again to form a new universe each time the old one had worn out. Similarly, the later Greek philosophers maintained that matter is eternal, so they too knew

---

*   The author, Dr. Magnus Verbrugge, is a Fellow in the Royal College of Surgeons of Canada.

no creator. They believed there had to be some power inside of matter that could make it come alive. This "religious" conviction was expanded into a complete philosophical system by the Greeks known today as *materialism*.

Man also knew that he himself has spiritual functions, including the ability to abstract concepts from the things he sees. Not knowing the Creator, however, many people began to see some hidden power or invisible spirit behind natural phenomena. This belief today is called animism. Jacques Monod, a Nobel Prize winning microbiologist, defines animism as the " . . . projection into inanimate nature of man's awareness of the . . . functioning of his own central nervous system . . . . the hypothesis that natural phenomena can and must be explained in the same manner . . . as subjective human activity . . . . "[1] Plato believed that the power which forms all things from chaotic matter was the Demiurg, the personified abstraction of his own power of thinking.

The great naturalist Aristotle declared life to be a special power behind every living thing, called *anima* ("breath") in Latin. This animistic projection of a life-force into inanimate matter became his substitute for the Creator. Aristotle's materialism thus took the form of *vitalism,* which has been advocated in modified form by many scientists and philosophers since, including Bergson, Driesch, and de Chardin.

Today most materialists have rejected vitalism, however, because vital forces cannot be measured with physico-chemical methods and instruments. Materialists claim that only physical forces are real: gravity, electromagnetism, and nuclear forces. They can be measured. What cannot be measured is considered by them to be a product of human imagination and is declared "supernatural." The world-famous Marxist biochemist, A. I. Oparin, declares that " . . . life, like all the rest of the world, is material . . . but its properties are not limited to those of matter in general . . . . it is a special form of the movement of matter . . . . "[2] Thus the materialist denies that life is really different from physical energy, maintaining it to be merely a special form of physical energy *to which it can be reduced.* Neither is there anything truly distinctive about human life. "With the appearance of man, however, there arises a new social form of motion of matter . . . . "[3]

Scientific Data on Living Things

We have long known that our body consists of at least 80% water, with the rest composed mainly of carbon, nitrogen, oxygen, phosphorous, and, to a smaller extent, a few other elements. Yet our body somehow makes complex molecules out of what we eat (mostly proteins, fats, and starches), after we have first broken these down into smaller molecules. Enzymes, for example, are special proteins that can speed up chemical reactions in our body by many thousands of times. Each of hundreds of thousands of different proteins has its own special structure and function. We know some functions of DNA, RNA, and others which are related to cell division and propagation of individual organisms. Each type of molecule has its own characteristics which the cell that has made them needs for its overall functioning. As soon as we take such a molecule out of the cell, it can still display the same chemical reactions as it does inside, but only in random fashion. Its directed activity is gone.

The Gap and the Leap of Science Fiction

Can materialists explain how matter brought forth living organisms without a Creator? Have their experiments given us any indication that life can ever be produced in the laboratory?

Billions of dollars have been spent on trying to bridge the gap between matter and life. We are told, however, that laymen must not concern themselves with these delicate problems. A. I. Oparin, and a spokesman for Marxist dialectics in Russia, wrote a very influential book, *The Origin of Life,* translated by Sergius Morgulis. In his introduction the latter wrote: "The biologist, unlike the layman, knows no line of demarcation separating plant life from animal life, nor for that matter living from nonliving material, because such differentiations are entirely conceptual and do not correspond to reality."[4] Thus Morgulis has arbitrarily declared that there is no gap. His master, Oparin, knows what power makes dead things come to life; it is motion: "Matter is in constant motion and . . . life came into being as a special form of motion."[5] This odd notion comes from Communist Friedrich Engels. Engels had discovered a new "law" of nature: "All qualitative differences in nature rest on differences of chemical composition or on different quantities or forms of motion (energy) or . . . both."[6] What the *anima* was for Aristotle as the creative power for living things, the physical forces (energy) are for Engels and his pupil Oparin. Monod called this "cosmic animism."[7] In principle, belief in cosmic animism is little different from worshipping gods of wood and stone.

Yet, dialectic materialism is quite popular among modern scientists. G. Montalenti uses it in *Studies in the Philosophy of Biology:* "The principle of dialectical materialism is well known, that a change in quantity determines qualitative change . . . . As the molecules become individually different and reproduce . . . the laws of physics and chemistry are the only ones that play a role . . . . what really matters, to start life is . . . the faculty of reproduction . . . . "[8] Dillon wrote a provocative scenario for this process of reproduction: " . . . two poly-amino acid chains accidentally came into contact which were mutually compatible in such a manner that each could replicate the other (or, alternatively, a single self-replicating peptoid molecule arose) . . . . This . . . was the first living being."[9] He does not mention that when two molecules join in a chemical bond we now have a new single molecule. Nor does he explain how a dead molecule can suddenly take on the function of self-replication. Physicist Elsasser feels that the random formation of poly-amino acid chains and their "accidentally" meeting are events that have a statistical probability of zero. But that does not deter Monod: " . . . the biosphere . . . is compatible with first principles [of physics] but not *deducible* from those principles . . . . it is unpredictable for the very reason . . . that the particular configuration of atoms constituting this pebble I have in my hand is unpredictable."[10] Bur once they arose, they were to be seen as "chemical machines."[11] How did they arise? Here is how: "Randomness caught on the wing, preserved, reproduced . . . and thus converted into order, rule, necessity. A *totally* blind process can by definition lead to anything; it can even lead to vision itself."[12] Thus "by definition," the impossible can happen!

Harold Blum helps the cause of materialism in a unique way. Why, he asks, did protein molecules originate "spontaneously?" Because " . . . they must have been if living systems were to evolve . . . [a fact] accepted by the great majority of biologists."[13]

An exquisite example of modern philosophical reasoning by Dr. L. Dillon defines life as " . . . the capacity for synthesizing proteins in at least sufficient quantities to replace those that are catabolized by normal processes."[14] This means that living beings are chemical entities. Next he concludes: " . . . it becomes amply evident that living things are chemical entities, whose fundamental properties are describable in ordinary physicochemical terms. Hence, to this degree the prevailing mechanistic view of the organic world is firmly supported."[15]

Science Regained

Materialists have been repeating over and over that Christians want to introduce supernatural forces into science. But it is really the materialists who want to introduce spirits and animism into science under the guise of creative forces hiding in dead molecules. Christians need no longer try to accommodate these spiritual inventions of pagan philosophy. It is now becoming well known that there are many scientific arguments that discredit evolution. Furthermore, the philosophical bankruptcy of materialism has been exposed by Herman Dooyeweerd, whose life's work has given Christians a mighty arsenal of philosophical weapons against the materialists. As summarized in his theory of the modal aspects of reality, this outstanding Dutch philosopher demonstrates that the various scientific laws of creation, which scientists can discover, cannot be reduced to each other. Each, rather, is a distinctive, irreducible, and specifically created aspect of reality.

He showed that all humanists assign creative powers to some force *inside* creation, which in effect becomes their god. The different philosophical "isms" arose from whatever force various philosophers chose as the one to which all the others were to be reduced. Thus they worship idols of their own making—idols of dead matter, as helpless as the stone idols of the ancient humanists.

It is now possible for Christian scientists not only to show where materialism went wrong, but even more importantly to build a true scientific endeavor on a Biblical foundation instead of Greek mythology.

If we confess that the origin of this cosmos is " . . . the sovereign holy will of God the Creator, Who has revealed Himself in

Christ,"[16] we can search for these laws, this *cosmonomy* through which God maintains His world. Science can still be saved from the fictions to which it has fallen victim in so many areas. If we are faithful, it will again be an honor to be a scientist in search of the laws of God's creation.

References

1. Monod, Jacques, *Chance and Necessity,* NY: Alfred A. Knopf, Inc., 1972, p. 30.
2. Oparin, A. I., *Life, Its Nature, Origin and Development,* NY: Academic Press, 1962, pp. 5-6.
3. *Ibid.,* p. 7.
4. Oparin, A. I., *The Origin of Life,* NY: Dover Pub., 1938 Translation by Morgulis, S., p. viii.
5. Oparin, A. I., *op. cit.,* (1962) p. 6.
6. Engels, Friedrich, *Dialectics of Nature,* NY: International Pub., (1940), 1960, p. 27.
7. Monod, J., *op. cit.,* p. 31.
8. Montalenti, G. in *Studies in the Philosophy of Biology,* London: MacMillan, Ayala, F. J., and Dobzhansky, Th., Eds., 1974, pp. 12-13.
9. Dillon, Lawrence S., *The Genetic Mechanism and the Origin of Life,* NY: Plenum Press, 1978, p. 412.
10. Monod, J., *op. cit.,* p. 44.
11. *Ibid.,* p. 45.
12. *Ibid.,* p. 98.
13. Blum, Harold, *Time's Arrow and Evolution,* NY: Harper & Bros., 1955, p. 164 and 173.
14. Dillon, L. S., *op. cit.,* p. 411.
15. Dillon, L. S., *op. cit.,* p. 426.
16. Dooyeweerd, Herman, *A New Critique of Theoretical Thought,* Amsterdam and Philadelphia: H. J. Paris and the Presbyterian and Reformed Pub. Co., Vol. I, 1953, p. 101.

No. 95, May 1981
Summary of Scientific Evidence for Creation Part I*

By Duane T. Gish, Ph.D., Scientist and
  Richard B. Bliss, Ed.D., Science Educator
Reviewed by Wendell R. Bird, J.D., Attorney

Introduction

Public schools in many localities are teaching two scientific models—the creation model and the evolution model—of the origin of the universe, of life, and of man. There is apparent scientific evidence for creation, which is summarized in this pamphlet, just as there is apparent scientific evidence for evolution. The purpose of this pamphlet is to summarize the evidence that shows that: **"The creation model is at least as scientific as the evolution model, and is at least as nonreligious as the evolution model."**

This scientific evidence for both models can be taught in public schools without any mention of religious doctrine, whether the Bible or the Humanist Manifesto. There are text materials and teacher handbooks that have been prepared for a fair presentation of both models, creation and evolution. There are also seminars and audiovisuals for training teachers to offer both models of origins.

This scientific evidence both for creation and for evolution can and must be taught without any religious doctrine, whether the Bible or the Humanist Manifesto."

"Creation-science proponents want public schools to teach all the scientific data, censoring none, but do not want any religious doctrine to be brought into science classrooms."

---

*   This Impact pamphlet was written by a scientist and a science educator and reviewed by an attorney, to provide a brief summary of the scientific evidence supporting creation. The text materials and references listed at the end together give a more thorough discussion of this scientific evidence.

Definitions of the Creation Model and the Evolution Model

The scientific *model of creation,* in summary, includes the scientific evidence for a sudden creation of complex and diversified kinds of life, with systematic gaps persisting between different kinds and with genetic variation occurring within each kind since that time. The scientific *model of evolution,* in summary, includes the scientific evidence for a gradual emergence of present life kinds over aeons of time, with emergence of complex and diversified kinds of life from simpler kinds and ultimately from nonliving matter. The creation model questions vertical evolution, which is the emergence of complex from simple and change between kinds, but it does not challenge what is often called horizontal evolution or microevolution, which creationists call genetic variation or species or subspecies formation within created kinds. The following chart lists seven aspects of the scientific model of creation and of the scientific model of evolution.

I. The Universe and the Solar System Were Suddenly Created

The First Law of Thermodynamics states that the total quantity of matter and energy in the universe is constant. The Second Law of Thermodynamics states that matter and energy always tend to change from complex and ordered states to disordered states. Therefore the universe could not have created itself, but neither could it have existed forever, or it would have run down long ago. Thus the universe, including matter and energy, apparently must have been created.

The "big bang" theory of the origin of the universe contradicts much physical evidence and seemingly can only be accepted by faith.[1] This was also the case with the past cosmogonic theories of evolutionists that have been discarded, such as Hoyle's steady-state theory.

The universe has "obvious manifestations of an ordered, structured plan or design." Similarly, the "electron is materially inconceivable and yet it is so perfectly known through its effects," yet a "strange rationale makes some physicists accept the inconceivable electrons as real while refusing to accept the reality of a Designer." "The inconceivability of some ultimate issue (which will always lie outside scientific resolution) should

The creation model includes the scientific evidence and the related inferences suggesting that:	The evolution model includes the scientific evidence and the related inferences suggesting that:
I. The universe and the solar system were suddenly created.	I. The universe and the solar system emerged by naturalistic processes.
II. Life was suddenly created.	II. Life emerged from nonlife by naturalistic processes.
III. All present living kinds of animals and plants have remained fixed since creation, other than extinctions, and genetic variation in originally created kinds has only occured within narrow limits.	III. All present kinds emerged from simpler earlier kinds, so that single-celled organisms evolved into invertebrates, then vertebrates, then amphibians, then reptiles, then mammals, then primates, including man.
IV. Mutation and natural selection are insufficient to have brought about any emergence of present living kinds from a simple primordial organism.	IV. Mutation and natural selection have brought about the emergence of present complex kinds from a simple primordial organism.
V. Man and apes have a separate ancestry.	V. Man and apes emerged from a common ancestor.
VI. The earth's geologic features appear to have been fashioned largely by rapid, catastrophic processes that affected the earth on a global and regional scale (catastrophism).	VI. The earth's geologic features were fashioned largely by slow, gradual processes, with infrequent catastrophic events restricted to a local scale (uniformitarianism).
VII. The inception of the earth and of living kinds may have been relatively recent.	VII. The inception of the earth and then of life must have occurred several billion years ago.

not be allowed to rule out any theory that explains the interrelationship of observed data and is useful for prediction," in the words of Dr. Wernher von Braun, the renowned late physicist in the NASA space program.

II. Life Was Suddenly Created

Life appears abruptly and in complex forms in the fossil record,[2] and gaps appear systematically in the fossil record between various living kinds.[3] These facts indicate that basic kinds of plants and animals were created.

The Second Law of Thermodynamics states that things tend to go from order to disorder (entropy tends to increase) unless added energy is directed by a conversion mechanism (such as photosynthesis), whether a system is open or closed. Thus simple molecules and complex protein, DNA, and RNA molecules seemingly could not have evolved spontaneously and naturalistically into a living cell;[4] such cells apparently were created.

The laboratory experiments related to theories on the origin of life have not even remotely approached the synthesis of life from nonlife, and the extremely limited results have depended on laboratory conditions that are artificially imposed and extremely improbable.[5] The extreme improbability of these conditions and the relatively insignificant results apparently show that life did not emerge by the process that evolutionists postulate.

"One example of the scientific evidence for creation is the sudden appearance of complex fossilized life in the fossil record, and the systematic gaps between fossilized kinds in that record. The most rational inference from this evidence seemingly is that life was created and did not evolve."

III. All Present Living Kinds of Animals and Plants Have Remained Fixed Since Creation, Other than Extinctions, and Genetic Variation in Originally Created Kinds Has Only Occurred within Narrow Limits

Systematic gaps occur between kinds in the fossil record.[6] None of the intermediate fossils that would be expected on the basis of the evolution model have been found between single-celled organisms and invertebrates, between invertebrates and vertebrates, between fish and amphibians, between amphibians and reptiles, between reptiles and birds or mammals, or between "lower" mammals and primates.[7] While evolutionists might assume that these intermediate forms existed at one time, none of the hundreds of millions of fossils found so far provide the missing links. The few suggested links such as *Archaeopteryx* and the horse series have been rendered questionable by more detailed data. Fossils and living organisms are readily subjected to the same criteria of classification. Thus present kinds of animals and plants apparently were created, as shown by the systematic fossil gaps and by the similarity of fossil forms to living forms.

A kind may be defined as a generally interfertile group of

organisms that possesses variant genes for a common set of traits but that does not interbreed with other groups of organisms under normal circumstances. Any evolutionary change between kinds (necessary for the emergence of complex from simple organisms) would require addition of entirely new traits to the common set and enormous expansion of the gene pool over time, and could not occur from mere ecologically adaptive variations of a given trait set (which the creation model recognizes).

[This article is concluded in Impact No. 96.]

References

1. Slusher, Harold S., *The Origin of the Universe,* San Diego: Institute for Creation Research (ICR), 1978.
2. *E.g.,* Kay, Marshall & Colbert, Edwin H., *Stratigraphy and Life History,* New York: John Wiley & Sons, 1965, p. 102.
    Simpson, George G., *The Major Features of Evolution,* New York: Columbia University Press, 1953, p. 360.
    [Paleontologists recognize] that *most* new species, genera, and families, and that nearly all categories above the level of families, appear in the record suddenly and are not led up to by known, gradual, completely continuous transitional sequences.
3. Note 6 *infra.*
4. *E.g.,* Smith, Charles J., "Problems with Entropy in Biology," *Biosystems,* V. 7, 1975, pp. 259, 264. "The earth, moon, and sun constitute an essentially closed thermodynamic system . . . . "
    Simpson, George G., "Uniformitarianism," in Hecht, Max A. & Steeres, William C., eds., *Essays in Evolution and Genetics,* New York: Appleton-Century-Crofts, 1970, p. 43.
5. Gish, Duane T., *Speculations and Experiments Related to the Origin of Life (A Critique),* San Diego: ICR, 1972.
6. *E.g.,* Simpson, George G., "The History of Life," in Tax, Sol, ed., *Evolution after Darwin: The Evolution of Life,* Chicago: Univ. of Chicago Press, 1960, pp. 117, 149:
    Gaps among known orders, classes, and phyla are systematic and almost always large.
7. *E.g.,* Kitts, David B., "Paleontology and Evolutionary Theory," *Evolution,* V. 28, 1974, pp. 458, 467:
    Evolution requires intermediate forms between species and paleontology does not provide them. For examples of the lack of transitional fossils, Ommaney, F. D., *The Fishes,* New York: Time-Life, Inc., 1964, p. 60 (invertebrates to vertebrates); Romer, Alfred S., *Vertebrate Paleontology,* Chicago: Univ. of Chicago Press, 3d

ed., 1966, p. 36 (vertebrate fish to amphibians); Swinton, W. E., *Biology and Comparative Physiology of Birds,* Marshall, A. J., ed., New York: Academic Press, V. 1, 1960, p. 1 (reptiles to birds); Simpson, George G., *Tempo and Mode in Evolution,* New York: Columbia Univ. Press, 1944, p. 105 (reptiles to mammals); Simons, E. L., *Annals N.Y. Acad. Science,* V. 167, 1969, p. 319 (mammals to primates).

No. 96, June 1981
Summary of Scientific Evidence
Part II*
*By Duane T. Gish, Ph.D., Scientist,** and*
  *Richard B. Bliss, Ed.D., Science Educator****
*Reviewed by Wendell R. Bird, J.D., Attorney*****

IV. Mutation and Natural Selection Are Insufficient to Have Brought About Any Emergence of Present Living Kinds from A Simple Primordial Organism

The mathematical probability that random mutation and natural selection ultimately produced complex living kinds from a simpler kind is infinitesimally small, even after many billions of years.[8] Thus mutation and natural selection apparently could

---

* This is the conclusion of Impact Article No. 95, May 1981.

** Dr. Gish earned his Ph.D. from the University of California at Berkeley in Biochemistry. He has worked as a research biochemist with Cornell University Medical College, the Virus Laboratory, University of California (Berkeley), and The Upjohn Company. Dr. Gish collaborated with one Nobel Prize recipient in elucidating the chemical structure of the protein of tobacco mosaic virus, and with another Nobel Prize winner in synthesis of one of the hormones of the pituitary gland. He is presently Associate Director of the Institute for Creation Research. Other staff scientists at ICR who helped prepare this summary include Dr. Henry M. Morris, (Ph.D., University of Minnesota, Hydraulics); Dr. Kenneth B. Cumming (Ph.D., Harvard University, Biology); Dr. Gary E. Parker (Ed.D., Ball State University, Biology); Dr. Theodore W. Rybka (Ph.D., University of Oklahoma, Physics); and Dr. Harold S. Slusher (M.S., University of Oklahoma, Geophysics).

*** Dr. Bliss earned his Ed.D. from the University of Sarasota in Science Education, with

not have brought about evolution of present living kinds from a simple first organism.

Mutations are always harmful or at least nearly always harmful in an organism's natural environment.[9] Thus the mutation process apparently could not have provided the postulated millions of beneficial mutations required for progressive evolution in the supposed five billion years from the origin of the earth until now, and in fact would have produced an overwhelming genetic load over hundreds of millions of years that would have caused degeneration and extinction.

Natural selection is a tautologous concept (circular reasoning), because it simply requires the fittest organisms to leave the most offspring and at the same time it identifies the fittest organisms as those that leave the most offspring. Thus natural selection seemingly does not provide a testable explanation of how mutations would produce more fit organisms.[10]

V. Man and Apes Have a Separate Ancestry

Although highly imaginative "transitional forms" between man and apelike creatures have been constructed by evolutionists based on very fragmentary evidence, the fossil record actually documents the separate origin of primates in general,[11] monkeys,[12] apes,[13] and men. In fact, Lord Zuckerman (not a creationist) states that there are no "fossil traces" of a transformation from an apelike creature to man.[14]

The fossils of Neanderthal Man were once considered to

---

a cognate emphasis in curriculum, instruction, and evaluation in science education. He wrote his dissertation on teaching the two-model approach (comparing evolution-science and creation-science) in public schools. He taught high school physics, chemistry, and biology for many years and was the Director of Science Education for the large public school district in Racine, Wisconsin. He served as the science consultant for Educational Consulting Associates and for several major publishers of science textbooks, as well as for the University of Wisconsin Research and Development film series. He has written textbook materials for public school instruction in the creation model and the evolution model.

**** Mr. Bird earned his J.D. from Yale Law School with numerous studies in Constitutional Law, publishing legal articles in the *Yale Law Journal* and the *Harvard Journal of Law & Public Policy* on the constitutionality of public schools teaching the scientific evidence for creation along with that for evolution. He was an Editor of the Yale Law Journal and was the recipient of the Egger Prize of Yale Law School for his article published there.

represent a primitive subhuman *(Homo neanderthalensis)*, but these "primitive" features are now known to have resulted from nutritional deficiencies and pathological conditions; he is now classified as fully human.[15] *Ramapithecus* was once considered to be partially manlike, but is now known to be fully apelike.[16] *Australopithecus,* in the view of some leading evolutionists, was not intermediate between ape and man and did not walk upright.[17]

The strong bias of many evolutionists in seeking a link between apes and man is shown by the near-universal acceptance of two "missing links" that were later proved to be a *fraud* (in the case of Piltdown Man *[Eoanthropus]*) and a *pig's tooth* (in the case of Nebraska Man *[Hesperopithecus]*).[18]

VI. The Earth's Geologic Features were Fashioned Largely by Rapid, Catastrophic Processes that Affected the Earth on a Global and Regional Scale (Catastrophism)

Catastrophic events have characterized the earth's history. Huge floods, massive asteroid collisions, large volcanic eruptions, devastating landslides, and intense earthquakes have left their marks on the earth. Catastrophic events appear to explain the formation of mountain ranges, deposition of thick sequences of sedimentary rocks with fossils, initiation of the glacial age, and extinction of dinosaurs and other animals. Catastrophism (catastrophic changes), rather than uniformitarianism (gradual changes), appears to be the best interpretation of a major portion of the earth's geology.

Geologic data reflect catastrophic flooding. Evidences of rapid catastrophic water deposition include fossilized tree trunks that penetrate numerous sedimentary layers (such as at Joggins, Nova Scotia), widespread pebble and boulder layers (such as the Shinarump Conglomerate of the southwestern United States), fossilized logs in a single layer covering extensive areas (such as Petrified Forest National Park), and whole closed clams that were buried alive in mass graveyards in extensive sedimentary layers (such as at Glen Rose, Texas).

Uniform processes such as normal river sedimentation, small volcanoes, slow erosion, and small earthquakes appear insufficient to explain large portions of the geologic record. Even the conventional uniformitarian geologists are beginning to yield to evidence of rapid and catastrophic processes.[19]

VII. The Inception of the Earth and of Living Kinds May Have Been Relatively Recent

Radiometric dating methods (such as the uranium-lead and potassium-argon methods) depend on three assumptions: (a) that no decay product (lead or argon) was present initially or that the initial quantities can be accurately estimated, (b) that the decay system was closed through the years (so that radioactive material or product did not move in or out of the rock), and (c) that the decay rate was constant over time.[20] Each of these assumptions may be questionable: (a) some nonradiogenic lead or argon was perhaps present initially;[21] (b) the radioactive isotope (uranium or potassium isotopes) can perhaps migrate out of, and the decay product (lead or argon) can migrate into, many rocks over the years;[22] and (c) the decay rate can perhaps change by neutrino bombardment and other causes.[23] Numerous radiometric estimates have been hundreds of millions of years in excess of the true age. Thus ages estimated by the radiometric dating methods may very well be grossly in error.

Alternate dating methods suggest much younger ages for the earth and life. Estimating by the rate of addition of helium to the atmosphere from radioactive decay, the age of the earth appears to be about 10,000 years, even allowing for moderate helium escape. Based on the present rate of the earth's cooling, the time required for the earth to have reached its present thermal structure seems to be only several tens of millions of years, even assuming that the earth was initially molten.[24] Extrapolating the observed rate of apparently exponential decay of the earth's magnetic field, the age of the earth or life seemingly could not exceed 20,000 years.[25] Thus the inception of the earth and the inception of life may have been relatively recent when all the evidence is considered.[26]

"There is scientific evidence for creation from cosmology, thermodynamics, paleontology, biology, mathematical probability, geology, and other sciences."

"There are many scientists in each field who conclude that the scientific data best support the creation model, not the evolution model."

References

8. *E.g.*, Eden, Murray, "Inadequacies of Neo-Darwinian Evolution as a Scientific Theory," in Moorhead, Paul S. & Kaplan, Martin M., eds., *Mathematical Challenges to the Neo-Darwinian Interpretation of Evolution,* Philadelphia: Wistar Inst. Press, 1967, p. 109:

> It is our contention that if "random" is given a serious and crucial interpretation from a probabilistic point of view, the randomness postulate is highly implausible and that an adequate scientific theory of evolution must await the discovery and elucidation of new natural laws. . . .

9. *E.g.*, Martin, C. P., "A Non-Geneticist Looks at Evolution," *American Scientist,* V. 41, 1954, p. 100.

10. *E.g.*, Popper, Karl, *Objective Knowledge,* Oxford: Clarendon Press, 1975, p. 242.

11. *E.g.*, Kelso, A. J., *Physical Anthropology,* 2nd ed., Philadelphia: J. B. Lippincott, 1974, p. 142.

12. *E.g.*, *ibid.*, pp. 150, 151.

13. *E.g.*, Simons, E. L., *Annals N.Y. Acad. Science,* V. 102, 1962, p. 293; Simons, E. L., "The Early Relatives of Man," *Scientific American,* V. 211, July 1964, p. 50.

14. *E.g.*, Zuckerman, Sir Solly, *Beyond the Ivory Tower,* New York: Taplinger Pub. Co., 1970, p. 64.

15. *E.g.*, Ivanhoe, Francis, "Was Virchow Right about Neandert[h]al?" *Nature,* V. 227, 1970, p. 577.

16. *E.g.*, Zuckerman, pp. 75-94; Eckhardt, Robert B., "Population Genetics and Human Origins," *Scientific American,* V. 226, 1972, pp. 94, 101.

17. *E.g.*, Oxnard, Charles E., "Human Fossils: New Views of Old Bones," *American Biology Teacher,* V. 41, 1979, p. 264.

18. *E.g.*, Straus, William L., "The Great Piltdown Hoax," *Science,* V. 119, 1954, p. 265 (Piltdown Man); Gregory, William K., "Hesperopithecus Apparently Not an Ape Nor a Man," *Science,* V. 66, 1927, p. 579 (Nebraska Man).

19. *E.g.*, Bhattacharyya, A., Sarkar, S. & Chanda, S. K., "Storm Deposits in the Late Proterozoic Lower Bhander Sandstone of . . . India," *Journal of Sedimentary Petrology,* V. 50, 1980, p. 1327:

> Until recently, noncatastrophic uniformitarianism had dominated sedimentologic thought reflecting that sediment formation and dispersal owe their genesis chiefly to the operation of day-to-day geologic events. As a result, catastrophic events, e.g., storms, earthquakes, etc., have been denied their rightful place in ancient and recent sedimentary records. Of late, however, there has been a welcome rejuvenation of [the] concept of catas-

trophism in geologic thought.

J. Harlen Bretz recently stated, on receiving the Penrose Medal (the highest geology award in America), "Perhaps, I can be credited with reviving and demystifying legendary Catastrophism and challenging a too rigorous Uniformitarianism." Geological Society of America, "GSA Medals and Awards," *GSA News & Information,* V. 2, 1980, p. 40.

20. *E.g.,* Stansfield, William D., *The Science of Evolution,* New York: MacMillan Publishing Co., 1977, pp. 83-84; Faul, Henry, *Ages of Rocks, Planets and Stars,* New York: McGraw-Hill Co., 1966, pp. 19-20, 41-49. *See generally* Slusher, Harold S., *Critique of Radiometric Dating,* San Diego: ICR, 1973.
21. *E.g.,* Kerkut, G. A., *Implications of Evolution,* New York: Pergamon Press, 1960, pp. 138, 139.
22. *E.g.,* Faul, p. 61.
23. *E.g.,* Jueneman, Frederick, "Scientific Speculation," *Industrial Research,* Sept. 1972, p. 15.
24. Slusher, Harold S. & Gamwell, Thomas P., *The Age of the Earth,* San Diego: ICR, 1978.
25. Barnes, Thomas G., *Origin and Destiny of the Earth's Magnetic Field,* San Diego: ICR, 1973.
26. Slusher, Harold S., *Age of the Cosmos,* San Diego: ICR, 1980; Slusher, Harold S. & Duursma, Stephen J., *The Age of the Solar System,* San Diego: ICR, 1978

No. 97, July 1981
The Anti-Creationists
By Henry M. Morris, Ph.D.

There are many evolutionists who evaluate scientific data objectively, even in relation to the controversial subject of origins, and are, therefore, willing to allow *both* models of origins (creation and evolution) to compete freely in the marketplace of ideas.

There are many others who are not merely evolutionists, but are anti-creationists—dedicated at all costs to discrediting the creation movement. Unfortunately such attempts often include a very careless handling of facts.

In this article, we have listed a number of these false charges, with brief answers to them.

CHARGE: "The anti-evolutionists have been successful, [William G. Mayer] explains, because they now use a Madison Avenue approach and employ full-time staff while there is not one scientist who is funded to devote full-time to espousing evolutionary theory." *(Science News,* Jan. 10, 1981, p. 19)

FACT: There is to our knowledge no one who devotes full time to espousing creationism. The ICR has a staff of ten part-time scientists, each of whom has many other duties besides speaking on creation. On the other hand, large numbers of scientists on university faculties spend far more time on evolutionist research and teaching than anything creationists can afford. Creationism is anything but "well-funded" as Mayer charges, having no access to government funding as Dr. Mayer did, when his B.S.C.S. organization expended almost $20,000,000 of federal funds in developing its evolution-based biology textbook series.

CHARGE: "The creationist model does not have the same kind of scientific validity as the theory of evolution. This is not to say that it cannot be a true account of the origin of life. It could be." *(Today's Education,* April-May 1981, p. 58G)

FACT: The evolutionist's definition of "scientific" is "mechanistic" or "naturalistic," but this is misleading. *Science* means *knowledge,* and the essence of the scientific method is observation and repeatability. Evolution is not "scientific" since macro-evolution is neither observable nor repeatable. Evolutionists admit creation may be "true," so it is appropriate—indeed essential—to include it in the educational process if teachers sincerely desire their students to search for truth, as they claim.

CHARGE: " . . . creationists tend to be masters of the partial quote." *(Next,* March-April 1981, p. 68)

FACT: The author cited two alleged out-of-context quotations by creationists, one by Dr. Gary Parker supposedly intimating that Dr. Stephen Gould was "championing creationism," the other by this writer supposedly claiming that two evolutionary geologists had agreed that the strata of the great Lewis "overthrust" were all flat and undisturbed. The fact is that we are always careful *not* to quote out of context. Such quotations have to be brief, for reasons of space, and so cannot give the full scope of the author's thoughts on the subject, but they do *not* misrepresent their nature and significance. Out of the many thousands of such references that are included in our writings, critics have to search diligently to find even a handful that they can interpret as misleading. Even in the two that were cited, a careful reading of the *full context* in each case will demonstrate that the reporter was himself guilty of distortion. Dr. Parker made it quite clear that Dr. Gould is a committed evolutionist (in spite of his arguments against certain Darwinian tenets). In the Lewis overthrust discussion, there was ample mention of the physical evidences of disturbances, and the quote (actually appearing only in a minor footnote) certainly did not affect the evidence developed in the particular section against the "overthrust" explanation. In no way did it misrepresent the beliefs of the authors quoted.

CHARGE: "[Creationists] have shown a certain genius for couching their arguments in scientific terms . . . . But their viewpoint remains dogmatically fundamentalist and profoundly anti-scientific." *(The Sciences,* April 1981, p. 18)

FACT: Whether or not the scientific creation model is compatible with the Biblical record is irrelevant to the question of whether the actual scientific data fit the model. Most creationist scientists do believe that the tenets of Biblical creationism are compatible with the tenets of scientific creationism, but it is only the latter that we believe should be taught in the public schools. The fact that the scientific model of creation can be used to support Christian theism is parallel to the fact that the scientific model of evolution can be used to support Marxist atheism or Religious Humanism or Theological Liberalism. All this is irrelevant to the fact that creation and evolution can both be discussed and compared simply as scientific models.

CHARGE: "If the world view of fundamental Christians is presented as science, why not that of the Hindus or the Buddhists?" *(American School Board Journal,* March 1980, p. 32)

FACT: There are only *two* world views—evolution and creation. Each of these has many variants. Hinduism and Buddhism are variants of the typical evolutionary world view, beginning as they do with an eternally self-existing universe (the same is true of Confucianism, Taoism, and all the other ancient pagan pantheistic religions). Creationists do *not* want the Biblical record of creationism taught in the public schools, but only the general creation model as a viable scientific alternative to the general evolution model.

CHARGE: "The creationist movement boasts a number of adherents who have been trained in science. Significantly, few are biologists. Creationists have done almost no original research." *(Time,* March 16, 1981, p. 81)

FACT: There are thousands of well-qualified creationist scientists today, a large percentage of whom are in the life sciences. Over half of the present and past members of the Board of Directors of the Creation Research Society, for example, are in biological fields. In addition, of the 29 scientists associated directly with ICR (including the ten staff members, plus trustees, advisory board members, and regional representatives), 17 are in the life sciences. At least 15 scientists in these two groups have regular Ph.D.'s in Biology from leading universities, and the others all have terminal degrees in closely related fields (biochemistry, medicine, etc.). As far as research is concerned, the ICR staff may be typical. These ten scientists (H. Morris, Gish, Bliss, Barnes, Slusher, Parker, Cumming, J. Morris, Austin, and Rybka) have published at least 150 research papers and ten books in their own scientific fields—all in standard scientific refereed journals or through secular book publishers—in addition to hundreds of creationist articles and perhaps 50 books in creationism and related fields.

CHARGE: "The basic premise, the basic dogma, is the existence of a divine creator. What they espouse as academic freedom to teach creationism is the academic freedom to teach the flatness of the earth." *(Discover,* Oct. 1980, p. 94)

FACT: No creationist scientist teaches a flat earth nor, for that matter, is such a notion taught in the Bible. The "dogma" of the existence of a divine creator is not one bit more "dogmatic" than the evolutionist's assumption of "no creator" and of the preexistence of matter as the source of this marvelous universe and its infinite array of complex systems.

CHARGE: "ICR is apparently well-funded. This money is used to advance their cause through lobbying and publication. They lobby at all levels of government, and have attempted to introduce a bill in the U.S. Congress to obtain money, time, and space equal to that awarded to concepts involving evolution." *(Geotimes,* Jan. 1981, p. 12)

FACT: The Institute for Creation Research is *not* well-funded. ICR has five major divisions with many functions and activities, and a current full-time equivalent staff of at least 20 persons. This large and complex operation is financed on a very modest budget of $650,000—which is considerably less than the financing available to many university departments of biology, for example. ICR never has initiated or lobbied for any creation lawsuit or legislation, believing that education and persuasion are more appropriate and effective than compulsion. ICR staff members occasionally serve as expert consultants or witnesses in such situations, but these actions are wholly initiated and financed by local groups of concerned citizens.

CHARGE: "The Institute stood to make $2 million a year in textbook sales, with a contract renewal option, if HB 690 were enacted. To achieve its ends, it distributes a kit to creationist lobbies with a sample resolution drafted by 'Dr.' Henry Morris, who cautions users not to reveal its source." *(The Humanist,* May/June 1980, p. 59)

FACT: The above statement was in reference to the creation bill currently stymied in the Georgia legislature due to such distortions as this. ICR's sample *resolution* (not "creation bill") was prepared in response to many requests from local groups, in order to help keep such actions focussed on science and education rather than religion and social issues. The suggestion that those who might adapt the resolution for their own uses should try to keep ICR out of the picture was simply to emphasize that it was the *local* groups of citizens, not ICR, who were the sponsors. As far as profits from potential book sales are concerned, this may well be the reason behind much of the opposition to bringing creationist literature into the schools. Evolutionist writers and publishers have for many years reaped tremendous profits from their monopolistic control over school-adopted book sales. Such publishers, in the past, have refused even to examine creationist (or two-model) textbook manuscripts. Accordingly, some of us had to pool our own very limited resources in order to get ICR books published. Rather than being profitable, however, this operation has been at a significant loss to all its investors, each of the six years it has been in existence. If, perchance, school boards actually should begin to specify a two-model approach in their schools and begin to look for appropriate textbooks, one can be *certain* that the big publishers would finally begin to publish such books themselves. We would have no objection to this, of course; they have the resources to do it and, if they treat the subject properly, we will cooperate in every way we can to help them.

In all their polemics, the anti-creationists invariably avoid discussing the actual scientific *evidence* for macro-evolution. If there *were* any such evidence, they could easily settle the whole conflict merely by presenting the evidence! Instead, they seem compelled to resort to bombast, ridicule, defamation, intimidation, and distortion. Surely that great body of working scientists, largely uninvolved so far in the creation/evolution conflict will soon begin to see that a two-model approach to all scientific study is salutary and will persuade their more emotional brethren to open their minds to potential truth wherever it might be found.

No. 98, August 1981

Springs of the Ocean

By Steven A. Austin, Ph.D. *

A Challenge

One of the most profound and moving experiences in the life of the Old Testament patriarch Job must have been his encounter with a whirlwind. At a time when Job's undeserved suffering led him to a point of despair, God questioned Job from the whirlwind concerning his knowledge of Creation (see Job, Chapter 38). God confirmed his sovereignty and justice by giv-

---

*   The author, Dr. Austin, is a Research Associate in Geology and head of the Department of Geology at ICR.

ing what must rank as the greatest science test of all time.

Among the most thought provoking of God's questions to Job was, "Have you entered into the springs of the sea?" (Job 38:16a). The word for "springs" is *nebek* (transliterated from Hebrew), an unusual word referring to the places where water issues or bursts out of the earth. Job must have pondered this question with amazement, for although he had seen many springs on the land, he had no experience with *undersea* springs. Today we know why. The ocean is very deep; almost all the ocean floor is in total darkness; the pressure there is enormous. It would have been impossible for Job to have explored the "springs of the sea."

Other Old Testament passages refer to springs of the sea. Genesis 7:11 describes the cause of Noah's Flood and says that the "fountains of the great deep were broken up and the floodgates of heaven were opened." In the phrase "fountains of the great deep," the word "fountains" is *mayanoth* in the Hebrew and refers to "springs" or something similar in many other passages in the Old Testament. The phrase also mentions the "deep." The "deep" is the Hebrew *tehom* that is mentioned in Genesis 1:2, where God's Spirit brooded upon the face of the "waters," or the "deep."

Psalm 33:6-9 describes springs in the ocean relating them to their creation. The Psalmist says, "By the Word of the Lord were the heavens made, and by the breath of His mouth all their host. He gathers the waters of the sea together as a heap; He lays up the deeps in storehouses. Let all the earth fear the Lord, let all the habitants of the world stand in awe before Him; for He spoke and it was done, He commanded and it stood fast." So, from the beginning of the creation, this passage is saying that the waters of the sea were heaped together. In characteristic Hebrew style this is rephrased in Psalm 33:7b as, "He lays up the deeps in storehouses." So, there is some vessel which is containing a portion of the deeps from the original creation.

Proverbs 8 contains an interesting personification of wisdom, where Wisdom speaks. Beginning at verse 22 we read, "When there were no depths, I [Wisdom] was brought forth; when there were no springs abounding with water, before the mountains were settled, before the hills, I was brought forth." Then verse 28 of Proverbs 8 says, "When he made firm the skies above, and the springs of the deep became fixed." Here is another direct reference to springs being in the ocean.

There are four main points in this matter that the Old Testament affirms. First, the Old Testament asserts positively that springs do exist in the ocean. The source of this knowledge claims omniscience and is allowing that omniscience to be tested by scientific investigation of the ocean floor. Second, the undersea springs are said to have been established at the earth's creation. Third, the Flood of Noah is claimed to have been caused, at least in part, by an unusual activity of ocean floor springs. Finally, springs are mentioned so we can marvel at the wisdom and power of God.

The Discovery

The discovery of ocean floor springs represents a great milestone in the scientific investigation of the earth. Before 1930 little was known about the ocean floor. Volcanoes were observed to break the sea surface and this provided evidence of undersea volcanism. Because modern volcanoes on land emit steam, scientists suggested that water might be coming out of volcanoes on the ocean floor.

Vent in the seafloor where hot water issues from the earth into the ocean.

The deep sea dives of William Beebe's bathysphere in the 1930's provided a close look at the ocean floor, but no springs were observed. In the 1940's mapping of undersea topography was under way using the echo sounder. Thousands of undersea volcanoes called "seamounts" and "guyots" were recognized and speculation about undersea springs increased. In the 1960's metal-rich, hot brines were discovered using sonar in the bottom of the Red Sea. This brine was an indirect evidence of water coming out of the ocean floor. Aided by reports from Mexican abalone divers, scientists using scuba equipment located shallow-water hot springs along the coast of Baja California in the late 1960s.

Deep diving research submarines have been constructed to withstand the three-tons-per-square-inch pressure at the ocean floor. These submarines have carried scientists into the deep. The first direct observations of deepsea springs, or their mineralized vents, appear to have been made on the Mid-Atlantic Ridge by Project FAMOUS in 1973. Spectacular hot springs were then discovered on the Galapagos Rift in the Pacific Ocean by the 23-foot long submersible *Alvin* in 1977. *Alvin* also explored, photographed, and sampled hot springs on the East Pacific Rise just south of the Gulf of California in 1979. The research continues.

Several nontechnical magazine reports present photographs and descriptions of these recently discovered seafloor springs. The Galapagos Rift springs are described in the November 1979 issue of *National Geographic*. The article is titled "Incredible World of the Deep-sea Rifts" and bears the caption: "Scientists explore rifts in the seafloor where hot springs spew minerals and startling life exists in a strange world without sun."

The East Pacific Rise springs are shown in *Science News*, January 12, 1980. This article is titled, "Smokers, Red Worms, and Deep Sea Plumbing" and is followed by the caption: "Sea floor oases of mineral-rich springs and amazing creatures fulfill oceanographers' dreams." The discovery of these deep ocean springs is said to be the "most significant oceanographic find since the discovery of the Mid-Atlantic Ridge."

The hot springs have been called "black smokers." The "smoke" is the dark, mineral-laden, hot (up to 400 °C) water spewing from "chimneys" up to 15-feet tall atop mounds of minerals up to 60-feet high. The minerals coating the vents are largely sulfides of copper, iron, and zinc precipitated instantly as the hot geysers contact the cold seawater. The vents provide the habitat for the first community of animals to be discovered which does not obtain energy by way of photosynthesis. Animals collected include red-tipped tube worms, giant clams, mussels, sea worms, crabs, and limpets. The *Science News* article describes the East Pacific Rise springs:

> . . . the researchers found about two dozen hot springs stretched along 6 km of the half-kilometer wide spreading center. But next to these angry-looking, superheated geysers—called "smokers"—the Galapagos Rift vents looked like tepid sprinklers. Not only was the gushing water about 300°C hotter (the first attempt to measure the water temperature melted *Alvin's* heat probe), but around the chimneys lay mounds of minerals including copper, iron, zinc, and sulfur, with lesser amounts of cobalt, lead, silver, and cadmium. Like the Galapagos, however, the same animals, with the exception of the mussels, were clustered in fields near the vents.

Although scientists have examined only a small portion of ocean floor, seafloor springs appear to be common along the 40,000-mile Mid-Oceanic Ridge system. Dr. John M. Edmond of MIT suggests that water circulation through oceanic springs is a major geologic process; he estimates that 40 cubic miles of water flow out of earth's oceanic springs each year. If this is so, then mineralization must be an important process on the sea floor, and study of ocean springs may promote understanding and location of ore deposits. Ocean springs are also a vast, untapped source of geothermal energy, which, unfortunately, is located far from the major population and energy demand areas.

The discovery of ocean springs ranks as one of the foremost scientific accomplishments of the last ten years. Let us remember, however, that their existence was known thousands of years ago. Surely, God spoke through men by means of His Holy Spirit.

Short Bibliography on Springs of the Ocean

Ballard, Robert D., and Grassle, J. Frederick, "Incredible World of Deep-sea Rifts," *National Geographic*, V. 156, No. 5, November 1979, pp. 680-705.

West, Susan, "Smokers, Red Worms, and Deep Sea Plumbing," *Science News,* V. 117, No. 2, January 12, 1980, pp. 28-30.

Corliss, John B., et al., "Submarine Thermal Springs on the Galapagos Rift," *Science,* V. 203, No. 4385, March 16, 1979, pp. 1073-1083.

No. 99, September 1981
An Answer for Asimov
By Henry M. Morris, Ph.D.

One of the most widely circulated anti-creationist articles to appear in many years was recently published in the *New York Times Magazine.* There was nothing new or significant in the article, but it has nevertheless been reprinted in whole or in part, under various titles, in newspapers from coast to coast and overseas, and has probably turned many people against creationism.

The reason for its impact is certainly not its contents, which feature the usual evolutionary distortions and pseudo-logic. However, the author is Dr. Isaac Asimov, the most prolific and widely read science writer of our generation, and this fact has assured a wide audience for his opinions. He is the author of over 230 books on all kinds of scientific subjects, including even a few books on the Bible, and many people consider him an authority on anything about which he chooses to write.

Asimov does, indeed, have impressive academic credentials and is a brilliant writer. It is, however, impossible for any scientist to be a real "authority" on anything outside his own limited field of special study and research (which, in Isaac Asimov's case, consists of certain aspects of enzyme chemistry), so that he owes his reputation more to his exceptional ability in the techniques of exposition than to his accomplishments in scientific research.

Furthermore, Dr. Asimov has his own religious axe to grind. He was one of the signers of the infamous *Humanist Manifesto II,* promulgated by the American Humanist Association in 1973.

Among other statements, this Manifesto includes the following anti-theistic affirmations:

> As in 1933, humanists still believe that traditional theism, especially faith in the prayer-hearing God, assumed to love and care for persons, to hear and understand their prayers, and to be able to do something about them, is an unproved and outmoded faith.
>
> As nontheists, we begin with humans not God, nature not deity.
>
> No deity will save us; we must save ourselves.

Asimov and other humanists decry the teaching of creationism as "religious" while, at the same time, their Manifesto proclaims their own set of beliefs to be "a living and growing faith."

The quasi-scientific basis of their humanistic faith, of course, is evolution. *Humanist Manifesto I* (published in 1933) made this clear. Its first four tenets were as follows:

> *First:* Religious humanists regard the universe as self-existing and not created.
>
> *Second:* Humanism believes that man is a part of nature and that he has emerged as the result of a continuous process.
>
> *Third:* Holding an organic view of life, humanists find that the traditional dualism of mind and body must be rejected.
>
> *Fourth:* Humanism recognizes that man's religious culture and civilization, as clearly depicted by anthropology and history, are the product of a gradual development due to his interaction with his natural environment . . . .

It is significant that Asimov, in his anti-creationist harangue, does not attempt to offer even one slight scientific evidence for evolution. Nevertheless he proclaims: "To those who are trained in science, creationism seems like a bad dream, a sudden reliving of a nightmare, a renewed march of an army of the night risen to challenge free thought and enlightenment." Asimov, as a prize-winning writer of science fiction, is a master at the use of emotional rhetoric to intimidate and frighten, and this essay is a skillful masterpiece of alarmist propaganda. He warns about those previous "societies in which the armies of the night have ridden triumphantly over minorities in order to establish a powerful orthodoxy which dictates official thought.'' He concludes with an Asimovian prophecy: ''With creationism in the saddle, American science will wither . . . . We will inevitably recede into the backwater of civilization . . . . '' The ''prophet'' Isaac never mentions the fact that most of the great founding fathers of modern science (e.g., Newton, Pascal, Kelvin, Faraday, Galileo, Kepler, etc.) were theistic creationists, nor that thousands of fully qualified scientists today have repudiated the evolutionary indoctrination of their school days in favor of the much stronger scientific evidences for creation.

Although Asimov gives no arguments or evidences for evolution, he does attempt to identify and refute what he thinks are the seven most important arguments for creation. These he denotes as follows:

1. The Argument from Analogy. Since no one would question that the existence of a watch implies an intelligent watchmaker, by analogy the much more intricate and complex universe implies an intelligent universe-maker. Asimov makes no attempt to answer this unanswerable argument, except to say that ''to surrender to ignorance and call it God has always been premature.'' Such an answer is foolishness. The principles of mathematical probability and scientific causality certainly do not constitute a ''surrender to ignorance,'' but provide a compelling demonstration that complex systems do not originate out of chaotic systems by random processes.

2. The Argument from General Consent. By this term, Asimov means the widespread belief among all peoples that the world must have been brought into its present form by some god or gods. Asimov maintains that the ''Hebrew myths'' of creation are no more credible than all these other beliefs and that ''such general consent proves nothing.'' Actually this so-called ''argument from general consent'' is rarely, if ever, used by creationists. However, it is almost always used by evolutionists to prove evolution! That is, since they can cite no *scientific* evidences for evolution, they use the argument that ''all scientists believe evolution'' as the main proof of evolution.

3. The Argument from Belittlement. Here Asimov incorrectly accuses creationists of failing to understand scientific terminology and of belittling evolution as ''only a scientific theory." As a matter of fact, creationists maintain that real "vertical" evolution is not even a scientific theory, since it is not testable. There is no scientific experiment which, even in imagination, could suffice either to confirm or to falsify, either macro-evolution or creation. The proper term to use is not "scientific theory" or even "scientific hypothesis," but "scientific model" or "paradigm," or some such title. The creation model can be used far more effectively than the evolution model in predicting and correlating scientific data (the laws of thermodynamics, the character of the fossil record, etc.).

4. The Argument from Imperfection. Creationists are often accused of mistaking disagreements among evolutionists as evidence that evolution itself is false. Actually, all creationists are well aware of this distinction, but it does seem odd, if evolution is a sure fact of science, that it is so difficult to describe how it works! How does it happen that, if evolution is such a common process in nature, its mechanics remain so obscure? Yet, as Asimov says: "However much scientists argue their diferring beliefs in details of evolutionary theory, or in the interpretation of the necessarily imperfect fossil record, they firmly accept the evolutionary process itself." Evolutionists walk by faith, not by sight!

5. The Argument from Distorted Science. One of the main creationist arguments against evolution is its apparent conflict with the second law of thermodynamics, but Asimov says this argument is "distorted science," since it ignores the fact that the earth is an open system. Of course, it does *not* ignore the fact that the earth is an open system; evolutionists such as Asimov seem to have a strange blind spot at this point, perversely continuing to ignore the fact that this naive charge has been repeatedly answered and refuted. Asimov should know, as a chemist, that the mere influx of external heat into an open system (such as solar energy entering the earth-system) would *not* increase the order (or "complexity" or "information") in that system, but would actually increase its entropy (or "disorder" or "randomness") more rapidly than if it were a closed system! If "order" or "complexity" is actually to increase in any open system, the latter must first be *programmed* to utilize the incoming energy in some organizing fashion and then be provided also with a complex energy *storage-and-conversion* mechanism to transform the raw heat influx into the specific useful work of increasing the organized complexity of the system. Since the imaginary evolutionary process on the earth possesses neither such a directing program nor organizing mechanism, the second law of thermodynamics does indeed conflict with it and, to all intents and purposes, renders it impossible.

Asimov also makes the arrogant charge that creationist scientists "have not made any mark as scientists." The fact is that a cross-section of the records of the scientists on the ICR staff, for example, or of the Creation Research Society, would compare quite favorably with those of most secular colleges and universities (including Asimov's own record).

6. The Argument from Irrelevance. This criticism is merely a caricature of the concept of a completed creation, which Asimov thinks would be "deceptive." The fact is that a genuine creation would necessarily require creation of "apparent age," the only alternative being eternal matter and no true creation. There is no deception involved at all. As a matter of fact, the world does not even *look* old, except to the distorted vision of an evolutionist. The fossil record by its very nature speaks clearly of a recent worldwide cataclysm, and there are far more physical processes which yield a young age for the earth than the handful of processes which, through arbitrary and unreasonable assumptions, can be forced to yield an old age.

7. The Argument from Authority. Asimov insists, as do many other evolutionists, that the only real evidence for creationism is from the book of Genesis. The Bible does, indeed, teach creation and its literal authority was accepted by most of the founding fathers of our country and by our country's first schools. That ought to count for something, especially with those who deliberately chose to come to this country from other countries (Asimov came with his parents as immigrants from Russia in 1923). As a matter of fact, however, creationists are quite content to let the scientific evidence speak for itself in the public schools, with no reference whatever to the Bible. Many of us, in fact, are quite insistent on this point, appalled at the prospect of a humanist teacher such as Asimov teaching the Bible to a class of impressionable young people.

Dr. Asimov opposes creationism in the schools with the following astounding concluding argument: "It is only in school that American youngsters in general are ever likely to hear any reasoned exposition of the evolutionary viewpoint. They might find such a viewpoint in books, magazines, newspapers, or even on occasion, on television. But church and family can easily censor printed matter or television. Only the school is beyond their control."

Unfortunately, his last statement is mostly correct. Parents have indeed largely yielded control of their tax-supported schools to the educational establishment and its *de facto* religion of evolutionary humanism. However, the increasing incidence of such tirades as this from Dr. Asimov indicates that the creation movement has become a serious threat to this powerful and pervasive system.

No. 100, October 1981
Depletion of the Earth's Magnetic Field
By Dr. Thomas G. Barnes

There are three important force fields associated with planet earth, a *gravitational field,* an *electric field,* and a *magnetic field.* The *gravitational field* attracts us to the earth, preventing us from flying off into space as the earth rotates. The earth's *electric field* is very unstable, producing electric storms from place to place and at unpredictable times.

The earth's *magnetic field* is due to a huge electric current, billions of amperes, circulating in the core of the earth. But the main complication lies in the fact that there are a multitude of extraneous sources which produce distortions in the magnetic field. As a consequence, the earth's magnetic field is very complex. The instability sometimes shows up as tremendous magnetic storms, blocking out transoceanic radio transmissions. There are all kinds of anomalies resulting from distortions in the magnetic field. There are many unpredictable variations in the magnetic field with time and location.

Navigators do not depend on their magnetic compass as much

now as in early days. When navigators do use the magnetic compass they have updated magnetic charts to provide corrections for gross deviations in the earth's magnetic field from place to place over the globe. This helps them correct their bearings for "false" directions indicated by the compass, but the charts cannot correct for all the distortions.

In spite of all the distortions of the magnetic field there are modern data-reduction methods of taking an epoch of worldwide data and "washing" out the "noise" (distortions) and obtaining the basic field. The basic field is that field produced by the current circulating in the core of the earth. This basic field is called the *dipole field.* It is similar to the magnetic field of a single magnet located near the center of the earth and having a north and south pole, hence the name *dipole.* It is sometimes referred to as the earth's *main magnetic field.* The dipole magnetic field is the magnetic field of interest in this paper.

Rapid Decay of the Earth's Magnetic Field

It is known that the earth's magnetic field is decaying faster than any other worldwide geophysical phenomenon. A comprehensive ESSA Technical Report[1] gives the values of the earth's magnetic dipole *moment* (the vector which gives the strength and direction of the magnet) ever since Karl Gauss made the first evaluation in 1835. The evaluations have been made about every 10 or 15 years since then. Each evaluation required accurate worldwide readings over an epoch (a year or so) and special mathematical reduction to "wash" out the "noise." These reliable data clearly show this relatively rapid decay. The report stated that on a straight line basis the earth's magnetic field would be gone in the year 3991 A.D. But decay is exponential and in this case has a half-life of 1400 years.

A relatively recent NASA satellite preliminary report shows a rapid decay in the earth's magnetic field. No knowledgeable scientist debates the fact of the rapid decrease in the earth's magnetic field, nor does he question that the associated electric current in the core of the earth is using up energy. The present rate of loss is seven billion kilowatt hours per year. The earth is running out of that original energy it had in its original magnetic field.

Predictable Depletion of the Earth's Magnetic Field

The original source of the earth's magnetic field was the original electric current circulating in the core of the earth. No one knows how that electric current got started any more than one knows why the earth was originally spinning on its axis. The two are not related but they are both original states of the earth.

The electric current and its associated magnetic field have been decaying every since the origin of the earth. One might ask why the current did not die out faster? Faraday's induction law prevented it from dying out faster. As the magnetic field diminishes it induces a voltage which opposes the decay, extending its lifetime. The large scale of this phenomenon accounts for such an extended life. The radius of the core of the earth is 3.473×10^6 meters. The total physics of this problem is formidable but it has been solved.[2,3] The solution predicts the decay. It yields the half-life equation:

$$\text{Half-Life} = 2.88 \times 10^{-15} \text{ (Conductivity) (Radius}^2)$$

where the half-life is in years, the radius in meters, and the conductivity is in mhos/meter.

Sir Horace Lamb came up with the equivalent of this equation in 1833. As mentioned in the previous section, statistical analysis of the data yields a half-life of 1400 years. Lamb did not have a good value for the conductivity and therefore could not make a good prediction, but he did know that it would last for thousands of years, and that it was a plausible explanation of the earth's magnetic field. It is still the only good theoretical/mathematical explanation. Now it can be used to evaluate the electric conductivity of the core of the earth, because the data show a 1400 year half-life. The value of the electric conductivity of the core is, from this equation, equal to 4.04×10^4 mhos/meter. This is a very reasonable value for molten iron under the temperatures estimated for the earth's core. This is the only good means of making that evaluation of the conductivity of the earth's core.

Working backward in time many thousands of years, this equation yields an implausibly large value of the magnetic field and of the electrically generated heat stored in the earth's core. (See ICR Technical Monograph No. 4: *Origin and Destiny of the*

Earth's Magnetic Field.[4]) A reasonable postulate was shown therein to yield an upper age limit of 10,000 years.

Refutation of the Reversal Hypothesis

To protect their long-age chronology, evolutionists hold to a reversal hypothesis. The magnetic field is said to have remained at essentially the same value during geologic time, except for intervals in which it went through a reversal, dying down to zero and rising up again with the reverse polarity. The last reversal is supposed to have taken place 700,000 years ago.

The reversal hypothesis has no valid theoretical support. That is acknowledged in a recent *Scientific American* article: "No one has developed an explanation of why the sign reversals take place. The apparent random reversals of the earth's dipole field have remained inscrutable."[5] Neither are there any dependable data to support the reversal hypothesis. Reference has already been made to the multitude of magnetic disturbances, "noise," that make it so difficult to evaluate the earth's magnetic dipole moment, even when using absolute measurements over the whole earth. Yet it is absolutely essential that one evaluate the earth's magnetic moment if he is to claim to know the state of the earth's magnet at that time.

The tremendous amount of data on magnetic anomalies is important in exploration because they are evidences of the nonuniformities where one might expect minerals, etc. But they are useless insofar as history of the earth's dipole magnet is concerned.

In reference to the claims that the magnetization patterns on the sea floor relate to a history of the earth's magnetic field and continental drift, A. A. and Howard Meyerhoff give a lengthy refutation and very firmly conclude: "The so-called magnetic anomalies are not what they are purported to be—a 'taped record' of magnetic events during the creation of the new ocean floor between continents."[6]

One of the factors that makes rock magnetization completely undependable as evidence for the so-called reversals is the *self-reversal* process that is known to exist in rocks, totally independent of the earth's magnetic field. Richard Doell and Alan Cox state that: "The reversed magnetization of some rocks is now known to be due to a self-reversal mechanism. Moreover, many theoretical self-reversal mechanisms have been proposed . . . . However, in order definitely to reject the field-reversal hypothesis it is necessary to show that all reversely magnetized rocks are due to self-reversal. This would be a very difficult task since some of the self-reversal mechanisms are difficult to detect and are not reproducible in the laboratory.'"[7] It is interesting to note that these authors attempt to shift the burden of proof to the opponents of the reversal hypothesis but in so doing they demolish the reliability of the very data upon which they depend.

J. A. Jacobs states that: "Such results show that one must be cautious about interpreting all reversals as due to a field reversal and the problem of deciding which reversed rocks indicate a reversal of the field may in some cases be extremely difficult. To prove that a reversed rock sample has been magnetized by a reversal of the earth's field, it is necessary to show that it cannot have been reversed by a physico-chemical process. This is a virtually impossible task since physical changes may have occurred since the initial magnetization or may occur during certain laboratory tests."[8]

A strong conflict is exposed when a direct comparison is made between (1) the real-time evaluations of the magnetic dipole field by Gauss, et al, and (2) the magnetic "field" evaluations deduced following evolutionary assumptions about the magnetization in rocks and artifacts.

Over the last two centuries the work of Gauss, et al, has shown a continuous depletion of the earth's magnetic field. That is generally accepted as fact, whereas the magnetized rock-artifact method fails to show any trace of this trend.[9]

Conclusion

The only valid theoretical mathematical explanation and the only tenable data support the conclusion that the earth's magnetic field was created with a sizeable amount of original magnetic energy and has been continuously decaying ever since and that it is headed for extinction in a few thousand years. Looking backward in time there is a limiting age because there is a limit as to how much magnetic energy the earth could have had originally. Reasonable postulates as to the maximum magnetic field the earth could have had limit its age to a few thousand years.

The reversal hypothesis which has been proposed to extend the magnetic field back billions of years has neither a valid theoretical/mathematical basis nor observational support. The paleomagnetic data upon which it depends for support do not correlate with the state of the earth's magnetic field, namely its magnetic moment.

References

1. McDonald, K. L. and R. H. Gunst, *Earth's Magnetic Field 1835 to 1965*, ESSA Tech. Rept. U.S. Dept. Com. 1967, pp. 1 & 15.
2. Lamb, H., Phil. Trans. *London* V. 174, 1883, pp. 519-549.
3. Barnes, T. G., *Creation Research Society Quarterly*, Vol. 9 (1), 1972, pp. 47-50.
4. Barnes, T. G., *Origin and Destiny of the Earth's Magnetic Field*, ICR Tech. Mono. No. 4, 1973.
5. Carrigan, C. R. and David Gubbins, "The Source of the Earth's Magnetic Field," *Sci. Amer.*, Feb. 1979, p. 125.
6. Meyerhoff, A. A. and Howard, "The New Global Tectonics," *Amer. Assoc. Petr. Geolo.*, Bul. V. 56 (2), 1972, p. 337.
7. Doell, Richard and Allan Cox, *Mining Geophysics*, V. II, Soc. Expl. Geophysicists, 1967, p. 452.
8. Jacobs, J. A., *The Earth's Core and Geomagnetism*, MacMillan, pp. 105-106.
9. Burlatskaya, S. P., "Change in Geomagnetic Intensity in the Last 8500 Years," Inst. of Terrestrial Physics, *USSR Acad. Sci.*, 1969, p. 547.

No. 101, November 1981
Origin of Mankind
By Gary E. Parker, Ed.D.

Children lined up row upon row, mouths open and eyes agog, as they look up at a museum's hairy half-man, club in hand, and listen to their group leader repeat:

Four million years ago, a few apelike animals began to

walk upright, taking the first faltering steps toward becoming human beings. Time, chance, and the struggle for survival continued shaping us. As Carl Sagan put it: "Only
through the deaths of an immense number of slightly
maladapted organisms are we, brains and all, here today."[1]

Along the way, social groups became the key to survival,
and the human family evolved as the pleasure of sex was offered in return for food and protection.[2] Now we are
capable of directing our own further evolution, but to
avoid extinction we must understand our animal origins
and instincts. Truly, evolution is the science of human
survival.

So goes the lecture, often replete with compounded speculation and sexually explicit detail, and always with the subliminal
soft-sell, "science is salvation." Our children are told this "old,
old story" over and over again in children's science magazines,
high school science textbooks, Saturday morning TV cartoons,
talk shows, news specials and documentaries, and, of course, in
museum after museum. Sometimes they hear the words "perhaps" or "theory" or "may have been," but the whole thrust of
constant repetition by "experts in the field" could not have been
designed any better to overwhelm our young people into believing that "evolution is a fact, like apples falling out of trees."[3]

But what are the facts? Tragically, the facts are virtually inaccessible to most students. Museums rarely point out which parts
of their displays are real and which are reconstructions and ar-
tistic imagination. Textbooks, encyclopedias, and scientific
journal articles, the normal sources of student information,
rarely report the facts admitted by an international conference
of leading evolutionists, namely that the missing links between
man and apes, like the supposed links between other plant and
animal groups, are still missing (see ref. 3). In fact, it is really
only in creationist works that students can get a scientifically
critical look at the so-called "facts" behind evolutionist
museum displays and textbook pictures of our supposed "family
tree."[4]

Now, thanks to two new displays, ICR's Museum of Creation
and Earth History gives students and other visitors a close look
at the facts regarding the origin of mankind. One display
features life-size replicas of famous fossil skulls, and the second
includes film and casts of dinosaur and manlike tracks from the

Paluxy River in Texas. Students are encouraged to put their science process skills into action and to examine *all* the relevant features and facets of each specimen. The "facts" evolutionists cite are included, but so are points missing from the ordinary, evolution-only display. Consider the following as examples.

Neanderthals were once pictured by evolutionists as "beetle-browed, barrel-chested, bow-legged brutes," a link between apes and man. It is now possible to diagnose the several bone diseases common among Neanderthals, and we now know that creationists were right all along on this point: Neanderthals were just people—fully human.[4]

Unfortunately, Neanderthals have not been the only people once considered subhuman by evolutionist authorities. Dr. Down named his well-known syndrome "Mongoloid idiocy" because he thought children born with this condition (an extra 21st chromosome) were "throwbacks" to the "Mongolian stage" in human evolution.[5] Even sadder, Henry Fairfield Osborn once argued that "unbiased" scientists would classify "mankind" into several distinct species, if not different genera. Thus, he wrote, "The standard of intelligence of the average adult Negro [who evolutionist Osborn placed in a distinct subhuman species] is similar to that of the eleven-year-old youth of the species *Homo sapiens*."[6] These ideas, rejected by evolutionists today, were, nevertheless, the "facts of evolution" in Osborn's time and are crucial to understanding world events of the 1930's and 1940's.

Piltdown. Almost everyone now knows that Piltdown Man was a deliberate hoax. But for over 40 years, from 1912 until the 1950's, the subtle message of scientific authority was clear: "You can believe in creation if you want to, but the facts are all on the side of evolution." The facts in this case turned out to be an ape's jaw with its teeth filed and a human skull, both stained to make them look older.

At least Piltdown answers one often-asked question: "Can virtually all scientists be wrong about such an important matter as human origins?" The answer, most emphatically, is: "Yes, and it wouldn't be the first time." Over 500 doctoral dissertations were done on Piltdown, yet all this intense scientific scrutiny failed to expose the fake.

Students may rightly wonder what today's "facts of evolution" will turn out to be in another 40 years.

Too Much From Teeth? One of our museum displays shows what happened when people were too eager to interpret meager data. All scientists, whether creationist or evolutionist, are embarrassed by *Hesperopithecus haroldcookii* ("Nebraska Man"), reconstructed flesh, hair, and family, from a single tooth. Touted as another "fact of evolution" at the time of the Scopes trial, "Nebraska Man" turned out to be just the tooth of an extinct pig.

Evolutionists today are much more cautious about such zealous over-extrapolation. Yet it was not until 1979 that *Ramapithecus*—"reconstructed as a biped on the basis of teeth and jaws alone"—was written off as a "false start of the human parade."[7] Even now *Aegyptopithecus* is being pictured as mankind's "psychological ancestor" (what Elwyn Simons called "a nasty little thing") on the basis of highly imaginative "behavioral analysis" of the canine teeth of the males.[8]

"Lucy" and the Australopithecines. Current speculation about human ancestry centers around a group of fossils called australopithecines, especially a specimen called "Lucy."[9] Students visiting ICR's Museum see a picture of Lucy's skeleton, plus a full-scale reconstruction of a skull.

Next to this gracile australopithecine skull, however, the student also sees a life-size model of a chimpanzee skull. The similarities are striking. In fact, the similarities between gracile australopithecines and chimpanzees are so striking that "modern chimpanzees, by this definition [Richard Leakey's] would be classified as *A. africanus* [australopithecines]."[10] Lucy's discoverer, Donald Johanson, made that statement about Leakey's definition, and he goes on to say that Lucy is even more "primitive" (i.e., more apelike) than Leakey's australopithecines. Perhaps the most logical inference from our observation—certainly one students should be allowed to consider—is that Lucy and her kin are simply varieties of apes, and nothing more.

An evolutionist might object, "But here is the crucial difference: Lucy walked upright, and that makes her the evolutionary ancestor of man." But let's make sure our students hear both sides of that story, too. First, as leading evolutionary anthropologists point out, the living rain forest chimpanzee spends a lot of time walking upright,[11] so that feature alone makes Lucy only manlike or chimplike—and all her other features argue for chimplike.

Secondly, we have evidence that people walked upright before Lucy was fossilized—the Kanapoi hominid, Castenedolo Man, perhaps even the Laetoli footprints discovered by Mary Leakey, and most especially the manlike tracks preserved with those of dinosaurs in the rocky bottom of the Paluxy River in Texas.[12] The ICR Museum's superb new Paluxy display (donated by Paul and Marian Taylor) features film of the research in progress and casts of the manlike tracks that young people can try on for size. If people walked upright before Lucy was fossilized, then of course she could not have been our ancestor.

But did Lucy really walk upright anyway? " . . . anatomical features in some of these fossils provide a warning against a too-ready acceptance of this story," says anatomist Charles Oxnard in a published address to biology teachers.[13] On the basis of multivariate analysis, an objective computer technique for analysis of skeletal relationships, Oxnard reaches two conclusions. His scientific conclusion: the evidence is clear that the australopithecines did not walk upright, at least not in the human manner. Then, to the assembled teachers, he expressed his educational conclusion: "Be critical." We must teach our students to be critical, to examine the facts that lie behind popular theories, and to test ideas and assumptions against the evidence at hand.

It is impossible for students to think critically about origins, however, if they are only presented with evolution in some form as the only idea acceptable in science. Teachers with no special interest in creation realize that presenting only evolutionary ideas is neither good science nor good education, and it must make students wonder how science can be called an open-ended search for truth. An increasing number of teachers, parents, and especially students are realizing that true academic freedom must involve not only the freedom to discuss *how,* but also *whether,* evolution occurred—and, even more importantly, the freedom to discuss its one and only logical alternative, the scientific concept of creation.

No scientist has trouble distinguishing the kind of order in objects shaped by time and chance (e.g., a tumbled pebble) and those created with plan and purpose (e.g., an arrowhead). According to creation scientists, the evidence of anatomy, physiolgy, and genetics enables us to recognize human beings and apes as separately created kinds. The fossils found so far indicate that apes and human beings existed as separate kinds with large but limited variability in the past as they do today. On the basis of such evidence, many scientists are now developing and defending creation as a scientific model, well able to compete with evolution in the marketplace of ideas.

We know that acceptance of either view strongly affects the way a person lives. But let's lay aside our personal preferences for the moment and simply ask: which concept better fits the facts—evolution or creation? "The good ole American fair play system is to show 'em both sides and let 'em make up their own minds." That simple and fair-minded view was expressed by Wayne Moyer during a television interview with Richard Threlkeld.[14] That is the approach we are trying to take in the "two model" section of ICR's Museum of Creation and Earth History: " . . . show people both sides and let them make up their own minds."

Paradoxically, Moyer does not believe the rules of fair play can be applied to the creation/evolution question. Why? "It's like mixing apples and oranges; you're working from two sets of assumptions." That is the "official position" of the anti-creationists, but it simply cannot be true. First, nothing is more crucial to good science and good education than the ability to compare critically two sets of assumptions. Our students do it in social studies, they do it in literature, they do it in real life—why not in science, where comparing fact and assumption ought to be the backbone of the open-ended scientific approach to problem solving? Second, when it comes to the scientific aspects of origins, any open-minded individual and all scientists—creationist, evolutionist, or undecided—work from the *same* assumption: respect for logic and observation and the time-tested procedures of science.

Surely we can all benefit from full and free discussion of this basic question: What is the most logical inference from our observations of human fossils: creation or evolution? Certainly our students deserve the freedom to choose and the freedom to look at *all* the data needed to make an intelligent choice.

References

1. Carl Sagan, as quoted in "The Cosmic Explainer," *Time,* Oct. 20, 1980, p. 68.
2. Rensberger, Boyce, "Our Sexual Origins," *Science Digest,* Winter, 1979 (Special Ed.), ("Sexual intercourse evolved into 'making love' . . . "), pp. 46-47.
3. Stephen Gould, as quoted in "Is Man a Subtle Accident?" *Newsweek,* Nov. 3, 1980, p. 96.
4. See for example, Duane T. Gish, *Evolution? The Fossils Say NO!* Creation-Life Publishers, San Diego, 1979, pp. 106-162.
5. Gould, S., "Dr. Down's Syndrome," *Natural History,* Apr. 1980, pp. 142-148.
6. Osborn, Henry, "The Evolution of Human Races," *Natural History,* Jan./Feb. 1926; rpt. Apr. 1980, p. 129.
7. Zihlman, Adrienne, and Jerold Lowenstein, "False Start of the Human Parade," *Natural History,* Aug./Sep. 1979, p. 86.
8. Elwyn Simons, as quoted in "Just a Nasty Little Thing," *Time,* Feb. 18, 1980, p. 58.
9. Johanson, Donald, and Maitland Edey, "Lucy: The Beginnings of Humankind," *Readers Digest,* Sep. 1981, pp. 49ff.
10. Johanson, D. and T. D. White, "On the Status of *Australopithecus afarensis,*" *Science,* Mar. 7, 1980, p. 1105.
11. "The Case for a Living Link," *Time,* Dec. 4, 1978, p. 82.
12. Parker, Gary, *Creation: The Facts of Life,* Creation-Life Publishers, San Diego, 1980, pp. 108-119.
13. Oxnard, Charles, "Human Fossils: New Views of Old Bones," *American Biology Teacher,* May 1979, pp. 264-276.
14. CBS "Sunday Morning," Nov. 23, 1980.

No. 102, December 1981
The Mammal-Like Reptiles
By Duane T. Gish, Ph.D.

Introduction

The "mammal-like" reptiles were a highly varied, widely distributed group of reptiles that had a number of characterstics that are found in mammals. Assuming evolution to be a fact and that mammals must have arisen from reptiles, evolutionists thus quite logically assume that the presence of these mammal-like characteristics provide support for the theory that mammals arose from one or more groups of creatures within these mammal-like reptiles.

Creationists do not accept these assumptions, of course. They point out that the vertebrates are extremely varied. Some weigh less than an ounce, while others weigh several hundred tons. Some are restricted to the land, with considerable differences in mode of locomotion. Others are skillful fliers, while others live exclusively in the sea. Evolution or no, it would be surprising indeed if vertebrates from different classes did not share many characteristics in common.

Looking at the problem with a broad overview, we would have to say that the evidence is all in favor of the creationist view, since there is not a shred of evidence in the fossil record to link the vertebrates to any supposed ancestor among the invertebrates. Even though this transition is supposed to have taken 100 million years, not a single intermediate has ever been discovered. If vertebrates themselves have not evolved, as seems certain, evolution theory is dead, and it is foolish to speculate about evolution of groups within the vertebrates, or within any other division. If we look at the problem with a more limited perspective, if we confine our attention to the reptiles, mammal-like reptiles, and mammals, then there is evidence which supports each viewpoint.

The Evolutionary View of the Evidence

Let us first examine the evidence which supports the assumption that mammals have evolved from reptiles. In doing so, we will look at the geological column and time spans through the eyes of evolutionists, as must be done if the evidence is to be evaluated within the assumptions of the evolution model. "Primitive" mammal-like reptiles appear simultaneously in the fossil record with the "reptile-like" reptiles in the late Pennsylvanian Period. From the start these creatures possessed certain characteristics which are now associated with mammals, but other mammal-like characteristics, such as a secondary palate and a double occipital condyle, were lacking. Later, in the Permian and then in the Triassic "advanced" mammal-like reptiles appeared that possessed these and other mammalian characteristics, including highly differentiated teeth and an enlargement of the dentary bone of the lower jaw and a reduction in size of the other bones of the lower jaw. Finally, at about the Triassic-Jurassic boundary, or approximately 180 million years ago on the evolutionary geological time scale, a creature existed, it is maintained, which possessed all of these mammal-like characteristics and which, though it still retained a fully-functional reptilian type (quadrate-articular) jaw-joint, also possessed, side-by-side with this reptile jaw-joint a mammalian type (squamosal-dentary) jaw-joint. We then had a creature which evolutionists designate as the first mammal.

Some General Observations

When evolutionists wish to cite evidence for evolution, they almost always point to the alleged reptile-to-mammal transition, *Archaeopteryx* (a supposed intermediate between reptile and bird) and the horse series. Gould and Eldredge exclude *Archaeopteryx* as a transitional form, calling it a strange mosaic which doesn't count as a transitional form,[1] and Eldredge, although he does believe that horses have evolved, states that there are no transitional forms between the different types of fossil horses.[2] Thus, there seems to be pitifully little evidence for evolution if indeed millions of species have gradually evolved through hundreds of millions of years. If this has happened, our museums should be overflowing with vast numbers of unquestionable transitional forms. There should be no room for question, no possibility of doubt, no opportunity for debate, no rationale whatsoever for the existence of the Institute for Creation Research. Instead of these vast numbers of undoubted transitional forms that should exist, however, the case for evolution rests on a very few doubtful examples, one of which is the alleged reptile to mammal transition.

Let us now look at the so-called reptile to mammal transition from a critical viewpoint. We wish first to make some general observations. Does the possession by a creature of some characteristics which are possessed by a second class of creatures necessarily indicate that it is transitional between these two classes? To answer that question in the negative, we can cite numerous examples. *Seymouria* was a creature that possessed some characteristics found in amphibians and some characteristics found in reptiles. It should therefore constitute a "perfect transitional form" between amphibians and reptiles. It could not possibly have been such an intermediate, however, since it appeared at about the beginning of the Middle Permian, which is at least 20 million years too late on the evolutionary time scale to be the ancestor of the reptiles, which had already made their appearance in the preceding Pennsylvanian Period.

Another example is the living duck-billed platypus. This creature is a mammal, and yet it has a duck-bill, webbed feet, and lays eggs, in addition to possessing other characteristics that might be called reptilian. It has characteristics of mammals, reptiles, and birds, and perhaps could be called a "primitive" mammal. It could not possibly be ancestral to mammals, however, because it appeared very recently, about 150 million years too late to be the ancestor of mammals! In fact, this unique combination of structural features renders it impossible to suggest that it arose from any particular class of vertebrates or that it could have been an intermediate between any two classes. Many similar examples could be cited. Thus the existence in a single creature of characteristics possessed by animals of two different types does not necessarily indicate that this creature is an intermediate between these two types.

Mammal-like reptiles appeared supposedly right at the start of the reptiles, gradually became more mammal-like through the Permian and Triassic, and finally culminated in the appearance of the first real mammals at the end of the Triassic. At this time the mammal-like reptiles essentially became extinct, even though earlier they had been amongst the most numerous of all reptiles, world-wide in distribution. Since evolution is supposed to have involved natural selection, in which the more highly adapted creatures reproduce in larger numbers and thus gradually replace the less fit, we would now expect the mammals, triumphant at last to flourish in vast numbers and to dominate the world. A very strange thing happened, however. For all practical purposes, the mammals disappeared from the scene for the next *100 million years!* During this supposed vast stretch of time, the "reptile-like" reptiles, including dinosaurs and many other land-dwelling creatures, the marine reptiles, and the flying reptiles, swarmed over the earth. As far as the mammals were concerned, however, the "fittest" that replaced the mammal-like reptiles, they were almost nowhere to be found. Most of the fossil remains of mammals recovered to date from the Jurassic and Cretaceous Periods, allegedly covering more than 100 million years, could be contained in two cupped hands. Most such mammals are represented by a few teeth. If evolution is supposed to involve survival of the fittest, and the fittest are defined as those that reproduce in larger numbers, the origin of mammals represents something very strange, indeed. Since they survived in very few numbers, evolution apparently occurred by survival of the unfit!

Now another very strange event (from an evolutionary viewpoint) took place. Very suddenly (on an evolutionary geological time scale), most reptiles, including all the dinosaurs, marine reptiles, and flying reptiles, disappeared and were abruptly replaced by a great variety of land-dwelling, flying, and marine mammals, which appear fully-formed. As documented in an earlier Impact article (No. 87, "The Origin of Mammals," September 1980), each specific type of mammal, such as bats, whales, primates, hoofed mammals, rodents, carnivores, insectivores, and monotremes (duck-billed platypus and spiny anteater) appear in the fossil record with their basic characteristics complete at the very start. It is strange that all that can be produced to document the evolution of the mammals are some generalized forms, but not one shred of evidence can be produced to document the evolution of a single specific mammal, such as bats, whales, rodents, or primates.

A Critical Review of the Evidence

The Jaw-Joint

Now let us consider the two creatures, *Morganucodon* and *Kuehneotherium* that supposedly represent the most definitive transitional forms between reptiles and mammals. These are the creatures that, it is claimed, possessed the mammal-type jaw-joint side by side with the reptile-type jaw-joint. In mammals there is a single bone in each half of the lower jaw, called the dentary, since it bears the teeth, and this bone articulates directly with the squamosal areas of the skull. Reptiles have six bones in each half of the lower jaw. Articulation of the jaw with the skull is indirect, with the articular (one of the bones in the jaw) ar-

ticulating with the quadrate bone of the skull, a bone not found
in mammals. Another fundamental difference between reptiles
and mammals is the fact that all reptiles, living or fossil, have a
single bohe in the ear, a rod-like bone known as the columella,
which connects the eardrum to the tympanum. Mammals
possess three bones in the ear, the stapes, malleus, and incus
which connect the drum to the tympanum. Evolutionists maintain that the stapes corresponds to the columella and that the
quadrate and articular bones of the reptile somehow moved into
the ear to become, respectively, the incus and malleus bones of
the mammalian ear. No explanation is given how the intermediates managed to hear while this was going on.

Another difficulty with the above notion is the fact that while
thousands of fossil reptiles have been found which possess a
single ear bone and multiple jaw bones, and thousands of fossil
mammals have been found which possess three ear bones and a
single bone in the jaw, not a single fossil creature has ever been
found which represents an intermediate stage, such as one
possessing three bones in the jaw and two bones in the ear.

Morganucodon[3] and *Kuehneotherium*[4] each possessed a *full
complement of the reptilian bones in its lower jaw.* Furthermore, there was no reduction in the functional importance of the
reptilian (quadrate-articular) jaw-joint, even though these
creatures are supposed to be intermediates between reptiles and
mammals, allegedly possessing a mammalian (squamosal-
dentary) jaw-joint in addition to the reptilian jaw-joint. Kermack, et al., state "The most striking characteristic of the
accessory jaw bones of *Morganucodon* is their cynodont
character. Compared with such a typical advanced cynodont as
Cynognathus, the accessory bones present show no reduction,
either in size or complexity of structure. In particular, the actual
reptilian jaw-joint itself was relatively as powerful in the mammal, *Morganucodon,* as it was in the reptile *Cynognathus.* This
was quite unexpected."[3] (We would interject here that we emphatically reject the idea of calling *Morganucodon* a mammal.)

These authors relate that it has long been generally held by
evolutionists that there was a progressive weakening of the jaw
joint in passing from early to late cynodonts, which weakening
continued into the first mammals (the cynodonts were "advanced" mammal-like reptiles). This is what one would predict

if mammals evolved from reptiles and there was thus a gradual evolutionary replacement of the reptilian jaw-joint by the mammalian jaw-joint. Kermack and his co-workers now reject this idea since the reptilian jaw-joint of *Cynognathus* was extremely powerful and the lower jaw of *Morganucodon* closely resembled that of *Cynognathus*.

There is no doubt whatsoever therefore, that *Morganucodon* had a powerful standard reptilian type jaw-joint. Although almost all of the available material related to *Morganucodon* consists of disarticulated bones (the individual bones are scattered about) and almost all of the individual bones consist of fragments, a fragment of a jaw was recovered with the quadrate bone still in contact with the articular bone, leaving no doubt about the existence of a reptilian jaw-joint in this creature. But did *Morganucodon* and *Kuehneotherium* have, in addition to this reptilian jaw-joint, a point of contact between the dentary and squamosal and, if so, does this indicate the incipient formation of a mammalian type jaw-joint?

Kermack and his colleagues certainly believe that this has been established for *Morganucodon* and *Kuehneotherium* (it is also said to have been accomplished in several other groups of mammal-like reptiles[6]). What is the basis for this belief? Regardless of how strongly this belief is held, it rests on inference. The evidence is extremely fragmentary and no fossils are available showing the dentary in actual contact with the squamosal of the skull. In fact, not even a single intact lower jaw is available, all such specimens being reconstructed from fragments.

What is the evidence for a squamosal-dentary joint in these creatures? This evidence consists of an alleged condyle on the dentary. A condyle is a rounded process at the end of a bone forming a ball and socket joint with the hollow part (termed the fossa) of another bone. In mammals there is a very prominent condyle on the posterior end of the dentary which articulates to the squamosal bone of the skull. The squamosal contains a fossa for the reception of the condyle and the contact forms the jaw joint. With *Morganucodon* and *Kuehneotherium,* the dentary extends sufficiently posteriorly to encourage the belief that it made contact with the squamosal and the alleged point of contact on the dentary is called the condyle.

Whether the dentary bone of these creatures actually made contact with the squamosal can only be inferred. But if there had been a real contact between the dentary and squamosal, could it be said that this constituted a mammalian jaw-joint which existed alongside the reptilian jaw-joint? We must remember that these creatures had a fully-developed, powerful reptilian jaw-joint. The anatomy required for such a jaw-joint, including the arrangement and mode of attachment of musculature, must be quite different from that required for a mammalian jaw-joint. How then could a powerful, fully-functional reptilian jaw-joint be accommodated along with a mammalian jaw-joint?

The Reptilian vs. the Mammalian Ear

Furthermore, we cannot divorce the evidence related to the jaw-joint from that related to the auditory apparatus. As mentioned earlier, evolutionists believe that as the bones in the reptilian jaw, except for the dentary, gradually became relieved of their function in the jaw they were now free either to evolve out of existence or to assume some new function. Thus, the quadrate and articular bones of the jaw became free (they were, by the way, firmly attached to the dentary in *Morganucodon*) and somehow worked their way into the middle ear to eventually become the incus and malleus, respectively.

Now the anatomical problems associated with such a postulated process are vastly greater than merely imagining how two bones precisely shaped to perform in a powerfully effective jaw-joint could detach themselves, force their way into the middle ear, reshape themselves into the malleus and incus, which are precisely engineered to function with a remodeled stapes in a vastly different auditory apparatus, while all at the same time the creature continues to chew and to hear! As insuperable as this problem appears to be, it pales into relative insignificance when we consider the fact that the essential organ of hearing in the mammal is the organ of Corti, an organ not possessed by a single reptile, nor is there any evidence that would provide even a hint of where this organ came from.

The organ of Corti is an extremely complicated organ. It is suggested that the reader consult one of the stardard texts on anatomy for a description. One cannot help but marvel at this complex and wondrously designed organ. It has no homologue in reptiles. There is no possible structure in the reptile from which it could have been derived. It would have had to have been created de novo, since it was entirely new and novel.

According to evolution theory, all evolutionary changes occur as the result of mistakes during the reproduction of genes. These are called mutations, and each change brought about by such mutations which survived must have been superior to preceding forms. Thus, if evolution is true, we must believe that a series of thousands and thousands of mistakes in a marvelously coordinated fashion gradually created the organ of Corti to function in an ear which at the same time had to be reengineered accordingly while dragging in two bones from the jaw which had to be redesigned. Furthermore, each intermediate stage not only had to be fully functional, but actually must have been superior to the preceding stage. And after all this was accomplished, we still have reptiles and birds today with the same old-fashioned reptilian auditory apparatus which is just as efficient as the corresponding mammalian apparatus.[7]

Other Required Changes

Furthermore, while all of the above miraculous changes were occurring, these creatures also invented (by genetic mistakes) many other marvelous new physiological and anatomical organs and processes, including a new mode of reproduction, mammary glands, temperature regulation, hair, and a new way of breathing.

The structure of the thoracic girdle of the mammal differs fundamentally from that of the reptile. In the reptile it articulates with the breastbone by means of the coracoid bones and forms part of the thorax. This is not the case with mammals. In reptiles the fore part of the thorax is rigid and incapable of expansion. In mammals the thorax is expansible. In mammals the thoracic and abdominal cavities are partitioned by the diaphragm, a fibro-muscular organ. Since reptiles have no diaphragm, their thorax is not a closed box. As a consequence of the above, reptiles cannot breathe as mammals do. They cannot alternately expand and contract the thorax as is the case with mammals. They must breathe buccally.

There is no structure in a reptile that is in any way similar or homologous to the mammalian diaphragm. There is no structure found in a reptile from which it could have been derived. Again, a complicated structure had to be created de novo (and by mistake!) to perform a function that was already being very satisfactorily performed in a different manner in the assumed reptilian ancestor.

Summary

Whatever one chooses to call them, *Morganucodon* and *Kuehneotherium* possessed the full complement of reptilian bones in the jaw, a powerful, fully-functional reptilian jaw-joint, and the standard single-bone reptilian ear. On the other hand, all mammals, living or fossil, have a single jawbone, a fully developed mammalian jaw-joint, and a vastly different auditory apparatus involving three bones in the middle ear and a totally unique and extremely complex structure, the organ of Corti. As described briefly above, there are many other fundamental differences between reptiles and mammals. It is argued here that these changes could not possibly have occurred gradually, and thus the notion that a reptile gradually evolved into a mammal is scientifically unacceptable.

References

1. S. G. Gould and Niles Eldredge, *Paleobiology,* V. 3, p. 147 (1977).
2. Niles Eldredge, as quoted by Boyce Rensberger (New York Times News Service) in the *Houston Chronicle,* Sec. 4, November 5, 1980, p. 15.
3. K. A. Kermack, F. Mussett, and H. W. Rigney, *Zool. J. Linn. Soc.,* V. 53, No. 2, p. 157 (1973).
4. D. M. Kermack, K. A. Kermack, and F. Mussett, *Zool. J. Linn, Soc.,* V. 47, No. 312, p. 418 (1968).
5. Ref. 3, p. 119.
6. A. W. Crompton and F. A. Jenkins, Jr., "Origin of Mammals" in *Mesozoic Mammals,* J. A. Lillegraven, et al., Eds., U. of California Press, Berkeley, 1979, p. 62.
7. G. A. Manley, *Evolution,* V. 26, No. 4, p. 608 (1972).

Other articles that may be consulted:
   A. W. Crompton and F. A. Jenkins, Jr., "Mammals from Reptiles: A Review of Mammalian Origins," *Ann. Rev. Earth and Plan. Sci.,* V. 1, pp. 131-153 (1973).

   A. W. Crompton and Pamela Parker, "Evolution of the Mammalian Masticatory Apparatus," *Am. Sci.,* V. 66, pp. 192-201 (1978).

Chapter 2

In the Debate Arena

Nowhere is the creation/evolution issue brought more sharply before public attention than on the debate platform. In view of the heated nature of the confrontations that often develop, the term *arena* may be more appropriate than *platform*.

The first of these debates, at least in relation to the current creationist revival, was held on October 11, 1972, at the University of Missouri (Kansas City) between Dr. Robert Gentile, Professor of Geology at UMKC and ICR Director Henry M. Morris. Since that time, ICR scientists have participated in at least 110 other such debates, not counting an unknown additional number involving creationist scientists not connected with ICR.

Debates sometimes generate more heat than light, although ICR scientists make every effort to maintain a good-natured and purely scientific approach to the subject, being more concerned to win a hearing for creation than to win a debate. In this aspect, the debates have been highly successful, usually drawing large crowds, including many who would never go to a religious meeting or even to a straight lecture on creation. Most observers believe the creationists actually "win" the debates, but in any case, the debates have probably served more effectively than anything else to bring creation to the attention of the news media, the scientific and educational establishments, and the public in general.

IN THE DEBATE ARENA

AAAS EVOLUTIONISTS MEET GISH AND PARKER

Two of the leaders of the anti-creationist cadre in the American Association for Advancement of Science engaged ICR scientists in a formal debate at Palomar College near San Diego on November 7, 1980.

Recent articles in science journals have emphasized that creationists usually win debates with evolutionists, but then they often ascribe the creationist victory to poor preparation and lack of speaking skill on the part of the evolutionists. The latter could not have been the case when Drs. Frank Awbrey and William Thwaites, San Diego State University biologists, debated Drs. Duane Gish and Gary Parker of ICR before a crowd of over 1,000. Drs. Thwaites and Awbrey have debated creationists on many occasions.

In their initial presentations, Drs. Parker and Gish offered evidence of creation related to the origin of life, the origin of adaptation and variability, fossil diversity, embryology and homology, and the origin of man. They also offered the evidence of "downhill" changes and catastrophe since the time of creation as reflected in the Second Law of Thermodynamics and in the deposition of fossil-bearing strata around the world.

The evolutionists then stressed a model of variability based on allelic variation and recombination within interbreeding populations, which actually seemed to reinforce rather than to challenge the creation model (which was supported by several journal articles on population genetics appearing in the three months immediately preceding the debate.)

As evidence that random mutations could produce new, beneficial structures, the evolutionists presented a picture of a two-winged fruit fly with small, wing-like flight control organs called *halteres*. A second slide showed how radiation-induced mutations had changed the halteres into a broader, though wrinkled, "wing," thus, presumably, changing a two-winged insect into one with four wings. Dr. Awbrey did point out (as Dr. Bliss had pointed out to him in a previous debate) that the new fly could not fly, but argued that the experiment showed at least that wings could evolve into halteres. His example, however, seemed to show the opposite—that finely tuned flight-control structures like halteres could degenerate.

Dr. Gish emphasized that the "sudden appearance" of complete, fully functional wings of the modern type offered strong support for creation—and such wings appeared not only in insects, but also in birds, flying reptiles, and flying mammals (bats). Commenting on the thousands of tons of fossil evidence of variation within created kinds, Dr. Gish predicted the evolutionists would have to resort to *Archaeopteryx* as practically the only candidate for an evolutionary transition. They did, saying that no amount of quoting could erase the reptilian-like character of some of the bones. However, no amount of evolutionary rhetoric seemed to erase the evidence of fully developed feathers (no scale-feather transition), fully developed wings (no leg-wing transition), an extremely robust furcula (wishbone, found only in birds), and the asymmetric feathers characteristic of strong fliers.

Perhaps the most positive outcome of the debate was the *agreement* of both parties that *both* creation *and* evolution deserve to be treated in science classrooms, in the interests of both good science and good education. The generally cordial atmosphere of the debate should help to convince people that the scientific data related to origins can be discussed with mutual respect and keen attention to scientific detail, even when the persons involved come to radically different conclusions.

GISH DEBATES IOWA STATE UNIVERSITY PROFESSOR

Dr. Duane Gish and Dr. John W. Patterson, Professor in the Department of Materials Science and Engineering at Iowa State University and an outspoken evolutionist, debated the proposition "Scientific evidence justifies the presentation of the theory of special creation in public schools along with the theory of evolution as an explanation of origins." Two debates were held, one on the campus of Des Moines Area Community College, Ankeny, Iowa, on Wednesday afternoon, January 16, and the other was held on the campus of Graceland College, Lamoni, Iowa, on Thursday evening, January 17, 1980. The debate at Des Moines Area Community College was moderated by Professor Frank Trumpy, who also had made the arrangements for the debate. At Graceland College the debate had been arranged by Dr. Ralph Bobbitt, Professor of Psychology at the College, and the moderator was Robert W. Greenstreet, the Forensics coach of the college. The attendance at each debate was about 200.

Patterson's main thrust in both debates was his contention that evolution is science and creation is based solely on dogmatic unchangeable religious convictions. He maintained that science excludes the acceptance of authoritarianism and demands that any proposition in science must be potentially falsifiable. In the first debate, Patterson spent most of the remainder of his time presenting evidence for the geological column and the theory of continental drift, both of which he maintained supported evolution theory, the latter particularly vindicating Darwin. In the second debate, Patterson marshalled as his evidence for evolution mainly the geological column and radiometric dating.

Dr. Gish began his discussion at Ankeny by expressing a stand against authoritarianism, since this should indicate that he would not be dogmatic and thus should be in favor of exposing students to all the evidence on both sides of the question on origins. After pointing out that most evolutionists are very dogmatic as to the so-called "fact" of evolution, Gish emphasized that evolution was no more scientific nor less religious than creation.

Since Dr. Patterson had stated in correspondence with Dr. Gish that he considered himself expert in thermodynamics and that, furthermore, creationists were distorting the problem of evolution and thermodynamics, Gish chose as one of his main thrusts in both debates the evidence against a mechanistic, naturalistic evolutionary origin of the universe and of life, based on the Second Law of Thermodynamics. His other main thrust was the sudden appearance of plants and animals in the fossil record without ancestors or transitional forms, maintaining that this evidence is remarkable support for creation, but contradictory to evolution.

The initial presentations were followed by rebuttals and questions from the audience. During the discussion at Ankeny, one student addressed Dr. Patterson rather impatiently, stating, "Dr. Patterson, you haven't even made an attempt to answer Dr. Gish's arguments based on the Second Law of Thermodynamics." Dr. Patterson, in reply, stated that perhaps someday the Second Law will be shown not to be a natural law after all. Both debates were conducted in a friendly and congenial atmosphere at all times.

Those who attended the debate at Graceland College were asked, following the debate, to indicate their conviction concerning the subject being debated, that "scientific evidence justifies the presentation of the theory of special creation in public schools along with the theory of evolution as an explanation of origins." The vote was: Strong disagreement 13; moderate disagreement 4; neutral 2; moderate agreement 12; strong agreement 131. The vote was thus 88.3% in favor, with 10.5% opposed. During his final rebuttal at the debate at Ankeny, Dr. Gish asked for a showing of hands to a series of questions. Twenty voted in favor of teaching evolution exclusively, six voted in favor of teaching creation exclusively, and the remainder voted in favor of teaching both in public schools.

CHARLESTON DEBATE CLIMAXES
SOUTH CAROLINA TOUR

A debate in the Municipal Auditorium of Charleston before an audience in excess of 1000 people, some who had driven several hundred miles to attend, on Saturday, February 10, 1980, climaxed a week-long series of creation science lectures in the state of South Carolina by Dr. Duane Gish. The series began on Tuesday evening before an overflow crowd of 400-500 on the campus of the University of South Carolina in Columbia. The lecture was well-received and was followed by an hour of questions and answers. The meeting was moderated by Dr. Terry Spohn, biology professor in the Department of General Studies.

On Wednesday evening Dr. Gish lectured on the Columbia Bible College campus. A snow storm the night before had caused cancellation of classes on Wednesday and the reduced attendance of 250 perhaps reflected the weather conditions. Dr. Gish also spoke in Dr. Raymond Scott's class on Tuesday and was interviewed on radio stations WMHK and WQXL while in Columbia. He also met with several creationist biologists on the USC faculty and addressed a local ministerial association.

On Thursday evening Dr. Gish spoke to an audience of about 600 on the Clemsen University campus that overflowed into an adjoining room. The lecture and question period was conducted in an excellent spirit. On Friday afternoon on the same campus, Dr. Gish conducted a three-hour lecture and discussion with about 150 students and faculty. Alleged evolutionary mechanisms were dissected in detail.

On Friday evening Dr. Gish presented a creation-science lecture at the Shannon Forest Presbyterian Church before an audience of 200, including science students from Furman University.

Dr. Gish's opponent in the debate on Saturday night was Dr. E. Roy Epperson, Professor of Chemistry at High Point College, North Carolina. The moderator was Adrian Munzell. Dr. Epperson, who was the first speaker, outlined the standard evolutionary scenario, beginning with the "Big Bang" theory of the origin of the universe, and continuing through the origin of life and finally the origin of man. He also cited the theory of embryological recapitulation, homologous structures, and so-called vestigial organs in support of evolution. He cited the peppered moth and the production of domesticated plants and animals through artificial selection as evidence of evolution in action.

Dr. Gish, in his initial presentation, documented the fact that the universe, which is an isolated system according to Dr. Epperson and most evolutionists, could not possibly have created itself if science is science and the Second Law of Thermodynamics is a law of science. He further documented through a series of slides and citations from the scientific literature that the fossil record contradicts evolution but admirably supports creation.

In his rebuttal, Dr. Epperson prophesied that the missing transitional forms will be found on the as yet inaccessible ocean floor. He maintained that, as far as probability considerations were concerned, time was the hero of the plot. He finally suggested that people ought to accept what the majority of scientists believe.

In his rebuttal, Dr. Gish documented that the theory of embryologic recapitulation is a thoroughly discredited theory, having been abandoned by embryologists long ago, and should not be used to shape plastic minds. He refuted arguments based on homology and vestigial organs, using no less than evolutionist Sir Gavin de Beer to refute the homology argument. He pointed out that no paleontologist expects to find the missing transitional forms on the bottom of the ocean. Dr. Gish pointed out that time could not be the hero of the plot because, under natural processes operating today, the more probable state of matter is always the disordered state, and the more time that is available, the more certain it is that any natural system will be in its more probable state. He further pointed out that no evolution at all is represented by the peppered moth or domesticated plants and animals.

ASHLEY MONTAGU CONFRONTS GISH AT PRINCETON

Over 2,000 people filled the Princeton University gymnasium on April 12 as Dr. Duane Gish of ICR and Dr. Ashley Montagu debated the relative scientific merits of creation versus evolution. Dr. Julian Jaynes, Professor of Psychology at Princeton, was the moderator. The debate was the climax of a three-day creation seminar held on the Princeton campus, with Dr. Gish and Dr. Henry Morris as speakers. Paid registrants for the seminar totaled about 400, with Drs. Gish and Morris each bringing three lectures on various aspects of creationism.

Dr. Montagu is one of the world's best-known evolutionary anthropologists, author of 65 books and widely acclaimed as a writer and lecturer. This fact, and the location of the debate on the prestigious campus of Princeton University, made the debate one of unusual significance. The format of the debate was somewhat unusual with each debater speaking first for thirty minutes, then for twenty minutes. Then, following a period of audience questioning, each speaker presented an eight-minute summation.

Dr. Gish, for the affirmative, first defined the creation and evolution models, stressing that the debate was to deal solely with scientific considerations. He stressed the significance of the law of increasing entropy as conforming explicitly to the creation model, but as posing a serious problem to evolution. He further pointed out that natural random processes, by the laws of statistical probability, could never produce higher degrees of organization in living things, and especially could never generate a living system from the nonliving.

Dr. Montagu, in his first presentation, stressed the preponderance of scientific opinion favoring evolution, also rehearsing the history of Darwinism. He said (without evidence) that increasing disorder was the very environment in which evolution thrives, and thus that the second law of thermodynamics supported evolution.

Dr. Gish then pointed out that the neo-Darwinian theory, which Dr. Montagu had supported, had been repudiated even by many evolutionists, on the basis of probability and thermodynamics. The fossil record, with its complete lack of transitional forms, also poses a serious problem for evolutionism, he said, while it precisely conforms to the predictions of creationism. Dr. Montagu insisted that many transitional forms were known, citing the "horse series," along with the standard textbook primate series from the insectivores to man, as the primary examples. He further defined evolution as "the maximization of the improbable." He then acknowledged that the fossil gaps "looked like" special creation, though they did not require it.

After a question-and-answer period which explored a variety of controversial topics, the two scientists gave brief summations. Dr. Montagu's remarks were general, except that he attributed the lack of fossil transitions to the scarcity of fossils in general, and stressed again the fact that most scientists accept evolution. Dr. Gish, in his summation, urged that education be opened to the consideration of both models of origins, instead of the present system of evolutionary indoctrination. He concluded that the absence of transitional fossils, in view of the tremendous number of known fossils, is very real and is inconsistent with evolution.

The seminar which had preceded the debate attracted large numbers of Princeton students, along with students from Rutgers, Drexel, and other universities in the area, plus other registrants from New York and even from Boston.

On Sunday, April 13, Drs. Gish and Morris spoke at four morning church services in the area. The Princeton Evangelical Fellowship, founded by Dr. Donald Fullerton and currently directed by Wayne Wever, sponsored all meetings. Altogether a strong and positive impact for creationism was made at Princeton.

EUREKA HOSTS EVOLUTION DEBATE

Drs. Harold Slusher and Duane Gish debated Humboldt State College professors Drs. Timothy Lawler and Richard Stepp before an audience of about 700 at the Eureka High School auditorium on Friday evening, February 14. Dr. Lawler, with a

Ph.D. in biology from the University of Michigan, is Professor of Biology and Dr. Stepp, who gained his Ph.D. in physics at Pennsylvania State University, is Professor of Physics.

In his initial presentation, Dr. Lawler, stating that evolution was totally mechanistic, gave the standard textbook story of evolution, emphasizing the biological aspects of the theory, such as mutation, natural selection, and species formation.

Dr. Stepp stated that he had spent 2½ months studying for the debate, but even that was not enough time, since the subject was so complex. He highly recommended the ICR book *Scientific Creationism*. While emphasizing that evolution was speculative and one may or may not choose to believe it, he stated that if one assumed evolution to be the process God used, then that gave the scientist the advantage of having something about origins to investigate and speculate about.

In his presentation, Dr. Gish suggested that a comparison of all available theories with the laws of probability would absolutely exclude the possibility of a mechanistic, naturalistic, evolutionary origin of life. He then compared the fossil record to the creation model and the evolution model, pointing out the fact that this evidence supports creation, but contradicts evolution. Dr. Gish also pointed out that the so-called theories of embryological recapitulation and of vestigial organs have been thoroughly discredited.

Dr. Slusher contrasted various aspects of evolution theory, such as those related to the origin of the universe and the origin of life, to the Second Law of Thermodynamics, documenting the fact that this natural law excludes any possibility of a naturalistic origin of the universe and of life. He also summarized scientific evidences supporting a short time chronology for the earth and the universe.

In the rebuttal, Dr. Lawler stated that the theories of embryological recapitulation and vestigial organs had indeed been proven false and that it was unfortunate that they are still found in textbooks. In his rebuttal, Gish pointed out that evolution did not qualify as a scientific theory, since it involved postulated events that were unobservable and ideas that were untestable.

Dr. Slusher in his rebuttal reinforced his Second Law argument and cited additional evidences for a young age for the universe and for the earth.

DEBATE RECORDED FOR CHRISTIAN TELEVISION

On Friday evening, March 7, 1980, Dr. Duane Gish debated Dr. Vincent Sarich before an audience of 300-400 in a television studio in Kansas City, Kansas. The debate was taped for later nationwide telecasts on CBN, and will be seen on the 700 Club, PTL Club, and other Christian television programs throughout the U.S. Dr. Sarich is Professor of Anthropology at the University of California, Berkeley, and is well-known for his "protein-clock," the suggestion that it is possible to date the time of divergence of various animals from their common ancestors by comparison of the structures of proteins common to these animals.

The format of the debate was unique. The two debaters and the moderator-interrogator, John Ankerberg, were on a circular platform surrounded by the audience. The debate began with a series of questions directed to both debaters by Mr. Ankerberg. Each debater was then given seven minutes to outline his position concerning origins in general. Several specific topics were then discussed, such as the fossil record, human origins, and the origin of life, with each debater being given five minutes and a two to three-minute rebuttal. For about 20 minutes the debaters then directed questions to one another, with a free-wheeling debate following each response. During the final 45 minutes of the program, the debaters were questioned by members of the audience, with each allowed to comment following the initial response.

During the debate Dr. Gish stressed the evidence for creation from thermodynamics, probability laws, and the fossil record, including the special creation of man. Dr. Sarich's arguments were based mainly on the similarities of proteins from various animals, particularly those of man and apes, his claims for some examples of transitional forms, particularly among the primates, and the distribution of fossils in the geological column.

GISH DEBATES DOOLITTLE AT IOWA STATE

The origin of life was the subject of the debate before a paid audience of approximately 1,500, held on the evening of Wednesday, October 22, 1980, in the C.Y. Stevens Auditorium of Iowa State University. The debate was arranged by Students for Origins Research, an I.S.U. creationist organization headed by John Meyer. Participants were Dr. Duane Gish and Dr. Russell F. Doolittle, who holds a Ph.D. in biochemistry from Harvard University and is Professor of Biochemistry at the University of California at San Diego. The moderator was Richard Hudson, the Forensics Debate Coach at I.S.U.

Dr. Gish, the first speaker, maintained that a naturalistic, evolutionary origin of life is impossible. Thus, the only alternative—the special creation of life by an intelligent creator—is the only answer.

Using thermodynamic principles and the laws of probability, Dr. Gish presented evidence which he contended showed that not even a single complex molecule, such as DNA, RNA, or protein, could have arisen spontaneously on the hypothetical primitive earth. Chemical, thermodynamic, and kinetic data showed that no significant quantity of even relatively simple organic molecules, such as amino acids, could have arisen spontaneously under hypothetical primordial earth conditions. He closed by pointing out that no life of any kind had been detected on Mars or the moon. This was contradictory to evolutionary expectations.

Dr. Doolittle began his presentation by asking those in the audience who were convinced that life had arisen by evolution to stand up. No more than 10% responded. Doolittle then presented an evolutionary view of the origin of the universe, beginning with "mysterious forces" which control the universe, and continuing through the hypothetical "Big Bang" start of the universe, the origin of stars, and finally culminating in the origin of life.

Doolittle argued that there was no difficulty producing considerable quantities of amino acids and other substances. He showed a hypothetical cycle involving "activated" nucleotides, a polypeptide catalyst, a coded polynucleotide template, and "activated" amino acids. He said that later gene duplication led to greater diversity. Doolittle also attempted to counter Gish's probability argument by asserting that if one would calculate the probability of all 2,000 of us being here in this auditorium tonight the odds would seem to be impossible, and yet here we were!

In his rebuttal, Gish pointed out that the 2,000 people would never have been there if their presence had depended on chance (as does evolution), but were there precisely because they did not get there by chance! Each had made his way to the auditorium deliberately!

Gish pointed out that chemists can obtain significant quantities of amino acids and similar products only by the use of a trap to isolate the products, since the rates of destruction of the products by the energy sources that produced them exceed the rates for formation by a millionfold and more. Even if a trap were available on the hypothetical primordial earth, this would also be fatal since no energy would thus be available to promote the next step up the ladder.

Gish asserted also that the production of "activated" amino acids and nucleotides would have been excluded under primordial earth conditions (ATP and other phosphorylated substances required for the synthesis of activated compounds are very unstable to water), and that Doolittle's scheme simply assumed the existence of a protein enzyme and a polynucleotide template rather than explaining their origin in the first place.

On Tuesday evening preceding the debate, Dr. Gish debated science writer Robert Schaddewald for two and one-half hours on WHO Radio, Des Moines.

DEBATE HELD AT WESTERN WASHINGTON

On Thursday evening, October 9, 1980, a debate was held between Dr. Duane Gish and evolutionist Dr. Donald C. Williams, who holds a Ph.D. in biochemistry at Western Washington University. The moderator was Dr. Richard Mayer of W.W.U.

Dr. Williams said he considered Dr. Gish to be a theologian, not a scientist. He stated that we are accidents of nature, and that evolution is a fact. The scientific portion of Dr. Williams' first 30-minute presentation consisted of a brief description of his ideas concerning the evolution of prokaryotes (bacteria and blue-green algae), and eukaryotes (higher cells). He suggested early life forms consisted of autotrophic prokaryotic anaerobes and that eukaryotes evolved from prokaryotes.

During Dr. Gish's first 30-minute presentation, he presented evidence based on thermodynamics and probability which he contended rendered a naturalistic evolutionary origin of the universe and of life impossible. Dr. Williams' second 30-minute presentation consisted almost entirely of an attempt to answer Dr. Gish's arguments. He asked why, if Dr. Gish believed in the Second Law of Thermodynamics, didn't he believe in the "law of evolution?"

In Dr. Gish's second 30-minute period he presented the evidence from the fossil record which he maintained is contradictory to the evolution model, but which can be admirably correlated with the creation model.

In his rebuttal Dr. Williams claimed that intermediate forms do exist, and accused Gish of using selected quotations. He suggested that perhaps proteins were not needed in the beginning, since RNA can act as a catalyst.

In his rebuttal Dr. Gish emphasized that he used testimony from well-respected evolutionists to document the absence of transitional forms, and there should be no difficulty in recognizing transitional forms if some actually exist. He characterized Williams' claim that RNA can act as an enzyme as "absurd," since no known RNA has enzymatic activity, and that enzymatic activity is limited to proteins. Dr. Gish also cited recent scientific research in which the investigators claimed that the mode of synthesis of messenger RNA rendered untenable the idea that eukaryotes had evolved from prokaryotes. Williams, Gish contended, was "out of date" as well as "out of step" with good science.

DEBATE FEATURES WISCONSIN SEMINAR

A creation-evolution debate between Dr. Newtol Press, Professor of Zoology at the University of Wisconsin (Milwaukee), and Dr. Duane Gish of ICR was the highlight of a creation seminar held on October 24-26, 1980, at the University of Wisconsin Center in Baraboo, Wisconsin (home of the Ringling Brothers Circus). Approximately 250 paid registrants attended the debate, held at Baraboo's downtown Civic Center on Friday night.

The seminar sessions on Saturday (with 150 paid registrants from many different communities in the area), featured two lectures by Dr. Henry Morris and two by Dr. Gish. On Sunday Dr. Gish spoke at the 8:30 a.m. service of Baraboo's First Baptist Church (whose Minister of Education, John Thompson, had organized the debate and seminar), while Dr. Morris spoke at the 9:45 and 11:00 a.m. services.

Dr. Press, who confessed that he was participating in the debate against the strong advice of his colleagues, paid his respects to the ICR scientists as men of integrity fighting a courageous uphill battle. His affirmative statement supporting evolution, however, consisted entirely of an attack on the position and writings of creationist scientists, with no specific scientific evidences offered for evolution. Dr. Gish, in his negative statement, gave much evidence from paleontology, thermodynamics, and probability which supported predictions from the creation model.

Dr. Press' rebuttal attempted to answer the creationist argument based on fossil gaps by citing biochemical studies indicating relationships corresponding to the traditional evolutionary phylogenetic trees. He closed with an emotional suggestion that genetic engineering was now creating new life forms, thus rendering all anti-evolution arguments obsolete. Dr. Gish replied showing that many more recent biochemical studies had exhibited numerous contradictions to the supposed phylogenetic trees and that genetic engineering could never create genuinely *new* life forms.

DEBATE AT UNIVERSITY OF WASHINGTON

Cultural anthropologist Dr. Eugene Hunn, Associate Professor of Social Anthropology at the University of Washington, was Dr. Duane Gish's opponent in a creation/evolution debate on campus before 1000 students and faculty at midday on Wednesday, November 19, 1980.

Gish, the initial speaker, described the predictions of the fossil record based on creation and evolution and then compared the actual data to the predictions of each model. He first described the general nature of the fossil record related to all animals, which he asserted strongly supported creation, but contradicted evolution. Using slides, he then reviewed the fossil record of primates and man, which Gish declared showed a separate origin for prosimians, monkeys, apes, and men.

In his presentation Hunn mentioned the refusal of anyone in the biology department of the University of Washington to debate, while offering himself as the "latest sacrificial lamb to the professional creationist debaters." Hunn then stressed the similarities between apes, monkeys, and man as evidence for descent from a common ancestor, using similarities between spider monkeys and man as an example. He described briefly the neo-Darwinian mechanism of evolution, starting with DNA as a *"self-replicating"* molecule. Most of the remainder of his time was spent on philosophical and religious implications, including quotations from Genesis.

In his rebuttal, Gish pointed out that the actual scientific evidence, including genetics, contradicts the idea that similarities in different animals are due to inheritance from a common ancestor. He also pointed out that neither DNA nor any other molecule can reproduce itself, and that they are replicated only by living cells, indicating that these molecules could not have preceded, nor existed independently of living cells.

In his rebuttal, Hunn asserted that new theories of evolution which are now being suggested predict gaps rather than transitional forms. He asked why, if God created, is the universe and its living things not now perfect.

Dr. Harold Slusher also debated Dr. Hunn on "KING—TV" for an hour on Wednesday morning. The consensus of those who heard and saw this debate agreed that Dr. Slusher was easily the winner.

SLUSHER DEBATES ILLINOIS GEOLOGIST

Dr. Harold S. Slusher participated in a creation/evolution debate on December 3, 1980, at College of Lake County, Grayslake, Illinois. This debate was sponsored by the Christian Life Fellowship and the College of Lake County. Dr. Slusher's opponent was Dr. Robert DeMar, Professor of Geology and Acting Head of the Department of Geology, University of Illinois, Circle Campus.

Dr. DeMar's main thrust regarding evidence allegedly for evolution was the geographical distribution of fossils. Dr. Slusher presented evidence for the creationist position from cosmogony, cosmochronology, the fossil record, and thermodynamics. Dr. DeMar repeatedly in rebuttal failed to discuss these or other scientific evidences and seemed to prefer to debate by use of unsupported assertions and evolutionary cliches, with no attempt at logical reasoning.

The debate was open to the public as well as to students. Almost a thousand were in attendance. The creationist position seemed to receive a very favorable reception.

2800 WITNESS DEBATE AT EDMONTON
Debate Highlights Canadian Tour

Nearly 2800 people crowded into the Jubilee Auditorium of Edmonton, Alberta, for the debate on the evening of Thursday, February 26, 1981, between the University of Alberta's Dr. Richard Fox and Dr. Duane Gish. Dr. Gish's 1981 Canadian tour began at Saskatoon, Saskatchewan, on Friday, February 20, and closed at the Prairie Bible Institute in Three Hills, Alberta, where he spoke to an audience of two thousand. The tour included other stops at Grand Prairie, Peace River, Lethbridge, Medicine Hat, Camrose, Calgary, and Red Deer, all in the province of Alberta. The visit to Saskatoon was sponsored by the Creation Science Association of Saskatchewan and the tour of Alberta was sponsored by the Creation Science Association of Alberta. Ivan Stonehocker, science teacher, and past president of the Alberta Teacher's Association, is president of the Creation Science Association of Alberta, and botanist Dr. Margaret Helder was director of the tour.

In Saskatoon, in addition to an evening lecture at the Circle Drive Alliance Church, Dr. Gish spoke before an overflow audience of nearly 600 on the University of Saskatchewan campus. After Dr. Gish's lecture, Dr. Taylor Steves, biologist, Dr. Willie Braun, geologist, and Dr. Peter Shargool, biochemist, all of the university faculty, each offered a 15-minute critique, and Dr. Gish followed each critique with a 15-minute rebuttal. An exchange between participants and the audience then followed. While in Saskatoon, Dr. Gish had four radio interviews and a television interview.

In Lethbridge, in addition to speaking to a large evening audience, Dr. Gish gave a noon lecture at Lethbridge University. Present was Dr. Job Kuijt of the university, whom Dr. Gish had debated six years ago during a visit to Lethbridge. During that debate Dr. Kuijt had presented practically no science but had devoted most of his time to a diatribe against Christianity and the Bible. On this occasion he rose to challenge Dr. Gish with "a long list of contradictions and distortions." When asked to be specific, he accused Dr. Gish of quoting Dr. E.J.H. Corner, a British biologist, out of context. Dr. Gish thereupon read the entire page of Dr. Corner's book from which he had taken the quote, and it was perfectly clear to the audience that Dr. Gish not only had *not* taken Corner's statement out of context, but the more he read of Corner's material the worse it sounded for evolution. Dr. Kuijt had little else to say.

The debate in Edmonton followed the usual format, with Dr. Fox leading off with a 60-minute presentation, followed by a similar presentation by Dr. Gish, and each responding with 15-minute and 5-minute rebuttals. The moderator was Bill Jackson, a popular radio personality in Edmonton. Dr. Fox, professor of geology and zoology, spent much time emphasizing that science is restricted solely to naturalistic phenomena with exclusion of supernatural explanations. He then insisted that the origin of the universe and of man occurred solely by naturalistic means. He strongly supported the neo-Darwinian mechanisms of evolution, that of slow, gradual change by mutation with natural selection, while not excluding minor influences due to other mechanisms.

Dr. Fox listed homology, extinctions, vestigial organs, geographical distributions, the geological column, and radiometric dating as evidences for evolution—for none of which, he declared, creation provided an explanation. He attempted to refute the creationist arguments based on thermodynamics.

In his initial constructive argument, Dr. Gish presented evidence based on the science of thermodynamics and the laws of probability that the universe could not have created itself by natural processes and that life could never have arisen by spontaneous mechanistic processes. He insisted that the nature of the universe and of natural laws and processes require a supernatural origin of the universe and of the living things it contains. He then illustrated via slides and quotations from current scientific literature his contention that the fossil record is remarkably in accord with creation but is strongly contradictory to predictions based on evolution theory. He closed by challenging Dr. Fox to explain, as evolutionists believe, that something like a cow, pig, or buffalo evolved into whales and dolphins.

In his rebuttal, Dr. Fox argued that it was the bias of the fossil record that produced the gaps, not the actual nonexistence of transitional forms. He insisted that all we are talking about in evolution in any case is the origin of species.

In his rebuttal Dr. Gish pointed out that neither the nature of the fossil record nor any bias in its collection could account for the universal absence of transitional forms. He insisted that the evidence related to homology, extinctions, and geographical distribution was either contradictory to evolution or difficult to understand, and that no real vestigial organs do, in fact, exist.

In Calgary, in addition to an evening lecture before an audience of 1300 in Calgary's Jubilee Auditorium, Dr. Gish had a mini-debate at the University of Calgary with geologist Dr. Val Geist and biochemist Dr. William Costerton, both of the university faculty. Geist and Costerton each made 17-minute presentations with 3-minute rebuttals and Gish had a 17-minute response to each plus 3-minute rebuttals. Dr. Geist had little to say except to express contempt for views other than his own with references to religion, philosophy, politics, Abscam, and the CIA. Dr. Costerton's presentation actually supported the creation view of the origin of life. He contended that as we are becoming more and more aware of the incredible complexity of life and its necessary coordination in all aspects, the complex repair mechanisms required for the survival of DNA, etc., a mechanistic evolutionary origin of life is becoming less and less acceptable. He strongly condemned creation-evolution debates, however, as "stupid" and even "immoral."

Gish presented briefly the scientific case for creation based on thermodynamics, probability laws, and the fossil record. After pointing out that Costerton's lecture supported the creationist position, Gish then stated that he was participating in the debate for precisely the same reason Geist and Costerton were there—each had been invited. He pointed out that debates were very common in science and did serve as a means of conveying information. The afternoon discussion closed with an interchange with the audience.

MORRIS DEBATES MILLER AT BROWN UNIVERSITY

One of New England's venerable Ivy League schools, Brown University in Providence, Rhode Island, was the scene of a creation/evolution debate on April 10, 1981, between biologist Kenneth Miller of the Brown faculty, and ICR scientist Henry M. Morris. The debate was sponsored by several campus organizations, as well as by the Dean of the College and the Dean of Student Life. Attendance, divided about equally between Brown students and people from the community, totalled nearly 1800.

Dr. Miller, who had previously served six years at Harvard University as director of the electron microscope laboratory in its biology department, proved an exceedingly knowledgeable and smooth speaker, the most effective evolutionist debater Dr. Morris had encountered to date. Dr. Miller had spent weeks in studying ICR debate tapes and literature and was well prepared, with two carousels full of slides covering almost every possible topic of discussion. Speaking very rapidly, he covered a wide range of topics superficially, but persuasively. As a Catholic, he claimed to be a "creationist," but nevertheless insisted natural processes accounted for the entire history of the universe and life. Unfortunately his remarks were laced with frequent sarcasm and *ad hominem* arguments (all audibly relished by many in the audience), especially ridiculing the concept of a recent creation. The bulk of his presentation consisted of attacks on the creation model rather than evidence for evolution. However, he did argue that similarities in certain chemical systems (especially Cytochrome C) indicated a close relation between man and chimpanzee and also that rubidium-strontium dating had conclusively proved an old earth.

Dr. Morris showed that the creation model predicted exactly: (1) the array of similarities and differences in living organisms (horizontal changes within kinds, clear-cut gaps between kinds); (2) ubiquitous gaps and lack of transitional forms in the fossil record; (3) the universal laws of thermodynamics; (4) the unity and catastrophic nature of the geologic record of earth history preserved in the rocks and fossil beds. All of these predictions were shown to be supported by firm scientific data and documented from authorities.

In rebuttal, Dr. Miller did not attempt to refute items (1) and (4) above (except by ridicule). However, he argued that the thermodynamic evidence against evolution was invalidated by the fact that certain organic chemicals had been shown to arise spontaneously in nature, and that the work of Eigen *et al* had opened the possibility of explaining thermodynamically the naturalistic origin of life. He did not question the fact that the laws of thermodynamics were explicit predictions of creationism. He also claimed that the horses, the pachyderms, the nautiloids, and the mammal-like reptiles provided examples of intermediate forms in the fossil record.

In his rebuttal, Dr. Morris showed that radiometric dating methods (including rubidium/strontium) were all based on nonprovable assumptions and always proved unreliable when checked against rocks of known age. He noted that many processes indicate a young age, with the same kinds of assumptions, also pointing out that "relative ages" in the geologic column were invalidated by the strong evidence of the formation of the entire column by a single hydraulic cataclysm, by the many examples of "sequence inversions" in the column ("old" formations on top of "young" formations, with no evidence that such reversals are mechanically possible), and by anomalous fossils (e.g., the well-documented evidence of human and dinosaur contemporaneous footprints in Texas—evidence which Dr. Miller dismissed as a "hoax"). He also pointed out that, while some chemicals may suggest man's genetic relationship with the chimpanzee, others suggest that he may be most closely related to the jackass, the garter snake, the glacial bear, the chicken, or the butterbean!

To his credit, Dr. Miller did agree that this was a scientific issue which deserved consideration in public institutions. Dr. Morris also urged that this type of "two-model" comparative evaluation should not only be aired in major public confrontations, but should be a daily exercise in every classroom where the subjects of origins and earth history were discussed.

SLUSHER AND MORRIS DEBATE GEOLOGISTS IN GEORGIA

"Resolved that evolution is a more effective model than creation as an explanation for the origin and history of life," was the topic for a debate at Columbus College in Georgia on May 6, 1981. Speakers for the affirmative were Dr. David Schwimmer (paleontologist) and Dr. William Frazier (sedimentologist), both on the geology faculty at the Georgia state college. Dr. Henry

Morris and Dr. Harold Slusher, both of ICR, took the negative, speaking for creationism. Approximately 1000 were in attendance.

Unfortunately, neither Dr. Schwimmer nor Dr. Frazier attempted to give any evidence supporting evolution. Dr. Schwimmer's talk was essentially a personal attack on creationists, especially Dr. Gish and Dr. Morris, alleging that their motives were bad, that they distort facts, quote evolutionists out of context, use outmoded data, etc. Dr. Frazier continued in the same vein except that he also attacked catastrophism and the concept of a young earth, again citing no actual evidences for evolution.

Dr. Morris, as first speaker for the creation side, showed that the stability and complexity of present kinds, the universal gaps in the fossil record, and the laws of thermodynamics all constitute explicit evidence both for creation and against evolution, using much "in-context" documentation from evolutionist writers. Dr. Slusher showed various astronomic and geophysical evidences against an evolutionary origin of the universe and for recent creation.

In his rebuttal, Dr. Schwimmer complained that astronomical evidence had no place in the debate and that Dr. Slusher's remarks were "gobbledygook" which neither he nor his colleague could understand. Dr. Morris attempted briefly to refute some of the *ad hominem* arguments of his opponents, since they had given no scientific arguments, showing that charges of outmoded data, out-of-context quotes, etc., were invalid. He also pointed out that, although catastrophism had not been the debate topic, there was indeed evidence of universal catastrophism in the geologic column.

Dr. Frazier's rebuttal again consisted of personal insults plus an acknowledgment that there was much catastrophism in geologic history. Dr. Slusher responded in kind, expressing surprise that the two geologists could not understand his astrophysical arguments, whereas he had experienced no difficulty in understanding *their* arguments, also noting that his freshman students always easily understood the astrophysical evidence. He concluded by reminding Drs. Schwimmer and Frazier that they had been utterly unable to answer the argument from thermodynamics showing evolution to be essentially impossible.

ASIMOV DEBATES GISH IN *SCIENCE DIGEST*

A written debate between famous scientist-science writer Dr. Isaac Asimov and Dr. Duane Gish appeared in the October, 1981, issue of *Science Digest*. Drs. Asimov and Gish each submitted 1200-word statements. Each was allowed to write a 435-word commentary on the other's contribution and then all of this material was published. Our readers are invited to obtain copies of the October issue of *Science Digest* and compare the creation/evolutionist arguments. This invitation to a creationist scientist from the editors of *Science Digest* to participate in this debate represents a highly significant breakthrough.

MORRIS/MILLER DEBATE
STIRS TAMPA COMMUNITY

A high degree of community involvement featured the debate between ICR President Henry Morris and Brown University biology professor Kenneth Miller on September 19. Moderator for the debate was Florida's State Commissioner of Education, Ralph Turlington. A crowd of approximately 1500 taxed all the facilities of beautiful Jefferson High School, with several hundred turned away, unable to find space even in adjacent rooms or on the floor. The debate was covered by six local television channels and seven radio stations. One of these, WPLP, broadcast the entire debate live, so that many thousands heard it who could not come to the auditorium. Station WTIS broadcast the debate tape later. Area newspapers, especially the Tampa *Tribune,* gave extensive coverage of the debate, quite favorable to the creationist position. Many local and state school officials were present, and a number of these, including Commissioner Turlington, commented later on the value of the debate, expressing sincere appreciation of scientific creationism. The Hillsboro school district has recently mandated a two-model approach in the Tampa schools and the Florida legislature is currently giving serious consideration to a two-model bill similar to those passed in Arkansas and Louisiana.

The debate was the second between Dr. Morris and Dr. Miller, the first having taken place last spring at Brown University in Rhode Island. Dr. Miller is a very personable and capable speaker, highly knowledgeable on the issues, and one of the few qualified evolutionists still willing to debate ICR scientists.

As the first speaker, Dr. Morris stressed that the debate was not on religious issues and also that the key question to be debated was the basic issue of evolution or creation—not flood geology or the age of the earth, which were important related issues, but not the essential question. He showed that real evolution (macroevolution) had never been observed and so was outside the scope of science. Such changes as *are* observed are either "horizontal within limits" (variation) or "downward" (mutations, extinctions), confirming explicit predictions from the creation model, and conforming to the principles of conservation and decay expressed formally in the two laws of thermodynamics. He then documented the universal absence of transitional structures in the fossil record, again conforming to the creation model, but presenting a serious problem to evolutionary gradualism. He closed by showing a tabulation of 35 great creationist scientists of the past, with their unique contributions to science, thus emphasizing that a commitment to creationism was not inimical, but helpful, to the advance of true science.

In his presentation, Dr. Miller concentrated primarily on attacking what he considered to be the key creationist concepts of flood geology and the young earth, discussing radiometric dating, the fossil sequences denoting the different geologic ages, and the significance of the travel time of light from distant galaxies. The only direct evidences cited for evolution were the genetic similarities between protein sequences of man and his near evolutionary relatives (especially emphasizing Cytochrome C) and the standard textbook "intermediate forms" (the mammal-like reptiles, the horse and elephant series, and the nautiloids). He favored the "punctuated equilibrium theory" and expressed his confidence that molecular biologists would soon be able to explain such phenomena genetically. Dr. Miller also brought the religious issue into the debate, stressing that, as a Catholic, he was a "creationist," and that evolution was merely the method of creation. He also insisted that the "special creationist" position was based on the Bible and not on science and that allowing it to be taught in schools would open the schools to other religions as well.

Each speaker also had a 15-minute rebuttal and a 5-minute

summary period. Dr. Miller accused Dr. Morris of intentionally lying when he claimed that the second law of thermodynamics negated evolution, insisting that the creationist insistence on a "code" and "mechanism" to produce increased complexity in an open system constituted invalid and misleading extensions of the second law and that in some systems (e.g., hurricanes) no codes were necessary. He insisted also that the hundreds of millions of documented fossils were all proofs of evolution. He again stressed that the presumed fact of different forms of life in different geological ages contradicted creationism and that the assumed creationist explanation of hydrodynamic sorting was inadequate as an alternative. Unfortunately, Dr. Miller frequently resorted to ridicule and insult, a tactic which had apparently worked well with the liberal Ivy League students at Brown but which was not appreciated by a general adult audience, most of whom seemed pro-creationist.

In his rebuttal, Dr. Morris said he was sorry that Dr. Miller had brought religion into the debate, but that since he had, it was necessary to correct the impression that evolution was an acceptable Christian position, citing a number of leading evolutionists to the effect that evolutionary ethics and Christian ethics were mutually contradictory, and that was one major reason why so many people objected to exclusive indoctrination in evolution. He also showed that genetic similarities were not a proof of common descent, but of common design and the apparent similarities had been greatly exaggerated. He pointed out also that chromosome numbers, which should be related to evolution if anything was, showed no such patterns whatever. The so-called transitional forms were shown to be either variants within the kind or mere "mosaics" of structures (e.g., the platypus, the mammal-like reptiles) and that there were *no* fossils anywhere of transitional *structures*.

The question period dealt with four major questions: (1) the meaning of the Paluxy River footprints of man and dinosaur; (2) the Big Bang theory and its implications; (3) the validity of the young-age calculation based on magnetic field decay; (4) Prigogine's supposed proof that life originated in spite of the entropy law. Dr. Miller had little to say about the Big Bang or Prigogine, but attempted to show that the Paluxy footprints were fakes and that the magnetic decay argument would be "laughed off the stage" by scientists who knew about paleomagnetic reversals. Dr. Morris showed that the human footprints were definitely genuine, and that the Big Bang theory is currently being seriously questioned by astronomers. He showed that the magnetic field argument was in no way undermined by the supposed field reversals and that it had been unanswered the many times it had been presented to scientific audiences. The Prigogine studies likewise had in no way subverted the second law argument against evolution or the naturalistic origin of life. Furthermore, Dr. Miller's charges about falsehood in this argument were not only in poor taste, but unfounded.

5000 HEAR GISH - DOOLITTLE DEBATE IN VIRGINIA

The debate at Lynchburg, Virginia, on Tuesday evening, October 13, 1981, between Dr. Russell Doolittle, Professor of Biochemistry, University of California at San Diego, and Dr. Duane Gish is now history, but the strongest reverberations are yet to be felt as this historic debate is scheduled to be televised throughout the U.S. on prime time television.

Approximately 5000 people (according to officials of Liberty Baptist College) crowded into the gymnasium of the College to witness the debate. In addition to the television crew that recorded the debate, local television cameramen and newspaper reporters were present.

Who won the debate? The best judge of this, of course, will be the response of the millions who will view the debate on television later. However, a front page story that appeared in the *Washington Post* on Thursday, October 15 (and published in many other newspapers in the U.S.) reported that "Dr. Doolittle agreed he had lost. 'I'm devastated,' he said afterward."

Chapter 3

The Strongholds of Evolution

The college and universities of the nation constitute the real nerve center of evolutionism. Public school teachers, of course, also teach evolution, but this is mostly because they themselves were taught it in their schools of education and because the textbooks which they use teach evolution. The textbooks were also written mostly by university professors. Not only are our future teachers all taught mostly by evolutionary humanists, but so are our future doctors and lawyers and people in every profession and vocation.

Therefore it is the students in the colleges and universities who need especially to learn the great reality of creation and the perverse unreality of evolution. Most of the debates described in the previous chapter, in fact, were held on the campuses of such schools, and they have had a profound effect on multitudes of students. Even though the audience will not usually be as large as for a debate, a regular creation lecture or seminar can be even more effective for those who do attend, since all of the available time can be devoted to a positive presentation of the evidence.

The accounts in this chapter describe a number of typical college and university meetings conducted by ICR scientists during 1980 and 1981. The impact of these and similar meetings at other schools (limited space precludes covering most of them here) has been profound and far-reaching.

THE STRONGHOLDS OF EVOLUTION

PARKER SPEAKS AT UNIVERSITIES OF
KANSAS AND MISSOURI

Few places have been as well-prepared for talks on creation science as those at the University of Kansas, in Lawrence, where Dr. Gary Parker of ICR spoke on October 25-27, 1979. Dr. Morris had addressed a large audience there in 1975, and he and Dr. Gish had debated two evolutionists there in 1976, before an audience of 3,000.

Students headed by Tom Dooley and New Life Forum had already been discussing points of creation science and challenging evolution by means of respectful but constant classroom questions and "open meetings" with students and professors at various places on campus. At the end of Dr. Parker's lecture and discussion before a university audience of perhaps 500, several science majors expressed real interest in pursuing creation science further, and many other science majors, already creationists, were ready to help them.

At the University of Missouri in Kansas City, Dr. Parker had the honor of speaking at the site of the first creation/evolution university debate (between Dr. Morris and a UMKC geologist in 1972). Dr. Parker shared reports from numerous recent science journals testifying unanimously that "creationists usually win the debates" and that, reflecting its success in the academic arena, creation will be around "in scientific circles for many years to come."

JOHN MORRIS SPEAKS AT UNIVERSITY OF IOWA

An important series of meetings was held October 26-28, 1979, on the University of Iowa campus at Iowa City under the able sponsorship of the newly formed Baptist Student Center. Speaker for the seminar was ICR scientist John Morris, who first presented and contrasted the basic creation and evolution models on Friday night at a "Favorite Professor Banquet."

An informal all-day creation seminar was held on Saturday at the BSU, where interested students studied such topics as the scientific aspects of Genesis 1-11, inability of uniformitarianism to explain the earth's geology, the Biblical model of geology, the search for Noah's Ark, and the Paluxy River footprint discoveries.

Two Sunday morning talks at the Central Park Baptist Church in Davenport and one evening meeting at the University Baptist Church in Iowa City were followed by a Sunday night meeting on campus attended by an overflow crowd of about 300 students, most of whom were not sympathetic to the creation cause at the start.

MISSISSIPPI STATE UNIVERSITY
HEARS CREATION EVIDENCE

An intensive emphasis on scientific creationism was focussed on Mississippi State University on February 16-18, 1980, as ICR Director Henry M. Morris spoke ten times at six locations to a total of over 2,100 students and others. The largest crowd was at the final meeting in Lee Hall on the campus on Monday night, where Dr. Morris lectured on "The Origin of the Earth and Man" to an audience of about 750. A standing ovation followed the message and extended question period. The meeting was sponsored by the M.S.U. Student Association, and the entire lecture and question periods were broadcast live over a local radio station.

Two important additional sessions were held on the campus on Monday. The Geology Club sponsored Dr. Morris' lecture on "The Creation Model of Earth History." In mid-afternoon, the Biology auditorium was the setting for his lecture on "The Creation Model of Human History," co-sponsored by Sigma Xi (the national scientific research honorary society) and the Biology Department. Although some faculty and graduate students expressed strong opposition, the reception at both forums was excellent.

The M.S.U. Creation Science Fellowship, led by Wyatt Gwin, made all arrangements and promotion. Many other students and faculty assisted, including Dr. Vistor Zitta, faculty adviser for Campus Crusade, and a former doctoral student in hydraulics under Dr. Morris at Virginia Tech.

FIVE HUNDRED HEAR MORRIS AT KANSAS STATE

"The Scientific Case for Creation" was the title of a lecture by Dr. Henry Morris which attracted 500 students and faculty members at Kansas State University, in Manhattan, Kansas, on October 10, 1980. Interest was high and potential follow-up looked promising after the two hours of lecture plus discussion. The meeting was sponsored by the KSU chapter of Campus Crusade for Christ.

Dr. Morris also conducted a one-day Creation Seminar, with approximately 100 paid registrants, the next day, held at the Grace Baptist Church of Manhattan. On Sunday morning, he was guest preacher at the three services of the church. Attendance for the three services totaled about 700. Rev. Horace Brelsford is pastor of the church and Jim Cook directs the KSU Campus Crusade work.

MORRIS AT LARGEST LUTHERAN SEMINARY

A warmly responsive audience of seminary students and faculty members heard Dr. Henry Morris deliver a special convocation message at Concordia Seminary (St. Louis) on February 4, 1981. Speaking on "Science, Scripture, and Creation," Dr. Morris urged his hearers to give creationism an important place in their ministries, stressing that it was "Scriptural, scientific, and significant."

Concordia Seminary is the largest Lutheran seminary in the world, with over 725 students, and serves the Missouri Lutheran

Synod. After almost losing the seminary to liberals in the early seventies, conservatives regained control in 1974, and the school is now firmly committed to special creation, as well as Biblical inerrancy, in all its teachings.

Most campus ministries of ICR speakers are on secular campuses, dominated by evolutionary thought. Concordia Seminary was a refreshing exception.

OVERFLOW AUDIENCE HEARS GISH AT ROCHESTER

Dr. Duane Gish presented the scientific evidence for creation before an audience of students and faculty in the Hubbell Auditorium of the University of Rochester on the evening of Tuesday, February 3, 1981. Many were sitting in the aisles and on the floor as an estimated 650 people crowded into the auditorium. Dr. Gish presented a slide-illustrated lecture, which included evidence based on thermodynamics, probability laws, and the fossil record. The lecture was followed by a question period. The lecture was sponsored by the University.

3000 JAM GYMNASIUM FOR
BROCK UNIVERSITY LECTURE

The gymnasium at Brock University in St. Catherines, Ontario, was jammed to capacity as 3000 people crowded into every available space on Monday evening, March 23, 1981, to hear a creation-science lecture by Dr. Duane Gish. Two to three hundred others were turned away at the door, as people came from many points in Ontario and from nearby New York State for the lecture. A search involving several weeks had failed to obtain an evolutionist willing to debate.

Following Dr. Gish's slide-illustrated lecture, in which he emphasized the evidence from thermodynamics, probability considerations, and the fossil record, questions were taken from the audience. Earlier in the day, Dr. Gish debated Dr. Jack Pasternak, Professor of Biology at Waterloo University, on the popular Tom Cherington television show originating in Hamilton.

ICR SCIENTIST LECTURES AT MICHIGAN TECH

Dr. Duane Gish presented a creation-science lecture in a crowded lecture hall at Michigan Technological University in Houghton, Michigan, on the evening of Thursday, April 9, 1981. After Dr. Gish's slide-illustrated lecture emphasizing thermodynamics, probability laws, and the fossil record, Michigan Tech biologists Drs. Janice Glime and Robert Stone and campus minister Rev. Jim Miller were given an opportunity to offer comments and ask questions. Dr. Gish was allowed to respond to each panel member.

Dr. Glime expressed her belief that at least some sort of limited union of evolution and theistic intervention can be achieved. She then defended organic evolution. She maintained that evolution was possible in spite of the entropy principle, using the order-disorder and open system arguments. Her answer to the lack of transitional forms in the fossil record was a resort to a sort of hopeful monster mechanism, citing the phthalidamide babies and experiments on fruit flies.

Dr. Stone was largely in agreement with Dr. Gish's position, pointing out that both the fossil record and embryology failed to produce the intermediate forms required by evolution. He recommended a position of suspended judgment on some of the questions generating differences between creationists and evolutionists. He stated that he indicated to his students that he believed in a Creator who had given the sciences to mankind.

Rev. Miller maintained that the error of creationists was their taking the Genesis account of creation in a literal sense. He did, however, maintain that God was dynamically related to the world. He expressed his belief in the immanence of God in all things while rejecting the supernaturalness of the Bible, which he maintained was introduced during the Middle Ages. Rev. Miller's view of creation is apparently whatever the current concensus of scientists may be, while rejecting, he said, a strictly materialistic, mechanistic view of evolution.

DR. GISH SPEAKS AT T.C.U.

Dr. Duane Gish presented a slide-illustrated lecture on creation science to an audience of about 500 students and faculty at

T.C.U. in Ft. Worth on April 30, 1981. Dr. Gish's lecture was followed by a 45-minute question period. The overall response was very positive.

The lecture had been arranged through the efforts of biology student Kim Mathews and Mr. Cullen Davis. Mr. Davis opened the meeting with a brief explanation of the implications and consequences of creation as it relates to the Bible and science.

DR. MORRIS FACES LARGE CROWD
AT AUBURN UNIVERSITY

The Auburn University Colosseum in Alabama was the scene of a significant meeting on May 7, 1981, when Dr. Henry M. Morris spoke on "The Scientific Case for Creation" to a large audience estimated at nearly 2000 people. The ICR Director's visit was sponsored by the Auburn University Religious Affairs Committee, and attracted wide coverage in area newspapers, radio, and television.

Dr. Ward, a theistic evolutionist and physics professor at Auburn, gave a short rebuttal to Dr. Morris' presentation. Dr. Ward had previously been a key witness against the "creation bill" that had been under consideration in the Alabama legislature. Dr. Morris then responded to Dr. Ward's critique, followed by a session of questions from the audience directed to both scientists.

ICR SCIENTIST AT UNIVERSITY OF ARKANSAS

Dr. Duane Gish served as the speaker for four morning and afternoon workshops on creation-science on Thursday and Friday, September 3 and 4, 1981, in the Student Union ballroom of the University of Arkansas in Fayetteville. The Thursday evening meeting featured State Senator Jim Holsted, the Arkansas legislator who introduced the legislation which was passed overwhelmingly by both houses of the state legislature and which mandates equal treatment for creation-science and evolution-science in the public schools, and State Senator John Lisle, a vigorous opponent of the legislation. Climaxing the conference on Friday evening, Dr. Gish presented a general overview of the scientific evidence for creation.

MORRIS LECTURES AT UNVERSITY OF ILLINOIS

The Lincoln Hall Theatre on the University of Illinois campus was the setting for a slide-illustrated lecture, "Creation versus Evolution," by Dr. Henry Morris, ICR President, on October 27. The audience of university students and faculty numbered over 450, with the lecture plus question period extending over two hours. The meeting was sponsored by the Basic Christian Fellowship and the Illinois chapter of Students for Origins Research.

Chapter 4

Creation and the World System

Although the evolutionary philosophy is especially dominant in universities and colleges, its influence has also permeated every other important center of influence. The politico-legal establishment and the news media are two prime examples. Both of these have been strongholds of evolutionism, but they are beginning to crack under the factual onslaughts of the creation movement.

Many legislative bodies have been considering the issue and even though ICR itself does not engage directly in political activities, it has been inadvertently and reluctantly drawn into the resulting litigation and other such activities by virtue of its leadership in creationism. Some of the accounts of these important developments are included in this chapter.

Similarly, creationism is increasingly receiving the attention of the news media, most of it quite hostile. The television networks, the leading magazines, and almost every paper in the country have carried feature articles dealing with the creation/evolution issue. The *Acts and Facts* periodical is too small to report many of these, but a few of the more significant television programs have been described. Furthermore, even though newspaper and magazine articles and editorials are almost always anti-creationist, the polls of their readers always turns out to favor creation, and some of these are included.

CREATION AND THE WORLD SYSTEM

A. Public Schools and the Law

THE ICR POSITION ON CREATIONIST
LITIGATION AND LEGISLATION

Because of the widespread news media attention being devoted to the creation movement these days—almost always heavily slanted and even deceptive in its bias against the introduction of creationism into the schools—it seems necessary once again for us to state clearly ICR's position on such matters as "creation laws" and "creation lawsuits." As a tax-exempt charitable organization chartered for purposes of education, research, and promotion of both scientific creationism and Biblical creationism, the Institute for Creation Research is precluded from "lobbying" for creationist laws or ordinances, and has always held the conviction that education and persuasion are more appropriate and effective in the long run than coercion.

The following summary items may help clarify ICR's position on such matters. On the negative side:

1. *ICR does not initiate, promote, finance, or lobby for so-called "creation laws."* Such legislation, if appropriate at all, should be entirely the responsibility of the citizens of each particular state.

2. *ICR does not initiate or finance lawsuits, either to restrain evolution or to introduce creation in public institutions.* For example, we were not involved at all in the recent widely publicized California lawsuit, despite widespread misunderstanding in this regard.

On the other side, however, we do strongly believe that teaching materials presenting the scientific evidences for creation and against evolution should be included in the programs of all tax-supported institutions, and a good part of our efforts (research, writing, and speaking) are directed toward that end. If such legislation or litigation actions are initiated, therefore (not by ICR but by others), we want them to be successful (every defeat in a lawsuit or failure to pass a proposed creation bill makes it all the more difficult to win a sympathetic hearing for creation anywhere else, since such defeats are inevitably well-publicized).

With this in mind, there are certain positive steps which ICR is prepared to take in such political matters whenever feasible, as follows:

1. *ICR personnel are willing as time permits to serve as consultants or expert witnesses on the scientific, educational, or legal merits of creationism.* However, political committees or litigants desiring such services are expected to reimburse those individuals for the costs of time and travel involved.

2. *ICR personnel do write and distribute materials advocating a "two-model" teaching approach in public institutions.* These are available for purchase by local groups as desired. Even though ICR does not encourage or endorse specific legislation or litigation, we do believe it is important for such actions (if they are going to be undertaken anyway) to

have text materials with a sound scientific and legal basis.

3. *ICR believes there is a distinction between "defensive" and "offensive" litigation.* That is, even though we would not file a lawsuit designed to *compel* teachers to teach creation, it is conceivable that a suit might be in order if a law were passed *banning* the teaching of creation. At present, however, there is neither constitutional nor statutory restriction against the teaching of scientific creationism in any school. It is also conceivable (though unlikely) that a libel action might sometime be justified if newspapers and periodicals continue printing untrue and defamatory statements about ICR and its staff.

SCOPES TRIAL IN REVERSE
(Teacher Dismissed for His Creationist Views)

On July 29, 1980, at 8:00 a.m. the Eighth Circuit Court of South Dakota convened where Mr. Lloyd Dale, a biology teacher for the Lemmon, South Dakota public school system, was to defend himself against dismissal by the Lemmon Board of Education. Lloyd Dale, the winner of the *South Dakota Outstanding Biology Teacher of the Year Award,* was condemned as incompetent by the Lemmon Board as they defended their action. Dale, holding a master's degree in science, and having taught biology for over 17 years, was declared to be an inadequate science teacher by two board of education members, two students (who claimed they did not think Dale was giving them a proper education), the superintendent of schools, and the Lemmon high school principal. All of these testified against Mr. Dale, affirming that he was a "bad teacher" and should have been dismissed.

How often was this "bad teaching" observed? Testimony by the principal, who was responsible for this evaluation, indicated that he visited Dale's class once. The principal also stated that he entered the classroom for a moment on several other occasions, but could not evaluate Dale as a biology teacher during these lab sessions. This kind of testimony, plus the complaints (one later withdrawn) that four students made to the principal (one student was the son of the president of the board) and two members of the board of education, incited the board to fire Dale.

There was another factor that kept coming up at the trial: scientific creation and evolution. Mr. Dale felt that the assigned textbook was highly biased on this subject and often scientifically misleading. When the topic of origins came up he approached it by using inquiry skills of science and discussed both models openly and objectively with the class. Dale presented the scientific data and suggested that the students make up their own minds on the matter of creation and evolution and suggested that scientists do not know for certain just how old the earth is or, from a scientific framework, how life came to be.

Testimony by other students in the class revealed that Dale respected their views, even though they did not always parallel his. Yet, contrary testimony from board members and the principal suggested it was inappropriate to discuss scientific creation and that since he was not following the textbook, he should be fired. Dr. William Mayer, a zoologist and Director of the Biological Sciences Curriculum Study in Boulder, Colorado, while acting as an expert witness against Dale, inferred that he was a bad teacher, therefore, vindicating the board's action. Dr. Mayer claimed that creation could not be scientific and that only evolution should have that distinction in the area of origins. When presented with the credible testing program conducted by Mr. Dale, Mayer stated that "standardized" testing and "criterion references" testing were not effective means for evaluating students in biology. He claimed that teachers always "teach to the test" and he implied that this was poor practice and that it did not make Dale a quality instructor.

During the trial proceedings it was pointed out that Lloyd Dale used chapter tests referenced to the criteria of the unit as well as giving his whole class a nationally standardized Nelson Biology Test pre (E form) and post (F form). Dale followed the exact procedures used by many biology teachers throughout the United States. In support of this procedure, testimony was given by Dr. Richard Bliss, the Director of Curriculum Development for the Institute for Creation Research, stating that he had observed quality science teachers use these procedures during his 26 years as a science and biology teacher and that many school districts used this testing program as one factor to denote the quality of their biology program. Bliss indicated that Lloyd Dale appeared to have carried out instruction in his biology class in an outstanding manner.

RULING GOES AGAINST CREATIONIST TEACHER

The Long-awaited decision in the famous South Dakota "Reversed Scopes Trial" (See *Acts & Facts,* October 1980) has rejected the appeal of biology teacher Lloyd Dale against his dismissal by the Lemmon South Dakota School Board. By all reasonable standards, Mr. Dale was a superior teacher, yet he was dismissed, apparently on the sole grounds that he taught creationism to his students as a valid scientific alternative to evolutionism, using an objective "two-model" approach. His appeal had been filed and supported by the South Dakota Education Association, which will also now carry it to the South Dakota Supreme Court.

In his decision, Judge Brandenburg ruled as follows:

> A teacher who is adversely affected by a decision of a school board is entitled to an appeal before the circuit court for a trial de novo. SDCL 13-46-t. Rather than a true trial de novo, however, the appeal has the limited function of receiving evidence solely for determining the legality, and not the propriety, of the school board's decision. *Moran v. Rapid City Area School District, 281 N.W. 2d 595 (S.D. 1979).* "Therefore, the judiciary may not invade the province of the school board's decision making unless such decision making is done contrary to law." *Id.* at 598. Being governed by the precedent of that case, we are limited to the question of whether the board acted lawfully in reaching its decision.

He apparently ignored the fact that the school board had repudiated Mr. Dale's rights under the First and Fourteenth Amendments. He had not disobeyed any directives from the school board or principal, his class had been visited by an administrator only once in 17 years, his students were not deprived of any biological information and did well on nationally standardized tests in the subject, and he had received numerous honors for his teaching skills. His dismissal could hardly have been based on anything but his nonreligious scientific presentation of creationism to his classes.

PRESIDENT REAGAN BACKS TWO-MODEL APPROACH

Republican presidential nominee Ronald Reagan has indicated his doubts about the so-called scientific theory of evolution and his support for the teaching of creation in the public schools at a news conference held before addressing a conference in Dallas sponsored by the Roundtable, an evangelical informational organization based in Washington, D.C. In an article in the San Diego *Union* on August 23, Governor Reagan is quoted as recognizing that evolution **"is a scientific theory only and in recent years has been challenged in the world of science."** He added: **"I think recent discoveries down through the years have pointed up great flaws in it."** He said that he himself had a great many questions about the theory.

Asked about the teaching of evolution in public schools, the former California governor said that if evolution is taught in public schools, creation also should be taught. With respect to schools in general, Mr. Reagan pointed out that as schools have tried **"to educate without ethics,"** there has been an increase in crime, drug abuse, child abuse, and human sufferings.

ACLU SUES TO OVERTURN
CREATION LAW IN ARKANSAS

What could well become the crucial anti-creationist lawsuit of the 1980's was filed in May by the American Civil Liberties Union against the state of Arkansas, challenging its new law for balanced scientific treatment of creation and evolution in the public schools of the state. If successful, this challenge could well initiate a domino effect that would preclude the teaching of scientific creationism in other states as well.

The ACLU will seek to have the Arkansas law (the first such law in the nation) declared unconstitutional on the grounds that it violates church/state separation, that it was enacted for religious reasons, that it violates academic freedom, and that its vagueness violates due process. Actually the law specifically forbids any religious instruction related to origins, requiring only balanced *scientific* treatment of the two basic models of origins, and forbidding discrimination against any student because of his belief in either creation or evolution.

LOUISIANA PASSES CREATION LAW

An act requiring scientific creationism to be taught in Louisiana schools as an alternative to evolution whenever the latter is studied was signed into law by Governor Dave Treen on July 21, 1981. The bill had passed both House and Senate by wide margins. Louisiana thus became the second state to enact such a law, with the latter structured in closely similar language to that in Arkansas, both states following a "model bill" developed by Paul Ellwanger and his associates in South Carolina. As in Arkansas, however, the American Civil Liberties Union immediately announced that it would challenge the law in court.

B. The Television View of Creationism

WALTER CRONKITE AND CBS DISTORT CREATION MOVEMENT

The CBS Evening news, featuring "genial and trustworthy" Walter Cronkite, attempted to stem the burgeoning creation movement in its telecast of March 6, 1980, portraying it as the **reactionary effort of a handful of fundamentalists to force the public schools to teach their religious beliefs in the classroom**. Throughout the entire news segment—depicting scenes from San Diego, New York, Georgia, and other places—the whole theme was that of fundamentalist religion attacking authentic science education, with **no reference at all to the fact that creation is better supported by science and that it is the "two-model" scientific approach, not a Biblical approach, which is being promoted by the creationists for public school.**

This distortion of the issue was completely deliberate, not one of misunderstanding. The CBS representative who filmed and narrated the sequence, John Sheehan, spent months reading creationist literature, interviewing creationist scientists, and thoroughly studying the issue. He was urged repeatedly to point out that most creationists, including thousands of well-qualified scientists, were stressing that creationism should be introduced into the public schools as a scientific model only, with the scientific evidence for and against both evolution and creation discussed fairly and objectively, with no reference to the Bible or religious literature. The news segment, however, completely ignored this whole dimension, emphasizing repeatedly that the fundamentalists were trying to legislate the Bible story of creation into the biology classroom.

Leadership of the movement was attributed largely to Henry Morris, "fundamentalist Baptist president" of a "non-accredited, religious" college. He was not identified as a scientist, nor was any mention made of the Institute for Creation Research or of the other scientists on its staff. One brief scene showed Dr. Gary Parker teaching a biology class at Christian Heritage College, but he was not identified.

Sheehan and his crew actually spent two days at the Institute for Creation Research, taping Dr. Parker's entire one and one-half hour class on the paleontology of the geologic strata and their deposition by the flood. Extensive footage was taken in ICR's Museum of Creation and Earth History, as well as interviews with Dr. Gish and others, none of which was shown on the segment.

Over an hour of continuous interview was filmed with Dr. Morris, practically all devoted to the scientific evidence for creation and the case for using a two-model approach in the schools. The only clips shown of the interview, however, were a couple of brief comments (responding to insistent questioning by Sheehan) regarding the moral and social effects of evolution.

In other segments, Nell Segraves of California spoke of her desire to get the Bible into the schools, Judge Braswell Deen of Georgia expressed his conviction that "creation laws" would eventually pass in all the states, and Luther Sunderland of New York was depicted as ridiculing evolution to an audience of teachers. Judging from ICR's experience, these segments may also have been taken badly out of context. Evolutionist scientists and teachers were shown expressing their opposition to being forced to teach religion in their classes.

Sheehan, knowing better, portrayed ICR and Dr. Morris as involved in a kind of conspiracy to get creation laws and ICR books introduced in the various states, not only for religious reasons but also for profit. The fact is, however, that ICR does not promote legislation or judicial action designed to *compel* creation teaching, favoring education and persuasion rather than coercion. Furthermore, the only reason ICR personnel are involved in getting creationist books published (through a specially-organized company, CLP Publishers) is because the standard textbook publishers will not publish and promote such books—the reason being that they involve too much financial risk. CLP functions very economically with only a small staff of dedicated personnel, but is still operating with regular annual deficits after its first five years of existence.

In spite of the disappointing nature of this national exposure, the very fact that CBS felt the creation movement warranted a "hatchet job" of this sort is testimony to its increasing importance.

One can anticipate that Mr. Cronkite and his team will receive much correspondence as a result. Hopefully, many will ask why no mention was made of the creation/evolution debates, the thousands of creationist scientists, any of the overwhelming scientific evidences for creation, or the fact that many statistically-controlled surveys show the great majority of Americans desire that both creation and evolution be taught in their public schools.

CBS "SUNDAY MORNING" SHOW GIVES FAIR TREATMENT TO ICR

Unlike the Walter Cronkite CBS Evening News Report, the "Sunday Morning" show which appeared on CBS stations on November 23, 1980, seemed to make a sincere effort to present the creation/evolution issue in a fair and objective manner. Although the program did emphasize the evolutionary position, using the testimony of Dr. Stephen Gould of Harvard, the treatment also featured the work of the Institute for Creation Research and its two-model approach for public school curricula.

The testimony of Dr. Richard Bliss, ICR's Director of Curriculum Development, was given a prominent and sympathetic part on the program. Also shown was a field class conducted in the Anza-Borrego Desert by Dr. Steve Austin and Dr. Gary Parker with their geology and biology students from Christian Heritage College. Although the program was hardly an ideal presentation of creationism, and although it showed that doctrinaire evolutionists such as Dr. Gould are entirely uncompromising in their commitment to evolution, it did provide a much more balanced treatment than is normally encountered in the national news media.

ICR SCIENTISTS APPEAR ON BBC-TV

Dr. Duane Gish, who has made several speaking tours of British schools and universities, was interviewed by Alec Nisbet for his "Horizons" program, broadcast on BBC-TV in Britain early in 1981. Dr. Morris and other members of the ICR staff were also photographed. Other creation scientists, as well as a number of prominent evolutionists were also interviewed for this broadcast.

ABC FEATURES ICR ON "20/20" PROGRAM

The popular network news program "20/20" on February 5, 1981, dealt with the creation/evolution issue in a series of interviews and review commentaries by ABC commentator Sylvia Chase. The program pin-pointed the Institute for Creation Research as the leader of the creation movement and did recognize the scientific emphasis in modern creationism, even though (in common with most other public news media treatments of the subject) it again attempted to portray the issue as partly one of Bible-waving fundamentalism versus objective science.

Repeating the tactics of the CBS Walter Cronkite show, Ms. Chase conducted lengthy videotaped interviews with ICR scientists, but the program only incorporated three very brief (and somewhat out-of-context) segments from these interviews. It also significantly distorted and overemphasized ICR's role in local attempts to mandate creation teaching in public schools. Nevertheless, although the program was clearly biased in favor of evolutionism, most creationists who saw it seemed to feel it was less one-sided than most such programs, and it did result in a flood of requests to ICR for more information about creationism.

Two significant features of the program were its beginning (a clip of President Reagan advocating the teaching of creation in the schools along with evolution) and its ending (Sylvia Chase stating that the new policy of the federal Department of Education was to leave the issue of implementing a two-model approach strictly up to local school boards).

C. Creation and Public Opinion

CREATION AND THE GALLUP POLL

Some interesting and helpful information has come to light in a recent survey of religious opinion conducted by top pollster Dr. George Gallup. The Poll was commissioned by the magazine *Christianity Today,* and many of the results are reported in its December 21, 1979, issue.

Of approximately 155 million Americans, 18 years of age or older, no less than one-half "believe God created Adam and Eve to start the human race." Out of the 155 million, 31 million (20%) consider themselves "evangelicals," and of this group Dr. Gallup says: "They believe, by almost an eight-to-one margin, that God created Adam and Eve to start human life."

Yet our public schools and other public institutions continue to teach dogmatically not only that Adam and Eve never existed, but that mankind was not created at all. Evidently the *public* still has little to say about what is taught in our public schools!

Also, in spite of the fact that God has been all but banned from the schools, and instruction has been purely humanistic for two generations, the Gallup Poll found that 94% of all adult Americans still believe in God, and only 4% are explicitly atheistic. More than 80% believe that Jesus Christ was the Son of God in a unique sense, and more than 40% believe the Bible to be the inerrant Word of God. Furthermore, 80% of all Americans (including practically all evangelicals) believe the Ten Commandments are still valid for today, so that the widespread propaganda for the "new morality" has not been so successful after all!

NEWSPAPER SURVEY OF SCHOOLS
FAVORS TEACHING CREATION

A significant newspaper questionnaire recently (May-June, 1980) provides important evidence that the teaching of the creation model in public schools is favored by a large majority of both parents and teachers.

The survey was conducted by the Tampa *Tribune—Times* for residents of Hillsborough County, Florida, where the teaching of the "two-model" approach (both creation and evolution) has recently been adopted by the school board. The questionnaire included many items of interest concerning the schools and their programs, with only one question dealing specifically with creation teaching. The survey was conducted at two levels: (1) a statistically controlled telephone survey of the community; (2) a questionnaire published in the newspaper for all readers who wished to respond.

The creation question was as follows: *"Do you feel that the subject of creationism, which is the study that man and the universe were created by a supreme being, should be taught in public schools?"* Replies to this question were as follows:

Parents: 77% "Yes"; 23% "No" or "Undecided"
Teachers: 73% "Yes"; 28% "No" or "Undecided"

The most interesting result of this survey was not the finding that most parents favor creation teaching (this has already been well documented), but the rather unexpected discovery that a large majority of public school teachers are also in favor.

SCHOOL BOARD MEMBERS FAVOR TWO-MODEL APPROACH

According to the *American School Board Journal* (March 1980, p. 52) a clear majority of school board members across the country (or, at least, of readers of the *Journal*) favor the teaching of creationism in the schools. In answer to the question: "How should public schools handle the teaching of the origin of man?", readers responded as follows:

1. Both creation and evolution explanations should be taught in a way that allows students to decide for themselves: 48%
2. Only creation explanation should be taught: 19%
3. Only evolution explanation should be taught: 25%
4. Neither should be taught: 8%

Thus, even among such an unlikely group as school board members and administrators, apparently at least two-thirds believe that the present practice of exclusive teaching of evolutionism should be stopped.

GLAMOUR MAGAZINE POLL FAVORS CREATIONISM

A poll conducted recently by a seemingly unlikely publication, *Glamour* magazine, resulted in a strong verdict in favor of creation, to the apparent surprise and chagrin of the magazine's editors. Over 53% of the magazine's readers indicated they did *not* believe in evolution, "despite the fact that Darwin's theory of evolution has been accepted for more than a half century as the explanation for the origin of life' (*Glamour,* August 1981, p. 29).

Furthermore 74% of the readers favored teaching creation along with evolution in the schools, and 56% said this would *not* be bringing religion into the schools. Over 61% said that textbooks and curricula should be revised to accommodate this change. The readers who responded were 50% Protestant, 20% Catholic, 5% Jewish, and 25% "Other."

Chapter 5

Creation Witness Everywhere

The Lord commanded His disciples to preach the gospel in all the world, witnessing "in Jerusalem, and in all Judea, and in Samaria, and unto the uttermost part of the earth" (Acts 1:8). Since the foundation and "cutting-edge" of the gospel is the great truth of creation (Revelation 14:6-7), people everywhere urgently need to know that evolution is the age-long deception of the anti-Christian world system, and that creation is not only taught in Scripture but by all the *real* facts of science.

Right from its beginnings over a decade ago, ICR has seen many doors open to this message—churches, schools, scientific associations, civic groups, etc.—not only near its home base, but also all across the country and around the world. The accounts in this chapter summarize some of these. During 1980 and 1981, as a matter of fact, ICR scientists spoke in over 35 states and 10 other countries, not including national and international outreach via radio and television.

The impact of all this testimony may never be directly measured, but the Lord opened the doors and can be trusted to bring forth good fruit from the seed sown, in His own proper time.

CREATION WITNESS EVERYWHERE

A. ICR's Jerusalem

LAWRENCE SCIENTISTS HEAR CASE FOR CREATION

Over 350 scientists filled the main auditorium at the internationally famous Lawrence Research Laboratories (Livermore, California) and listened attentively as ICR Director Henry M. Morris outlined "The Scientific Case for Creation" at noon on November 1, 1979. The lecture was sponsored by the Earth Sciences Division of the Laboratories. The newspaper account of the event the next day stressed the fact that the lecture had been entirely scientific rather than religious, as expected. A stimulating question period followed the lecture.

The Lawrence Laboratories comprise one of the most famous research installations in the world. Co-sponsored by the United States government and the University of California at Berkeley, the Laboratories have an annual research budget exceeding 330 million dollars. A weekly Bible study group among the lab scientists was instrumental in arranging the lecture by Dr. Morris, who was in the area for meetings sponsored by Livermore's First Baptist Church.

SLUSHER SPEAKS TO 3000 IN ORANGE COUNTY

On May 9, 1980, the Orange County (Calif.) Creation Science Association hosted the film "Footprints in Stone" in the Social Science Hall at the University of California (Irvine) and on May 16, Dr. Harold Slusher spoke to an enthusiastic audience also in Social Science Hall UCI. Many students and faculty members attended the talk on "Reconsider the Age of the Earth." On May 15, Dr. Slusher spoke to a capacity crowd of 3000 at the Calvary Chapel, Costa Mesa.

The crowd consisted of many young people and professionals. Dr. Slusher also appeared in several radio talk shows and had interviews with two local newspapers on the amazing evidence of the young age of the universe, the solar system, and the earth. Dr. Robert Peterson, the Superintendent of the Orange County Board of Education, enthusiastically supported the meetings. The Orange County Creation Science Association (Christopher Chui, President) believes that with time and hard work, both *creation* and *evolution* will soon be taught in science classrooms in California.

LIVERMORE MEETINGS ANSWER
COMMUNITY CONTROVERSY

Dr. Dean Kenyon, Profesor of Biology at San Francisco State University, and Dr. Henry Voss, Astrophysicist at Lockheed's Palo Alto Research Laboratory, were featured speakers at the

"Conference on Scientific Origins," February 6-8, 1981, in Livermore, California, along with ICR Scientists Richard Bliss, Henry Morris, and ICR Attorney, Wendell Bird. Six major evening lectures were held in addition to an all-day Educator's Workshop. Other participants at the latter included David Lewton, East Bay Parks Administrator and Head Naturalist; Louis Goodgame, Social Science teacher in Del Norte County; and Nancy Stake, Director of Citizens for Scientific Creation in Saratoga.

MORRIS FEATURED IN PROPHECY CONFERENCE

Dr. Theodore Epp of the "Back-to-the-Bible" broadcast, and Dr. Henry Morris of ICR were the featured speakers at the annual Conference on Prophecy, sponsored by the American Board of Missions to the Jews (A.B.M.J.) in the Southern California area on March 1-4, 1981.

B. All Across the Nation

NORTH CAROLINA RESEARCH TRIANGLE HOSTS CREATION SEMINAR

Dr. Gary Parker and Dr. Henry Morris were the speakers for a stimulating creation seminar at Raleigh, North Carolina, across from the campus of North Carolina State University, on March 21-22, 1980. Approximately 350 paid registrants, including an unusually high proportion of scientists, educators, and other professionals, attended the sessions. The seminar was sponsored by TASC (Triangle Association for Scientific Creationism), a group of about 20 scientists in the famous "research triangle" formed by North Carolina, North Carolina State and Duke Universities.

Dr. Morris also spoke at a faculty luncheon on the N.C. State campus and in church services at the Calvary Presbyterian and Friendship Baptist churches in Raleigh. Dr. Donald Hamann, Professor of Food Science at N.C. State and member of ICR's Technical Advisory Board, is the chairman of TASC

MORRIS ADDRESSES 600 TEACHERS IN TENNESSEE

Over 600 teachers and administrators of the Tennessee Association of Christian Schools heard Dr. Henry Morris at their annual convention on September 25-26, 1980, at the Bill Rice Ranch near Murfreesboro, Tennessee. The two featured speakers were the ICR Director and Dr. Bob Jones, III, President of Bob Jones University in South Carolina. Dr. Morris spoke twice to general sessions of the convention, bringing messages on the distinctive character of Christian education and, in addition, conducted four workshop sessions on various aspects of creationism.

ROCKY MOUNTAIN CHRISTIAN TEACHERS HEAR CREATION MESSAGE

Dr. Henry Morris of ICR was the featured speaker at the annual Rocky Mountain Conference of the American Association of Christian Schools. Meeting in Cheyenne, over 200 teachers and administrators of Christian Schools from Colorado, Wyoming, Idaho, Montana, and Nebraska heard Dr. Morris give four one-hour lectures on the general theme of "The Creationist Philosophy of Education." Dr. Al Janney, President of the American Association of Christian Schools, was also featured on the program.

SEATTLE ROUND ROBIN DRAWS OVERFLOW CROWDS

A three-night, three-church round robin of evangelistic creation messages in Seattle, attracted overflow crowds in each of the three churches each night, as ICR scientists Harold Slusher, Duane Gish, and Henry Morris presented Bible/science messages and personal testimonies to enthusiastic audiences each evening on November 18, 19, and 20, 1980. Host churches were Boulevard Park Presbyterian, Grace Baptist, and Des Moines Gospel Chapel. Dr. Robert Wheatley, pastor of the Presbyterian Church and organizer of the conference, had been a top engineering student in Dr. Morris' classes in 1945 at Rice University, and had been won to Christ through the Bible-science studies conducted on campus by Dr. Morris during the closing months of World War II. Approximately 1,500 people attended the three sessions each evening.

OVERFLOW AUDIENCE ATTENDS HOUSTON SEMINAR

The Spring Branch Community Church of suburban Houston, with a seating capacity of 450, set up closed-circuit television in an adjoining fellowship hall to accommodate the 700 who registered for the creation seminar on Friday evening and Saturday, February 6-7, 1981, with Dr. Harold Slusher and Dr. Duane Gish sharing the speaker's platform. Dr. Slusher presented evidence related to the origin of the universe and the age of the universe and of the earth, while Dr. Gish presented evidence for the special creation of living things, including the origin of man. Dr. Gish also spoke at all services at the church on Sunday. Dr. Joe Wall is pastor of the church, with the planning and implementation of the seminar under the direction of geophysicist Larry Cochran.

Dr. Gish also spoke at a noon meeting on Friday at the Texas Medical Center in downtown Houston under the sponsorship of the Baptist Student Union, Gerald Le Pere, Director. An overflow audience of about 550 medical, dental, and nursing students and faculty attended, with approximately 100 additional turned away for lack of seating.

ALABAMA HOLDS LARGE PUBLIC MEETING

The large Wernher von Braun Civic Center was the scene of a four-hour public meeting on scientific creationism on the evening of March 14, 1981, with ICR scientists Dr. Henry Morris and Dr. Harold Slusher as featured speakers. Auburn University scientists Dr. Malcolm Cutchens, Dr. John Burkhalter, and Dr. Bruce Gray also spoke briefly, as did Alabama University Professor Steven Underwood and Boeing Research Engineer Stan Swinney. The meeting was sponsored by the Alabama Citizens for Quality in Education, headed by Mr. Bryan Tabor. Attendance was estimated at over 800 and community interest was high, with Dr. Morris being interviewed on the local radio and television news programs as well. On Sunday, March 15, Dr. Morris and Dr. Slusher spoke in the services at four area churches.

CEDARVILLE COLLEGE HAS CREATION CONFERENCE

The annual In-Forum program of the Cedarville College student senate featured ICR scientists Henry Morris and Duane Gish in a three-day meeting on March 31-April 2, 1981. Speaking in chapel services and special evening meetings, the ICR speakers stressed the Biblical significance and scientific strength of creationism. Cedarville is a liberal arts college of 1500 students, supported by the General Association of Regular Baptists.

OHIO MEETINGS REACH LARGE NUMBERS

Over 800 paid registrants signed up for a very successful Creation-Science Seminar sponsored on April 3-4 by the Washington Heights Baptist Church of Dayton, with Dr. Duane Gish and Dr. Henry Morris as speakers. The ICR scientists also appeared on several radio and television programs while in the area, and spoke in the services of three churches: Westwood Baptist (Cincinnati), Southgate Baptist (Springfield), and Washington Heights Baptist (Dayton).

MORRIS SPEAKS AT THOMAS ROAD

ICR Director Henry M. Morris brought the Sunday message to an audience of 3,000 at the early service at the Thomas Road Baptist Church in Lynchburg, Virginia, pastored by Dr. Jerry Falwell, on March 8, 1981. At the 11:00 a.m. service, which was telecast over the 385 stations (largest number for any program of any kind in the nation) carrying "The Old-Time Gospel Hour," Dr. Morris gave a 5-minute report and challenge on the creation movement.

LEXINGTON CONFERENCE ATTRACTS WIDE INTEREST

Dr. Henry M. Morris of ICR was featured speaker at the annual Bible Conference of the Lexington Baptist College and the Ashland Avenue Baptist Church of Lexington, April 20-22, 1981, bringing six messages to audiences of about 600 in the mornings and 1,000 in the evenings. Dr. Morris also spoke at the three services of the South Lexington Baptist Church on Easter Sunday, April 19. Since, coincidentally, the Lexington School Board was currently considering incorporating scientific creationism into its school curricula, the news media gave an unusual amount of attention (mostly negative) to Dr. Morris' visits, with television crews and newspaper reporters at many of the services. Feature newspaper articles on the creation issue appeared several times before and during the meetings, with many segments also appearing on radio and television news broadcasts.

GISH SPEAKS AT INERRANCY CONFERENCE IN CINCINNATI

Dr. Duane Gish presented a lecture on the Bible and science at the International Council on Biblical Inerrancy conference in Cincinnati on Saturday, March 21. Speakers at the conference included Dr. R. C. Sproul, President of the Ligonier Valley Study Center in Pennsylvania, and Dr. Harold Hoehner of Dallas Theological Seminary. Over 900 registered for the conference. Dr. Gish emphasized the scientific accuracy of the Bible, citing several passages as examples and also emphasized the Biblical and scientific evidences for special creation. On Sunday afternoon, Dr. Gish presented a creation-science lecture at the White Oak Christian Church, Rev. David Roberson, pastor.

LARGEST CHURCH IN ARKANSAS HEARS ICR SPEAKER

The largest church in Arkansas, the First Baptist Church of Fort Smith, was host to four special lectures by Dr. Henry Morris on Sunday, May 24, 1981. Dr. Morris spoke to two interdenominational citywide Bible classes on Sunday morning, emphasizing scientific creationism, and to another on Sunday afternoon, emphasizing Biblical creationism. He also spoke for the evening services at the church. Total attendance at the four sessions was approximately 2000.

BIRD CONFRONTS ACLU IN BOSTON

Mr. Wendell R. Bird, general counsel to ICR, spoke by invitation at the American Civil Liberty Union's National Director's Conference on the campus of Tufts University in Boston on June 6, 1981. This was the annual meeting of top ACLU officials from across the nation. Mr. Bird began his lecture by quoting a statement that public school "material should never be excluded or removed simply because it expresses unpopular or controversial views or because it coincides with particular religious views [e.g. . . . on evolution]." After endorsing this statement, he identified its source as the Academic Freedom Committee of the ACLU in 1976. Mr. Bird then stated that the ACLU's current position in its Arkansas lawsuit contradicts academic freedom and civil liberties in opposing students' right to learn creation-science and defending indoctrination in evolution-science. He presented the legal reasons, with slide illustrations, why public schools do not violate separation of church and state by teaching creation-science along with evolution-science. A panel discussion then closed the morning's program with Mr. Bird, Dr. Niles Eldredge, curator of the American Museum of Natural History, and Mr. Jack Novik, an ACLU attorney in its Arkansas lawsuit.

C. To the Uttermost Parts

ICR SCIENTIST LECTURES IN SCANDINAVIA

The weekend of October 26-28, 1979, saw the first creation seminar to be held in Sweden. Dr. Duane T. Gish of the Institute for Creation Research gave five lectures on key issues regarding creation/evolution. Approximately 350-400 people participated, with a very large proportion of the audience below 25 years of age.

In addition to the seminar near Stockholm, Sweden, described above, Dr. Gish gave several lectures on scientific creationism in Oslo, Norway, and Copenhagen, Denmark, during the period of October 28-November 1.

In Oslo, Dr. Gish gave an evening lecture to which teachers

had been invited. His subject was teaching two models of origins in public schools. During this lecture Dr. Gish presented the scientific evidence for special creation and described the ICR approach to teaching origins in public schools. This lecture was translated, although most present were competent in English.

During the next morning, Dr. Gish presented a lecture on scientific creationism at the Institute of Zoology of the University of Oslo. The attendance was about 100. Interest was keen and questions were cordial. During the evening, Dr. Gish shared the platform with Carl Christian Hauge, Director of the Institute for Church and Society of Bergen, at a meeting at the Menighetsfakultetet (Free Theological Faculty of Norway). Mr. Hauge discussed (in Norwegian) the Biblical doctrine of creation and Dr. Gish presented (in English without translation) the scientific evidence for creation. A discussion period followed. The lectures in Oslo were arranged and sponsored by the Institute for Church and Society, Amalie Skramsvei 3, 5000 Bergen.

In Copenhagen, Dr. Gish presented the scientific evidence for creation in lectures at the College of Engineering and at the H.C. Orsteds Institute of the University of Copenhagen. He also lectured at Rygards High School and at the Copenhagen International High School (where he had lectured in 1977), and at the American Church. All lectures were in English. The reception at these lectures was cordial and interest was high.

DR. GISH LECTURES IN EUROPEAN SCHOOLS

Dr. Duane Gish lectured at the Capernwray Bible School at Carnforth, Lancashire, England; Tauernhof Bible School at Schladming, Austria; Bodenseehof Bible School near Friedrichschafen, Germany; Klostermuhle Bible School at Obernhof/Lahn, Germany; and the Torchbearer Bible School at Holsby Brunn, Sweden. These lectures took place during the period of October 7-24, 1979. The Capernwray or Torchbearer schools were founded by Major W. Ian Thomas, and now comprise about a dozen schools in nine different countries.

Dr. Gish gave from six to nine lectures at each school, presenting the scientific and Biblical evidence for special creation. Students attending these schools come from the U.S. and

Canada, as well as European and Scandinavian countries.

ICR SCIENTISTS CONDUCT FRUITFUL
SEMINAR IN KOREA

A unique opportunity to combine creationism and evangelism was afforded ICR scientists Henry Morris and Duane Gish in connection with the record-breaking '80 World Evangelization Crusade held in Seoul, Korea, on August 12-15, 1980. An overflow crowd of over 1,200 Korean students, faculty, and others greeted Dr. Morris for the opening lecture of a four-day Creation/Evolution Seminar, and a similar crowd attended Dr. Gish's final lecture. Other speakers for the seminar were Dr. Charles Thaxton, biochemist of Probe Ministries; Dr. Walter Bradley, Professor of Mechanical Engineering at Texas A & M University; and Dr. Young-Gil Kim, Associate Professor of Materials Science at the Korean Advanced Institute of Science.

The ICR scientists were among the 175 speakers from many lands who participated in the Crusade and its numerous seminars and special meetings. So far as known, this is the first international evangelistic crusade which has included an emphasis on creationism, and it has apparently made a significant impact on the nation's schools and professionals.

In addition to the Creation Seminar meetings, Dr. Morris addressed 200 professional men and women from many nations at one session of the Crusade's Professionals Seminar, speaking on the theme "Science and Christian Faith." A large number of these requested further help and information. He also spoke on "The Scientific Case for Creation" to over 100 science graduate students and faculty at the Korean Advanced Institute of Science. Finally, he spoke to over 1,000 Korean students and leaders in the Campus Crusade for Christ on the theme "Creation and Evangelism." Dr. Gish spoke for three hours to a packed auditorium at the Dae Bang Presbyterian Church. On the final Sunday night, he spoke to a large and responsive audience at the New Seoul Full Gospel Church.

The main evangelistic meetings of the Crusade were held at night in the giant Yoido Plaza (actually Seoul's evacuation airstrip) with over two million people present each night. The largest crowd, on the third night of the Crusade was at least 2.75

million! Approximately 400,000 indicated (by standing) that they were responding to various invitations to accept Christ.

These were undoubtedly the largest religious gatherings in modern history (and perhaps the largest gatherings of any kind in all of history). It was an almost incredible sight, completely without parallel, yet practically ignored by the American news media.

Seoul is one of the world's great cities, with a population of eight million, and Korea has made tremendous strides toward prosperity and an advanced technological economy in just a few years, even while living continually under the very real threat of sudden invasion from Communist North Korea. The seven million Korean Christians are praying that, under God, they may soon be able to make the Republic of Korea (population 35 million) the first truly Christian nation in the world. One difficulty is that evolution is universally taught in the schools and colleges and even in many of the theological seminaries.

An important result of the Seoul Creation Seminar was the formation of an association of Korean creationist scientists, dedicated to promoting creationism in the schools and other institutions of Korea. Also, the ICR scientists were given assurance by the nation's educational leaders that the "two-model" approach will be implemented as soon as possible in the Korean schools.

The Korea Herald newspaper, in a feature article summarizing the meetings on Sunday, August 17, noted that there were, in addition to the mammoth evening rallies, a total of 12 different Seminars for particular groups, plus lectures in 50 different churches. The only specific Seminar featured in the article was the Creation/Evolution Seminar, which it summarized as follows:

> The most attractive lecture meeting was the Creation and Evolution Seminar, which was held at the Campus Crusade for Christ of Korea auditorium in Seoul during the crusade. . . . The lecture meeting noted that in many states around the world, Christian parents were insisting that their children be given the privilege of choosing between the Creation Theory and Evolution Theory from an academic and scientific point of view. We, too, the lecture noted, should give our children a choice by presenting them with two theories while they are studying. It further said that our

desire was to present the scientific basis for the Christian's alternative—the Creation Theory—through this lecture meeting.

MORRIS SPEAKS FOR LONDON PASTORS' CONFERENCE IN SPURGEON TABERNACLE

Approximately 500 British conservative Christian pastors and full-time Christian workers met for the annual "School of Theology" in London on September 28-October 1, 1981. As main speaker for the conference, Dr. Henry Morris, president of ICR, gave six lectures on various aspects of scientific and Biblical creationism. This was the third annual such conference, with the 1980 speaker having been Dr. John Whitcomb. This strategic group of Bible-centered independent evangelical churches and pastors could well be the key to a future resurgence of Biblical Christianity in Great Britain. Under the leadership of Dr. Peter Masters, pastor of the Metropolitan Tabernacle, made famous in the 19th century by its great pastor, Charles Haddon Spurgeon, these churches have become strongly creationist and are backing the creation movement in Britain.

Dr. Morris also preached at both morning and evening services in the Spurgeon Tabernacle on Sunday, October 4.

FOR FURTHER READING

These books can be obtained at your local bookstore or ordered direct from CLP Publishers, P. O. Box 15666, San Diego, California 92115. Write for a complete descriptive catalog. Video catalog also available upon request.

What is Creation Science?
Henry M. Morris, Ph.D. and Gary E. Parker, Ed.D.
The question everyone is asking answered by outstanding educators and scientists in language you don't have to be a scientist to understand. Nearly 60 illustrations, with comprehensive indexes and bibliography. **No. 187**

Evolution? The Fossils Say NO! *Duane T. Gish, Ph.D.*
The most extensive treatment in print showing the universal and systematic gaps in the supposed fossil record of evolutionary history, including a thorough discussion of human origins, showing conclusively that man did not evolve from ape-like ancestors. Generously illustrated. Over 100,000 in print.
General Edition, No. 054; Public School Edition, No. 055

Evolution in Turmoil *Henry M. Morris, Ph.D.*
Sequel to *The Troubled Waters of Evolution*. Updating the status of evolutionary thought and actions in recent years. **No. 271**

Men of Science/Men of God *Henry M. Morris, Ph.D.*
One of the most serious fallacies of modern thought is that genuine scientists cannot believe the Bible. Illustrated, brief biographies of some major scientists who believed they were "thinking God's thoughts after Him." **No. 108**

Creation: The Facts of Life *Gary E. Parker, Ed.D.*
If you are an "armchair scientist" with a hunger for knowledge (but no Ph.D. to help you understand it!), this book was written for you. Clear explanations and "down home" examples of the basic concepts of creation and evolution **No. 038**

The King of Creation *Henry M. Morris, Ph.D.*
Places modern creation movement in its biblical perspective, emphasizing Christ as Creator and Sovereign of the world. **No. 096**

Acts & Facts/Impact Series Anthology
The past decade has seen a great increase in interest and controversy in the realm of creationism. These five books trace this growth through the compilation of significant articles and debates that have been reported in ICR's popular *Acts & Facts* publication. Although they may be ordered individually, the complete five-volume set provides a comprehensive record of the recent revival of interest in creation science.

Creation: Acts/Facts/Impacts, 1972-1973   No. 037
The Battle for Creation, 1974-1975   No. 013
Up With Creation, 1976-1977   No. 179
Decade of Creation, 1978-1979   No. 044
Creation—The Cutting Edge, 1980-1981   No. 272

Scientific Creationism *Henry M. Morris, Ph.D., Ed.*
The most comprehensive and up-to-date textbook or reference handbook now available covering all major aspects of the field of scientific creationism. Available also in a special Public School Edition in which all biblical references and discussions are omitted.
General Edition No. 140, Paper
Public School Edition No. 141, Paper; No. 357, Cloth

Many Infallible Proofs *Henry M. Morris, Ph.D.*
A complete reference handbook on all aspects of practical Christian evidences, for the strengthening of personal faith in the inspiration of the Bible and the truth of Christianity. Believed to be the most comprehensive and up-to-date textbook available on this subject. Evidence from science, history, prophecy, internal structure, philosophy, and common sense, with answers to the various alleged mistakes and contradictions of the Bible.
Cloth, No. 103; Paper, No. 102

The Bible Has The Answer (Expanded Edition)
Henry M. Morris, Ph.D. and Martin E. Clark, D.Ed.
Scientific, logical, and biblical answers to 150 frequent questions on the Bible and science, occultism, controversial doctrines, person and work of Christ, the practical Christian life, modern world problems, things to come, and many others. Baptistic and premillennial on doctrinal questions.   **No. 023**

The Genesis Flood *John C. Whitcomb, Th.D. and Henry M. Morris, Ph.D.*
The standard definitive text in the field of scientific biblical crea-

238

tionism and catastrophism; the most extensive and best-documented treatment available on both the biblical and scientific implications of creation and the flood. Largely responsible for the present revival of scientific creationism.　　　　　**No. 069**

The World That Perished　*John C. Whitcomb, Th.D.*
A sequel to *The Genesis Flood,* with refutations of criticisms and further evidences of a young earth and biblical catastrophism. Strikingly illustrated.　　　　　**No. 184**

The Genesis Record　*Henry M. Morris, Ph.D.*
Verse by verse scientific and devotional commentary on the book of beginnings.　　　　　**No. 070, Cloth**

The Early Earth　*John C. Whitcomb, Th.D.*
Studies of the origin and nature of man, the gap theory, the antediluvian world, and others. Illustrated. Dr. Whitcomb is Professor of Old Testament and Director of Post-Graduate Studies at Grace Theological Seminary.　　　　　**No. 051**

The Bible and Modern Science　*Henry M. Morris, Ph.D.*
An evangelistic presentation of evidences for the scientific validity of the Bible, including archaeological and prophetic confirmations. Over 300,000 in print.　　　　　**No. 333**

Dinosaurs: Those Terrible Lizards　*Duane T. Gish, Ph.D.*
Did dinosaurs live at the same time that humans did? Are dragons just imaginary creatures? In this beautifully illustrated book for children, Dr. Gish explains what dinosaurs were and why they no longer exist. The issue of creation vs. evolution is presented on a level that children can easily understand.　　　　　**No. 046, Cloth**

Dry Bones . . . and Other Fossils　*Gary E. Parker, M.S., Ed.D.*
What are fossils? How are they formed? What can we learn from them? These and many other questions are answered in conversational dialogue in this creatively illustrated book for children. Its educational value is enhanced by including references to the fall of Adam, the Flood, and the promise of a new earth. An explanation of fossils and their significance presented in a manner that children will understand and enjoy.　　　　　**No. 047**

Tracking Those Incredible Dinosaurs　*John D. Morris, Ph.D.*
What's the *real* story on those footprints in the Paluxy River bed? What do they really tell us? An eye-witness report documented by

nearly 200 photos. Dr. Morris, highly qualified in geoscience, examines the historical evidence, as well as the existing evidence found in a nearby river of the small Texas town of Glen Rose, which has recently become the center of much controversy. Did man and dinosaurs live together in ancient times? *Look at these photos and draw your own conclusions.*   **No. 173**

The Natural Sciences Know Nothing of Evolution
A. E. Wilder-Smith, Ph.D.
Examines the evidence and presents the conclusions in a comprehensive analysis of evolution from the viewpoint of the natural sciences.   **No. 110**

The Troubled Waters of Evolution *Henry M. Morris, Ph.D.*
Presents nontechnical study of the evidence for creation and traces the history of evolutionary thought, showing how our society today has been devastated by it.   **No. 170**

Biblical Cosmology and Modern Science *Henry M. Morris, Ph.D.*
Scientific and biblical expositions of many aspects of cosmology, covering origins, catastrophism, demography, sedimentology, thermodynamics and eschatolgy. Includes extensive critiques of day-age, gap, and allegorical theories of Genesis.   **No. 337**

Studies in the Bible and Science *Henry M. Morris, Ph.D.*
Sixteen studies on special Bible-science topics, including evidence of Christ and the Trinity in nature, the Bible as a scientific textbook, biblical hydrology, concept of "power" in Scripture, scientism in historical geology, and others.   **No. 377**

Institute for Creation Research Technical Monographs

No. 1 Speculations and Experiments Related to the Origin of Life (A Critique) *Duane T. Gish, Ph.D.*
An analysis and devastating critique of current theories and laboratory experiments which attempt to support a naturalistic development of life from nonliving chemicals   **No. 158**

No. 2 Critique of Radiometric Dating *Harold S. Slusher, Ph.D.*
Sound principles of physics are used to evaluate and refute the most important radiometric methods of determining geologic ages.
                                                              No. 159

No. 4 Origin and Destiny of the Earth's Magnetic Field
Thomas G. Barnes, M.S., Sc.D.

A technical exposition of one of the most conclusive proofs that the earth is less than 10,000 years old. **No. 161**

No. 5 Our Amazing Circulatory System . . . By Chance or Creation? *M. E. Clark, M.S.*

A technical study of the human heart and circulatory system, emphasizing the impossibility of evolution. **No. 162**

No. 6 Age of the Solar System
Harold S. Slusher, Ph.D. and Stephen Duursma, M.S.

Provides detailed mathematical evidence that the "Poynting-Robertson effect" (fall of interplanetary dust into the sun as a result of solar radiation pressures) requires a very young solar system. **No. 163**

No. 7 Age of the Earth
Harold S. Slusher, Ph.D. and Thomas Gamwell, M.S.

This in-depth study of evidence from the earth's thermal cooling and radioactivity shows that the earth cannot be old. **No. 164**

No. 8 Origin of the Universe *Harold S. Slusher, Ph.D.*

Examination of the Big-Bang and Steady State Cosmogonies. Shows convincingly that the universe could not have originated by naturalistic processes and favors a recent origin. **No. 165**

No. 9 Age of the Cosmos *Harold S. Slusher, Ph.D.*

Setting all assumptions and guesswork aside, this study looks at the physical indicators to the upper limits of the age of the cosmos.

No. 166